Praise for

HANDBOOK ON BUILDING A PROFITABLE BUSINESS

"I thought all the good books in this field had already been written. Klein's book does precisely what the title says. Entrepreneurs bright enough to win will benefit immensely by Klein's advice."

Joseph R. Mancuso, President, Center of Entrepreneurial Management, Author of seventeen books, New York, NY

"I found your new book packed with useful practical information. Not only have you included the 'how to-get-starteds', but also provided sound advice and guidance . . . for small business owners as well as consultants and instructors. I plan to keep it close by at all times as I instruct my students and consult with clients. Kudos to you, Mr. Klein!"

Fred Andrews, Business Service Coordinator, Middlesex Community College, Middletown, CT

"I highly recommend this book. Every chapter is clear, concise and easy to understand. The information contains a gold mine of practical information."

Melvin Powers, Author, How to Get Rich in Mail Order, North Hollywood, CA

". . . you have presented an incredible amount of *profitable* information. In fact, I was trying to find something, anything, you might have left out so I could comment on it. But this book is more complete and inclusive than any source I have ever seen. I only wish that it was available when I started my business many years ago. I would have avoided many headaches, heartaches and heartburn. Actually, I was able to pick up some helpful ideas . . . that will help me in my business today."

Paul Vaughn, President, Hooven Business Mail, Los Angeles, CA

"This book is great! It is a complete guide to establishing and running a profitable business. Regardless of what type of business you wish to start or buy, you should read and use this massive handbook. It is loaded with insights, techniques, and

factual information to help you achieve money-making success."
*Russ von Hoelscher, Author, Entrepreneur and Leading
Marketing Consultant, El Cajon, CA*

"A most informative and interesting approach to guiding the
new entrepreneur through the complexities of getting started. . . .
The content gets right to the heart of the issues."
*Richard T. Ward, Ed. D. Associate Professor of Manage-
ment, Hawaii Pacific College, Honolulu, HI*

"A monumental lifetime compilation of invaluable information -
hardly ever found in books."
*Ed Burnett, President, Ed Burnett Consultants,
Englewood, NJ*

"I was very impressed with the content, format and conversa-
tional writing style. This handbook is very thorough, but yet it is
not overwhelming. In my opinion, this would be an excellent
resource for vocational teachers and counselors who address
entrepreneurship as a viable career opportunity."
*Mary W. Hendrix, Director, Educational Development &
Training Center, East Texas State University, Commerce, TX*

". . . the book should be appealing to a broad audience."
Professor Fran Jabara, Jabara Ventures Goup, Wichita, KS

"This is a serious and substantial work. . . . the author writes in a
terse, no-nonsense style that sticks to the subject in each chapter
and on every page. . . . Throughout the book it is evident that his
business philosophy is one that keeps profit firmly in mind as a
goal of business. . . . It should become the definitive book on the
subject."
*Herman Holtz, Entrepreneur and Author of business-oriented
books, Wheaton, MD*

"The book covers so many of the subjects that we've all seen
young business fail at. . . . simply because they didn't have the
basic business rules and guidelines to get them operating soundly.
. . . It should be a tremendous aid in reducing that failure rate for
students that look at all aspects of starting and operating their own
business. . . . I'm really impressed."
*Harry Turner, Jr., President, Harry Turner & Associates, Inc.
Topeka, KS*

Handbook on Building A Profitable Business

FRED KLEIN

Entrepreneurial Workshops Publications
Seattle, Washington

First printing - July 1990
Second printing - October 1990
Third printing - January 1991

Published by:

Entrepreneurial Workshops Publications
4000 Aurora Building
Seattle, Washington 98103
(206) 633-5350

Library of Congress, Catalogue Card Number: 89-083407

Klein, Fred
    Handbook On Building A Profitable Business
    ISBN 0-940995-01-8

This handbook is designed to provide accurate and authoritative information on the subject matter covered. It is sold with the understanding that the author and publisher is not engaged in rendering legal, accounting, or professional services within the scope of the book. If such expert assistance is required, the services of a professional should be obtained.

*To my wife, Vera, for the
unwavering support she gave me in
developing and writing this book.*

CONTENTS

CONTENTS (cont.)

CONTENTS (cont.)

CONTENTS (cont.)

A Message to the Reader

I have prepared the *Handbook on Building a Profitable Business* to personally assist you in your search to know more - and to do more - about your role as an entrepreneur. While this manual is not intended to cover every aspect of business down to the smallest detail, it will give you all the information you will need to start and manage a business profitably:

- It will help you evaluate the talents and capabilities you possess that will enable you to become a successful entrepreneur.

- It will inspire you to develop new ideas and will offer you solid guidance on how to improve your chances for success.

- It will provide guidelines to help you make start-up decisions and to find the best financing for your venture.

- It will tell you how to operate a successful business. You will learn strategies to help you deal with banks and management techniques to help you make effective decisions regarding purchasing, pricing, marketing, advertising, sales, production, and personnel matters.

Individuals who purchase this book show by this very act they possess the desire and will to become more successful. If you are thinking about starting a new business, you will benefit from this approach because it will assist you and inspire you to generate your own winning ideas - ideas that you can apply immediately. If you are already in business, you will learn how an alert management style can help you increase your profits.

This is not a textbook filled with theories; it is based on actual experience. In this respect, it goes far beyond most instructional books. My intention is not to convince you to start a business, but to help you decide whether you are ready. The ultimate objective is to provide insight and guidance on how to put your newly acquired knowledge into practice. Too many people start businesses when they are not properly prepared because of emotional, financial, family, or vocational problems.

On the other hand, there are those who are ready to honestly confront these obstacles and have the will, stability, and resources to overcome them. This manual will help you to identify these obstacles and then it will provide suggestions about how to manage them. It will steer you toward the types of businesses compatible with your qualifications, personal characteristics, and background.

You will find no case histories in this book. Although they make interesting reading, they also tend to give the impression that anyone can be successful by merely imitating the accomplishments of others. Nothing can be further from the truth as no two situations or individuals are alike. Your success will solely be due to your own way of thinking and doing things based on your personality, capabilities, and experiences. I believe that people who can think for themselves, when provided with solid facts and guidelines, do a better job in reaching the right decisions than those who follow a variety of so-called "winning plans" or who do things according to the book. Success can't be copied; you must develop it from within.

To obtain the maximum benefit from this, I recommend that you first read the text from cover to cover, then go back and study the parts which are of immediate concern to you. On the initial reading, you will obtain a complete overview of what entrepreneurship is all about. You will discover whether you have an entrepreneurial personality. You will learn about different types of businesses and their characteristics. You will explore the many ways you can enter a business, how to finance it and how to operate it profitably.

While reading, you will find it helpful to reference or highlight the parts of immediate interest to you. I also suggest that you make notes of any ideas and thoughts which occur to you which you should pursue further.

Make this handbook a permanent part of your business library. Read and reread it as you make plans to start and manage your own business. Each time, you will find more nuggets of wisdom that should help you clarify your thoughts to make those decisions that will make your business a great success.

Fred Klein
Seattle, Washington

WHERE DO I START?

When an entrepreneur has made a firm decision to enter business, a number of questions immediately occur.

What kind of business should I choose?

Shall I incorporate?

What about capital?

Where should I locate?

What licenses are required?

What are my chances to succeed?

These are *all* good questions, and you will find the answers in this handbook.

If you have no clear idea which business is right for you, refer to Your Business and Its Location (Section 4) and your personal inventory (Section 9).

Answers to questions about finances can be found in Section 5.

A discussion on sole proprietorships, partnerships and corporations can be found under Types of Ownership (Section 4).

Considerations for selecting a site can be found under Your Business and Its Location (Section 4).

For licensing, look up Getting Ready to Do Business (Section 4).

To evaluate your chances as an entrepreneur, refer to Section 9 on the Entrepreneurial Traits and The Entrepreneurial Self-Test.

Please note: This manual contains references to services offered by the U.S. Small Business Administration (SBA). Bear in mind that government rules and regulations do change from time to time. For critical questions, it is advisable to contact one of their offices to obtain information on the most current policies.

Section 1

THE ENTREPRENEUR TODAY AND BEYOND

More and more Americans are living the dream of owning their own businesses. The opportunities to be gained in starting a business and having it succeed have never been greater.

The most recent available Bureau of Labor Statistics report that from 1970 to 1983, the number of self-employed Americans rose by nearly one-third - to 9.2 million people.

Business growth should continue for many reasons. One is the rapid growth of two-income families. If one family member holds down a regular job, the other is in a good position to take on the risk of a business venture. Businesses which deal in services alone account for nearly one half of all small enterprises - and they are on the rise. They also require less start-up capital than other businesses.

Technological innovation also plays an important role. Small business can move quickly - often outperforming big business in responding to our rapidly expanding technology. Start-up entrepreneurs are finding challenges in new fields and are putting their ideas and expertise to work. Governmental deregulations also make the process of entering and doing business easier.

How important is experience in starting a business? It is obviously a strong plus-factor. New entrepreneurs generally have experience in their fields as well as in business management. For those who do not have general business experience, additional training in workshops, reading, talking with successful business managers and owners, and formal education are very helpful. Also training and experience in the field of your choice will increase the chances for success.

In recent years, the average age of start-up entrepreneurs has steadily dropped; it is now in the early 30s. By the year 2000, this trend is expected to continue with an increase in the number of entrepreneurs in their 20s.

More women and minority entrepreneurs of all age levels are also expected to make an impact. In 1977 there were one million women-owned businesses. By 1986 this figure has quadrupled to over four million. Women entrepreneurs today are mostly found in retail business, in service sectors and in specialties such as law, public relations, information management and data processing. The Small Business Administration (SBA) has responded to this shift by directing several programs toward women and minority enterprises.

There is a trend toward longer life expectancy, based on medical advances. This will result in larger markets for services and products for elders. Other factors are shorter work weeks and a rise in leisure or disposable time for the average American. This in turn will lead to bigger markets for sports, entertainment, travel and other leisure time products and services. Older Americans will be holding a good part of America's wallets, and will be more likely to purchase quality products and services and ignore inferior and fad items.

Another current trend is toward specialization. Cable/pay television networks, catering to specialized markets, give stiff competition to the more conventional television networks. Large businesses are often too complex to change course without slow, deliberate effort. This gives the smaller but more maneuverable business a real edge in the rapidly changing specialized markets. It means that highly specialized companies can carve out niche markets that can be very profitable.

What will the "hot" new industries of the future be? Here are a few representative categories:

> Personal Computer Repair and Software Markets
> Leisure Products and Services
> Do-It-Yourself Products and Information
> Health Care Products, Services and Information with special   attention
>   to the aged
> Biotechnology/Bioengineering
> Trendy Clothing and Accessories
> Specialty Retail Stores
> Security Services for Homes and Businesses
> Pre-packaged Foods

Another interesting study conducted by the SBA shows that the business failure rates are lowest in these industries:

> Beer and Wine Wholesalers
> Drug Stores
> Fuel and Ice Dealers
> Funeral Services
> Laundry, Cleaning and Garment Repair
> Personal Services (consulting, secretarial, etc.)
> Service Stations
> Wood Products

and some of the fastest-growing businesses are:

> Carpentry and Flooring
> Computer and Data Processing Services
> Inner-city Bus Transportation (private)
> Masonry, Stonework and Plastering
> Painting, Paperhanging and Decorating
> Radio, TV and Miscellaneous Stores
> Roofing and Structural Work

In summary, business trends for the 1990s and beyond point to:

- Growth of business starts - especially in the retail and service industries.

- A split in ages of start-up entrepreneurs - an increase in numbers of entrepreneurs in their 20s, as well as those in their 50s and 60s.

- Entry of greater numbers of women and minority entrepreneurs.

- An increase in the level of education of entrepreneurs - both in business and technology.

- Longer life expectancy, creating new markets aimed at older Americans, and larger markets for leisure time products and services.

- Increased specialization - a move away from large, generalized businesses. There are opportunities for those who are willing and able to recognize them and take action - now.

What Successful People Say About Being in Their Own Businesses

Well-established entrepreneurs who often started with very little, and now own and operate their own firms, agree on the advantages of being in business. Here are the three big factors they almost always emphasize:

- Personal Satisfaction
- Power and Influence
- Security and Unbounded Income Potential

Personal Satisfaction: Your business mirrors your skills and knowledge. Today, small business demands expertise. You must know your field well in order to compete. Your know-how and educational experiences can give you a decisive competitive edge. This can mean the difference between merely holding your own or being a spectacular success.

Being an entrepreneur helps you achieve a level of personal satisfaction you may never have experienced before. It gives you an enormous sense of independence and a feeling of being your own person. As an independent business person, you forever escape the boredom, routine and frustration you may have felt in working for others.

While you may spend more time in your own enterprise than in any job you ever held before, your new venture will be more enjoyable and meaningful. You set your own schedules and forget about previous restraints. As a result, the time clock is no longer a driving force in your life.

There is one limit on this extraordinary new freedom: No matter how high you rise in business, you will always have an ultimate boss - your customer. Your customer covers your payroll and provides your income and profits. As long as you meet the needs of your customers and give them the best possible service, you really *can't fail* in a company of your own.

Power and Influence: Being an entrepreneur opens the doors of power and influence to you. Owning a business involves you in every aspect of the operation, and correspondingly commands the respect of others.

Instead of standing there pulling a single lever, you are now in charge of the whole machine. You have the power to influence the entire course of the business through your own judgment. This power to make your own decisions gives you another advantage: You can make changes and move with much greater speed and agility than "big business" with its need for committees and consensus, and its restraints of taking risks.

As mentioned earlier, entrepreneurs find personal satisfaction by making their businesses reflect themselves. Satisfaction also flows from being independent and calling their own shots, and by having the control to change their businesses and lives in their corner of the world.

Security and Unlimited Income Potential: Your successful business translates to financial independence. As an entrepreneur, you will find ways to protect yourself and your family financially in a way that big business can't come close to matching.

In a business of your own, you do not face the risks of layoffs, mandatory retirement, being fired from a job or locked into a situation by internal politics. You have a direct and clear voice in assuring your own well-being. You create *your own* security.

Owning your own company is a very good way to increase income by reducing taxes. Successful entrepreneurs expect much greater income than is possible when working for a salary. This income is even more significant when tax deductions for insurance, auto use, travel and entertainment are considered. Using your private residence for business purposes is one more tax break opportunity open to you.

It is unrealistic, however, to expect a start-up business to produce an immediate bonanza. It *does* happen, but more often a new operation needs time to work up a head of steam. While working toward profitability, you will experience the gratification of seeing your efforts produce rewards.

You can expect your income to rise when your business begins to grow since increased sales almost always result in higher profits. Another important factor is the steadily increasing net worth of a successful business. In fact, a growing company presents a tremendous investment opportunity to outsiders who are looking for investments. While passive investments like stocks or real estate may appreciate up to 100 percent or more in a given time period, a robust business may yield a return of *thousands* of percentage points during a comparable period! The reason for this is the entrepreneur's intense involvement in the business.

Best of all is the fact that the 1990s present unique opportunities for a move into your own business. According to most of the men and women who took the plunge and *made* it, *the time is right* to start a company and prosper.

Family Considerations: If your enterprise happens to be a family business, it can provide employment for some of your family members. Aside from the financial advantages, this arrangement provides a business training ground for children and a place to teach and test family values. What better way to teach cooperation, the value of hard work, honesty and basic job skills?

The business may also offer job opportunities tailored to family members who have special needs. For example, it can furnish work for a handicapped family member. It is also an option for individuals whose family responsibilities make a more flexible work schedule necessary or desirable.

Also, a business can be passed on to a spouse or children, to protect your dependents' financial futures, or sold later at a profit.

What disadvantages does entrepreneurship carry? Initially, while the business develops, finances may be strained. Your family will need to set priorities for spending, and understand that sacrifices and belt-tightening may be necessary. They must realize that operating a business means working long hours - time that may be taken away from usual family activities. Like you, your family should know about the advantages a small business can bring, as well as the sacrifices they may have to make. You will need their full support.

Why Businesses Succeed

Contrary to popular opinion, statistics show that not many businesses fail in their first year of operation, perhaps only 2%. By the second year the failure rate goes up to 10% to 15%. After five years it may reach between 50% to 60%. Depending upon the nature of the business, the total failure rate may reach 80% after ten years.

This shows that the first five years are particularly critical. From then on, chance of failure decreases sharply. After ten years, most businesses that survive can expect to continue almost indefinitely.

Retail and service businesses show the highest initial failure rates - perhaps because they are the easiest to enter. The opportunity of easy entry is an invitation to go in ill-prepared. On the other hand, at the ten-year mark, retail and service businesses are the best survival candidates.

There are many reasons for business failures. Dun and Bradstreet, a national business credit and research firm, defines a failure as "A business being involved in legal proceedings or bankruptcy as a result of a business inability to pay its creditors". The study does not include voluntary liquidations where creditors are paid in full. They also report that well over 90% of business failures are related to poor planning and bad decisions, and lack of experience or business expertise. Less than two in every 100 fail because of neglect, fraud or disaster. Generally speaking, most business failures are caused by poor management. One of the objectives of this manual is to bring into focus the differences between good and poor business management.

The most frequently cited reasons for failure lie in insufficient experience or capabilities in the following areas:

- Poor marketing strategies
- Ineffective advertising
- Poor merchandising
- Inadequate sales
- Inability to meet competition
- Poor location
- Lack of understanding basic accounting
- Inadequate financing
- Excessive fixed or operating expenses
- Difficulties with receivables
- Inventory problems
- Personnel problems

This manual deals with all of the above-listed problems. But if you still feel a need for a better understanding and knowledge in these areas, do not hesitate to enroll in classes dealing with these subjects. Contact trade organizations in the line of business you are planning to enter for further information. Talk to consultants in specific fields.

Spend enough time to research your proposed business. Is there a market for your goods or services now? What about its future prospects? Where should it be located? What problems should you anticipate internally or from your competition? Who will your competition be? One strategy to increase your chance for success is to discuss your plans with owners of businesses similar to yours. You will be surprised how helpful most of these people will be.

A great deal can be learned by joining trade organizations in your chosen field and staying active within those associations. Also, attend their meetings and conventions. Being in close touch with people in your field will increase your likelihood of success. Some of the most successful entrepreneurs attribute a large part of their success to a combination of all of those contacts.

Make realistic estimates of your start-up and continuing capital requirements. To obtain adequate financing and stay within your budget limits, you may enlist the help of your accountant.

Plan ahead by preparing a formal business plan. Such a plan gives you a useful summary of goals and keeps your business growing within your financial capabilities. By spelling out your objectives in writing, you will gain a better insight of what you want to accomplish now and in the future. These guidelines are also helpful during times of crises in reminding you to stay the course. Your banker and consultants can be helpful in giving you ideas on how your business plan should be structured.

We will later go into much more extensive detail on how to make your business successful.

Section 2

A PENETRATING LOOK AT THE POTENTIAL IN A BUSINESS OF YOUR OWN

This section gives you a broad overview on the risks and rewards a small business owner faces. It calls your attention to the critical areas to be considered by you, the entrepreneur. Based on your experience and financial resources, the following information will make it easier for you to evaluate your chances of succeeding in the business you choose.

Some of the key points discussed here, such as personnel management and financing, will be described in greater detail later in the handbook. We will also compare the small business environment with that existing in big business. This will be particularly helpful to you if you are accustomed to big business and not familiar with small company operations.

Small Business Compared to Big Business

An important aspect of small business lies in the ability of management to operate flexibly. Policies are not set in concrete and there are no rigid rules on how day-to-day operations are to be conducted. This enables you to put your ideas and plans into action quicker, particularly in times of rapidly changing business conditions.

One of the most commonly overlooked advantages of a small business is *size*. Working with a limited number of employees makes it possible for the owner to have closer one-on-one contact. By staying in touch with your people, you can give them more personal input, and therefore encourage increased involvement.

Experience shows that in small business, employees more often provide innovative ideas, and participate in the decision-making process. This results in a happier and more effective group of co-workers. Also interesting is the fact that employees lose less time due to illness or accidents.

If you know your employees' capabilities and trust their judgment, it will benefit the business in two ways:

- First, it provides you with the opportunity to delegate more tasks. This will reduce your routine workload and allows you to concentrate on planning and on other high-priority projects.

- It also increases your employees' skills, productivity and their desire to do a good job. This doesn't necessarily mean that every one of your employees would *want* a wider range of responsibility and more variety in their work. But those who do will respond positively to the trust placed in them.

In assigning authority and responsibilities, it is important to consider the abilities and limitations of your people. The end result of this approach will be a more productive workforce with fewer personnel problems that will almost certainly reflect favorably on the bottom line of your financial statement.

Close, personal relationships with your suppliers can likewise be a great advantage to a small business. As a result, you may obtain faster service, better prices and terms and other preferential treatment.

The entrepreneur should also stay in close personal touch with customers. In any business, small or large, the customer is the ultimate boss. He can make or break you. In a small business you have the opportunity to give your customers more personalized attention. If you keep them satisfied, they can be the source of some of the most effective word-of-mouth advertising for you. They also can give you new ideas for making changes and improving your products or services. The more you get to know them as individuals, the better you can respond to their needs. This will result in repeat business which is the lifeblood of *any* enterprise.

There are three major areas where we can compare advantages and disadvantages between small and big business:

- Competitive Strength
- Ability to absorb losses
- Hiring and retaining key personnel

The first item is *Competitive Strength*. Big business has more competitive power than a start-up, or even a well-established small business. The large firm also has greater financial resources and assets; a well-known record of performance; name-recognition, and a reputation that took a long time to build. But this does not mean that big business has a lock on the market. Small business has an almost unlimited ability to find niches or specialized markets that big business has failed to capture or has simply overlooked.

The second area where big business has an advantage over small business is *its ability in coping with reverses successfully*. By virtue of size and resources, a loss that can be absorbed by big business may cause a small business to fail. Big business simply has deeper pockets when a sales slump or credit losses occur. It also has better access to favorable financing for acquisition of equipment and expansion.

Third, small business often has difficulty in *hiring and retaining competent personnel* due to its limited resources. A small business can't always offer salary or benefit packages that rival those offered by big business. However, creative use of profit-sharing and other incentive plans can often make up for some of these differences.

Since management positions available in big business are limited, good management people often consider working for a small company and are willing to negotiate salary and benefits. The difficulty of hiring and keeping key people can be overcome by offering creative compensation packages, and paying careful attention to employee needs. It is also obvious that not everyone wants to work for a big business.

Other Challenges Small Businesses Face

It is well known that problems can be turned into opportunities. Most difficulties in small business can be traced to poor management and inadequate financing.

One of the most important factors in the successful management of your business is how you manage *yourself*. That is, how you use your time, energy, and how you set priorities. You have to decide on the areas you can personally impact the most to make your business function best. This handbook gives you the tools you need to begin shaping yourself into an effective manager.

One of the requirements in effective management - including self-management - is to possess the capacity to be in control of your time; also to set priorities that you and your employees must follow to achieve maximum results. It's the ability to decide who does what and to schedule the sequence of steps that must be taken to accomplish tasks within certain time-frames. It is the competence to delegate projects to the right people and follow up on their performance on a regular basis.

Let us take a brief look at financial concerns in a small business. The most common is a lack of adequate funds. This is often due to being unable to raise sufficient funds to cover anticipated and unexpectedly high start-up costs.

There are ways to minimize this problem by careful planning. Spending too much initially on fixed assets, such as equipment and supplies can be a pitfall. These expenditures may not leave enough money to cover the working capital required to operate the business. Poor management of inventory - buying too much or too little - is also a hidden danger. Even with careful planning, lack of experience in this area can put a business in a precarious situation.

Too-liberal credit terms to customers can create cash shortages. If your experience in credit management is limited, your accountant can assist you in deciding how much credit you can afford to extend, and under what terms. In retail and service businesses you can offer credit through the use of major credit cards. The companies that back these cards are responsible for their collections. You can cash the credit card slips signed by the customer at your bank in the same way as you would deposit cash or checks, but a fee will be charged for this service.

A problem that too often results from inexperience is improper pricing of goods. Keeping in touch with your suppliers and competitors can help you make better more profitable decisions in this area.

It is easy to underestimate the value of effective advertising. You must know where your markets are and the best ways to reach them. Do not hesitate to make use of consultants such as small advertising agencies or representatives of various media (magazines, direct mail, TV, newspapers, radio, etc.) to get ideas on the most cost-effective approaches.

Also important is your insurance planning. A small business is extremely vulnerable to losses. You cannot anticipate all the problems, but you should plan carefully to cover the business for ordinary and catastrophic losses such as fire, flooding, windstorms, and losses due to theft, vandalism, arson, or other criminal activity, as well as the liability for on-site injuries or damages tied to your product or service. Insurance is far less costly than having your business foot the bill for settlement of these claims, or repair of damages. Insurance is almost always a cost-effective expense. Under-insured businesses can go bankrupt due to claims caused by just one single incident.

Briefly summarizing, the major advantages of small business as compared to big business include:

Opportunities for personalizing employee, supplier, and customer relations, resulting in greater productivity and market control.

Flexible management, resulting in business that can respond rapidly to changing markets and allow personal innovation.

Focusing on markets small or specialized enough to escape attention and competition by big business.

Self-management, including time management, task delegation, and broadening your base of experience.

Financial management considerations include:

Raising adequate funds and allocating them wisely.

Proper handling of credit purchases.

Pricing, quality control, advertising and adequate insurance.

The Rewards

Rewards fall into two categories: Monetary and psychological. If your business is to be a success rather than merely a survivor, you will experience financial success and enjoy an excellent income. In fact, a thriving business can show profits to an extent you never thought possible before. It can become an excellent investment as its assets often will appreciate at an astounding rate. Securities and real estate investments appreciate in a somewhat predictable manner. A profitable business can, however, show a total return of 10 to 100 times over stocks and tangible asset investments in a comparable period of time. As a result, your business can provide you with a comfortable retirement income and an estate for your heirs.

What about the psychological rewards of a successful business?

First of all, they present you with a sense of freedom for personal accomplishment that overshadows all the other rewards. Again, money is the measure of accomplishment rather than a goal in itself.

Entrepreneurs are driven primarily by psychological rather than by financial needs. Business provides freedom from being confined to an assembly line type of job. It lets you make your own decisions without having to go through channels - and frequently being turned down - as it often happens in corporate managerial structures. This freedom to put ideas into action is the ultimate test of entrepreneurial accomplishment.

For most entrepreneurs, the business is an extension of themselves. It provides a way to test and re-test their self-worth and ability to use skills. The "game" of business competition also gives you the opportunity to measure your skills against the skills of others. It adds the excitement of a continuing challenge to your life. For the most part, entrepreneurs measure their self-worth by testing their abilities and showing accomplishments.

The Risks

First, what are some general risks? Failure rates for small businesses are low during the first year of a start-up, but can rise to as high as 80 in every 100 within ten years. Studies by business research firms tie greater than 90% of business failures to poor management and inexperience; that is, 9 out of 10 business failures relate to management problems. An individually owned and operated business is also more sensitive to the economy. A recession, or a surge of interest rates that big business can ride out, can hurt small businesses. You will need to carefully plan ahead and do all the research necessary to anticipate trends in order to help insure your venture's survival and success.

This picture may seem rather stark, but it is part of the reality of owning your own business. After we discuss risks in general, we will show how they can be turned into opportunities.

What personal risks does business ownership carry? One possibility is that your business may survive, but not show any profits. Your long-term success depends on its profitability. Even by showing profits, there are no guarantees that they will be sufficient to give you your projected income. You may be frustrated in trying to reach your personal financial goals if your business grows more slowly than you had expected. On the other hand, rapid expansion and uncontrolled growth (such as in premature opening of additional locations) can present a serious problem, too. It can lead to a shortage of working capital and loss of managerial control over the operation. Many entrepreneurs are initially thrilled when their business suddenly expands beyond their wildest dreams. But, unless they can move quickly in obtaining the right kind of financing and qualified personnel to handle the increased volume, they can find themselves unable to cope with that growth.

Another factor in a fast-growth situation is that it could put more stress on the entrepreneur than he can handle, adversely affecting his health and ability to function effectively.

Section 3

SPECIAL GROUPS OF ENTREPRENEURS

Even if you do not identify yourself with any of the special groups discussed here, you will benefit greatly by reviewing this section. If you, in that process, gain only *one* valuable idea, it will be worth the time it took to do it. Women, minorities, inventors, senior citizens and a host of others have found unique challenges in the world of business. What we are about to discuss here are challenges, opportunities and also some of the obstacles that special groups are facing in addition to those that all entrepreneurs encounter. You will also learn that being a member of a special group also holds certain advantages.

The groups this manual covers are:

- Women Entrepreneurs
- Minority Entrepreneurs
- School/College Age Entrepreneurs
- Entrepreneurial Mothers and Single Parent Entrepreneurs
- Husband/Wife Teams
- Inventors
- Handicapped Entrepreneurs
- Immigrants

Women and minority entrepreneurs face the same kind of challenges and obstacles as do white males - plus some additional ones. Some of these hurdles are real and some may be perceived. There are many women and minority entrepreneurs who have lifted themselves up by their bootstraps. How? By simply refusing to accept that there are any barriers to stop them from reaching their goals. It takes determination and persistence to overcome obstacles. It probably takes more effort and stubbornness than is typically put forth by some of their white male peers.

For those who succeed, there are great rewards. Successful women and minority entrepreneurs will suddenly find themselves just as respected and accepted as their peers are.

Women Entrepreneurs

The number of women managers and business owners is growing rapidly as more and more women enter business. Most women entrepreneurs start service or retail businesses. Service businesses have lower start-up costs than many other enterprises and are usually easier to finance. Women usually have a natural "in" to service and retail businesses because their job experience so often lies in one or both of these areas.

Opportunities and Rewards for Women Entrepreneurs

Many of the rewards you can expect as a woman entrepreneur are similar to those of other entrepreneurs: personal satisfaction, security, and financial success.

One aspect that has greater significance to most women is greater independence - knowing that you have not only the ability, but the opportunities to make your own decisions and have more control on how to run your life. Since self-esteem is an important need for most entrepreneurs, and studies show that many women have low self-esteem and a strong need to feel good about themselves, this reward seems all the more important. Self-esteem needs are met in two ways: Getting messages from others that you, and what you are doing, is important or valuable. And personally feeling and believing that you, and the things you do, are important.

Security is also important. It means being protected against risks such as being demoted or laid off. By becoming an entrepreneur, you provide your own security and protect yourself against any lack of chances for job advancement. You also need not be concerned about a well-paying job, or missing opportunities that could be open to you as a man but are closed to you as a woman. Despite legal attempts to help open more opportunities for women, equality in the workplace has not yet been achieved. However, becoming an entrepreneur makes you the manager and decision maker.

Special Challenges for Women Entrepreneurs

Women face the same difficulties as male entrepreneurs but sometimes have additional hurdles to clear. There are three areas of special challenge for women entrepreneurs - financial, educational, and psychological or cultural.

First, you may find that you have difficulty getting financing from lenders, especially banks and savings and loan associations. You may face the same difficulty in getting funding from relatives, friends or investors. Intentional sexual discrimination can be a part of this, but more likely it is based on attitudes toward women that are slow to change.

One way to bypass these road blocks is to find out where other women entrepreneurs in your community have obtained their funds, then concentrate on establishing strong business relationships with these institutions. Approach one or more of their loan officers, acquaint them with your ideas and plans and keep in touch with them until you are ready to make a loan application. You will also learn a great deal about alternate financing sources by talking with other successful women entrepreneurs in your area, and you may find that some of these women are willing to give you financial backing as well as advice.

Another promising possibility is to check with the closest women-owned/operated bank. Women's banks have been growing in numbers. They have standards similar to other banks for granting loans, but can offer you loans and services if you qualify, regardless of your sex. Many also offer financial planning and financial management workshops. For further information refer to SBA Loan Facts in Section 5.

If you are married, you may also find that your funding is tied to your husband's income or credit history, and he may be required to offer collateral or co-sign your loans. If you are unmarried or divorced, you will usually not be able to get financing without first establishing your own credit history. The credit history you shared with your former husband is not usually acceptable to lenders as your own. If you are married, you will want to begin establishing *a separate line of credit* as a matter of good business practice.

Another aspect of financing for women entrepreneurs is obtaining continuing commitments for financing from banks. So it is essential to develop good business relationships with your banker or other lenders so that, before your start-up funds are gone, you will have these other commitments in place. Again, check with the SBA, keep in close touch with your banker or loan advisor, and remain in contact with successful entrepreneurs (both male and female) about backing you or suggesting other funding sources.

You will want to ask local women in business about their funding sources, and check with your Chamber of Commerce for listings of local business associations, business groups, and community development corporations. Some, though not all, communities will have funds earmarked for women and minority businesses. National or regional women's business associations are also good sources for information about special financial programs which are financial grants that do not have to be repaid. The General Services Administration (GSA) can provide you with a current list of these national associations.

Education or experience can be another area of special concern for women. Younger women in general have had more formal education than older women, usually at least by finishing high school and often having completed some college courses. Younger women are also more likely to have some paid work experience.

For older women, much of their experience has been in home management or volunteer work. That experience is not always recognized as valuable by resume screeners or by potential lenders. So you may have to work harder to convince lenders that you have the skills and organizational capabilities to make your business a success and their investment less risky. It is not enough to be competent; you also need to be able to sell others on your ideas and abilities.

How do you convince institutions and lenders about your skills and abilities if you don't have much experience or formal education and may even have some doubts about yourself? Your Personal Inventory in Section 9 of this manual is a helpful reminder of the wide variety of abilities you already possess. Where you achieved abilities is not as important as the fact that you have them and can demonstrate how you have used them.

One area that women often need to strengthen is their math/accounting skills. Weakness in this area can lead to poor business planning and business analysis. If this is not one of your strong suits, back yourself up with outside help, and consider taking a math refresher or accounting class.

A final area of concern for women is psychological or cultural. Women often have smaller personal networks than men. That is, fewer people they regularly meet with. This is because women tend to separate their home, work and social or recreational contacts. With men, recreation and work contacts often overlap, as in sports activities, in meetings after work and in other social situations with the same people they work with. Women's friendships are usually on a one-to-one basis rather than in groups. This may mean fewer total opportunities to make meaningful connections with people who will later be useful in their businesses. You can, however, increase your chances of meeting with potential investors or advisors by searching out people who are in your field of interest and discuss with them your business ideas and needs. You can widen that network by beginning early to join local business, trade and social organizations and by attending conventions in your industry.

One characteristic of a successful entrepreneur is aggressiveness or "drive". This is sometimes thought of as a male trait. However, women have these traits, as well. Drive is the determined attitude that keeps you on-track toward goals and keeps you from quitting when the going gets tough. Assertiveness is important. By being assertive, you move toward your goals and stand up for yourself, but respect other people's rights as well. This makes assertiveness and drive very different from being obnoxious and pushy.

Most successful women entrepreneurs have strong emotional ties to their fathers, or to another supportive male in the family. He was important in at least two ways. First, he acted as a role model. He was looked up to, and his behavior or attitudes were in some ways copied. Second, most successful women entrepreneurs report that these men accepted them as people, and expected them to do whatever they were capable of, whether or not it "fit" for usually accepted female behavior.

Special Programs for Women

There are many national organizations for businesswomen and women entrepreneurs. Among the largest of these is the National Association of Women Business Owners - NAWBO. This organization has local chapters in most major cities, and offers the chance to broaden your range of business contacts and keep you in touch with local and nationwide business trends. It also offers seminars on business management and financing. Check with the SBA or your local library for a current list of national women's business groups. Most groups charge an initiation fee and dues. Before you invest in a membership, check out their activities with officers and members of the organization to determine if they meet your goals. The same holds true of local groups. They can be easily located through your local Chamber of Commerce.

Another avenue to help prepare yourself for your business career, or to strengthen your skills, is offered by the Center for Women's Opportunities of the American Association of Community Colleges and Junior Colleges. The Center offers courses nationwide through community and junior colleges, either individually, or as a 45 credit-hour package. Junior, community colleges or vocational schools can also offer relatively low-cost courses in communications, assertiveness training, stress management and other classes that can add to your regular business skills.

In summary, there are few significant differences in traits for male and female entrepreneurs, but women do face some extra challenges and obstacles to business entry and success. Main barriers fall into two groups:

Financial - getting the backing to start and provide ongoing financing for the business.

Cultural - dealing with or breaking down the stereotypes that women are less capable managers or "belong" only in certain business fields or job roles.

You can deal with the financial aspects in a number of ways. Take advantage of special loan programs, women's banks and conventional banks.

Begin to establish a credit history, even if you are married and assume you have a lengthy shared credit history. Finally, look for backing by relatives or business and other contacts.

Cultural barriers in accepting women in business change very slowly. Perhaps your best way to deal with this is to get family support, develop a support network that includes successful male and female role models, and work on improving your spoken communications skills.

As a woman entrepreneur, you will have all the rewards open to other entrepreneurs, plus special rewards in personal satisfaction and security.

Minority Entrepreneurs

The numbers of minority business owners are rising. Yet, there are still relatively few minority entrepreneurs. Like the stereotypes that exist for women, attitudes against minorities do not disappear with just a change of the law.

Opportunities and Rewards for Minority Entrepreneurs

Becoming an entrepreneur gives you a wide range of opportunities and rewards. As a minority entrepreneur, you have special concerns and needs that may make some rewards more important or meaningful to you than they might be for a person who is not a member of your minority group. You will confront all the obstacles other entrepreneurs face, and may experience more difficulties in obtaining financing. But remember, making your own opportunities is something you have in common with other minority entrepreneurs, and many of the other special groups of entrepreneurs we are discussing.

Being able to establish your own security and your own opportunities is an extremely important reward for you as a minority entrepreneur. You create your own management position, and have control over your tasks and income. Part of your security is being able to produce a comfortable or even outstanding income for your hard work.

By opening doors of opportunity for yourself, you may also make it easier for other members of your group or your family to follow in your footsteps in the future. As a minority group sees its members becoming successful, the more likely it is that they will set their personal goals for the same kind of success. Having successful role models encourages people to dream and follow a pattern for success.

Like opportunities for women, not all doors to minority business opportunities can be opened easily. But, if enough people try, they eventually will succeed. If you play down or ignore instances of discrimination, you may find that people will be more likely to notice your business skills rather than your minority status.

Finally, you will acquire a wide variety of rewards in personal satisfaction. One gain is in feeling that you have more power and control in running your own life and making your own breaks. Another is the knowledge that what you are doing is important, and that you are doing it well. Still another is having customers recommend you to others and give you their continued business. All of these things add to your personal satisfaction and can increase your self-esteem feelings of personal value. You may have more obstacles to overcome than your male counterparts, but you can gain the same or greater respect as other successful entrepreneurs.

Special Problems and Concerns for Minority Entrepreneurs

One of the obstacles you may face is difficulty in the area of financing. If you have not had an upper level management position in business, you may have little experience to show that you have the background to manage a business. For this reason, you may be turned down for loans as a poor risk even if your other qualifications for loans are acceptable.

If you have difficulties in getting financing, take advantage of government and private financial programs open to entrepreneurs in general, and any special programs for minority entrepreneurs.

One of the best ways to find local financing is by asking successful minority entrepreneurs about their funding sources. Also, check with your Chamber of Commerce and local community development corporations about funding and any special programs for minority entrepreneurs.

The General Services Administration (GSA) or the library can give you a current list of general and minority business associations and groups in your area who can give you further information on local funding. Your local branch of the Small Business Administration has information and descriptions of federal loan programs.

Getting involved in local and national business associations increases your business contacts and puts you in touch with a larger number of potential investors. Increasing your contacts with non-minority business people may also help you better understand their points of view, and make it easier for you to communicate well with customers and business contacts outside your minority group. At the same time, it gives these people a chance to see you as a person, and learn how different you are from any pre-conceived ideas they may have held.

Also think about attending communications or assertiveness training classes, and look for situations where you can be with people outside your group so you can observe how they communicate with each other.

You will need to keep in mind that it is advantageous and profitable to deal with non-minority suppliers and customers. But, if you do not feel comfortable with these people, you can target your own group as a market.

Special Programs for Minority Entrepreneurs

A good resource for minority women entrepreneurs is the National Association of Black Women Entrepreneurs, which is open to women entrepreneurs of all races. The NAACP (National Association for the Advancement of Colored People) is also a source for referrals to local and national programs. Finally, the GSA can provide a list of national minority business groups and associations.

In summary, the picture for minority business managers and entrepreneurs is getting brighter, but the change is slow since it is usually easier to change laws than ideas and prejudices. Business provides minority entrepreneurs with the chance to make a niche for themselves in the world of commerce.

Minorities may face discrimination in financing, but they can deal with this by increasing their business and social contacts, getting legal backup where necessary, and looking for minority lenders or lenders with a history of good relations with minority business people.

Minorities may also be limited by cultural and language differences, and for that reason face discrimination on the part of customers and suppliers. These problems can be lessened by working on communications skills and, on some occasions, by using non-minority individuals as go-betweens when dealing with sensitive accounts.

School/College-Age Entrepreneurs

At this time, over 100,000 companies in the United States have owners who are less than 20-years old. The number is probably much higher if one adds unlisted or unregistered businesses to that figure. Working your way through college is certainly nothing new. What *is* new, however, is that more and more of these businesses are not just for the purpose of paying for tuition. Their owners expect to continue with them even after finishing school.

Because of the ease of financing, most of these businesses are in service areas, and many are aimed at the school or college-age market.

Opportunities and Rewards for School/College-age Entrepreneurs

As a school or college-age entrepreneur, you have many of the same opportunities as other entrepreneurs. Your age can be a special door-opener, since the college or school environment exposes you to many potential customers in your age bracket, and your familiarity with other students' interests and needs.

You may be operating your business just to pay for school. In this case, the reward you will be most interested in is money. Your business can pay for itself almost from the word "go". You invest very little money, and begin to make profits quickly. Since your investment is small, your risks are low. However, you *do* need to make a big investment in energy; what you lack in money, you will have to make up for in enthusiasm and hard work.

Another reward in operating your own business is that it allows you to be more independent. You make your own decisions. Also, you may make not only enough money to put yourself through school, but to support yourself afterwards. This can give you the satisfaction and security of being more in charge of your own life.

Your business in school or college gives you some other kinds of assets to build on after you leave or graduate. First, you have business management experience at a very young age. Second, you will have a business track record or reputation, and business contacts. Third, you will have an existing business to continue, expand or sell. This is turn can help you pay to start another business.

Finally, it can provide the experience you need to begin establishing your credibility as a business person.

When it comes to financing your enterprise, it is important that you establish a solid credit history. This can be achieved by starting to take small loans and paying them off promptly. One other way is to get a co-signer. This person is usually a parent or relative who signs with you for your loan and guarantees repayment if you do not pay it back.

Another way to obtain a loan is to offer collateral. Collateral is something you own that can be sold, traded, or given to the lender to cover the amount of your loan if you do not repay it. Or, you can offer a lender, "matching funds". This means that you will take a loan for the same amount of money as you have on deposit in a bank or other lending institution.

Finally, your credit history is also built on how well you take care of expenses such as rent, telephone bills, car payments, credit card payments, and other obligations.

Special Concerns for School/College-age Entrepreneurs

Probably the biggest hurdle for you to overcome as a school or college-age entrepreneur is getting finances. For some businesses, however, you can really do without major financing. In a service business, you can often start off by simply covering the cost of a newspaper ad or photocopying your own brochure or advertisement. For a little more money, you can have business cards made. For some businesses - especially those dealing with food, you may need a special business license. Check this carefully with your city and state business licensing office for applicable licensing laws.

If your enterprise requires more financing than you can get on your own, think about taking on a partner, or applying at banks or savings and loan associations. Because of your age and inexperience, you will have to work extra hard to convince loan officers that your business plans are serious, workable, and that you will deliver what you promise.

Since you are in school, you may find that dividing your time between school and work can sometimes be difficult. It is important to control how fast your business grows and how you use your time so you get what you want out of school and your business. Sometimes this can mean turning down work and foregoing profits in order to protect your progress in school.

Programs for School/College-age Entrepreneurs

There are few financial programs aimed at school or college-age entrepreneurs. Refer to Section 5 under SBA Loan Facts for financing information. The SBA can also give you information on other local loan possibilities. Their SCORE counselors (Service Corps of Retired Executives) can also give you good general advice on starting and managing your business. These same options are open to *all* entrepreneurs.

If you are in junior high or high school, Junior Achievement Clubs take you step-by-step through starting, running and selling a business. You get hands-on experience in business with people your own age, and your club advisors have successful businesses of their own. Distributive Education Clubs of America - DECA - also gives you an early step into business as a high school student. If you are in college, check with your student-body association about entrepreneurs' associations and business clubs, which are growing nationwide. They get involved in business groups outside of your campus so that you have valuable outside business contacts when you leave school or graduate.

If you are in a community or junior college, take advantage of the special courses offered in Small Business Management, and related courses such as Time-Management, Stress-Management, and Communications.

In summary, recently more school or college-age people have been starting their own enterprises with the idea of creating business for its own sake, and not just to pay for school. One of your biggest hurdles may be to convince financial backers that you have or can put together a workable, profitable "legitimate" business. And that you will deliver on your promise to repay a loan. However, if you can't get adequate financing, you may have to start with a very small operation requiring a minimum amount of money, and begin building up your credit history and a base of solid business contacts.

A business, operated while you are in school or college, can reward you with more independence and security. And it can yield the finances you need for your education, plus seed money for starting another business.

Retired/Semi-Retired Entrepreneurs

The number of retired or semi-retired people becoming entrepreneurs is growing. Part of this is due to medical advances which lead to longer lives and a corresponding increase in the number of elders in our society. These people often retire in good health, and can expect to be productive far beyond usual retirement age.

Many of these retirees will be financially secure, with good pension plans and Social Security backup. Others will have to rely solely on Social Security. Most will find their reduced income shrink even further because of inflation, and they are vitally interested in earning additional income.

Other retirees want to continue working to meet their self-esteem needs by continuing to deal with challenges. These people make the most of their investment dollars and continue to enhance their lifestyles.

The experience gained over a lifetime of employment give retirees a good start in launching successful enterprises.

Opportunities and Rewards for Retired/Semi-retired Entrepreneurs

Retirees who are entrepreneurs can look forward to special rewards in three areas. One of them is personal satisfaction. As an older person in our society, you face many messages that you are no longer valuable, or that you are somehow worth less than a younger person with the same skills. This can be very hard on one's self-confidence; the more you hear this, the more likely you are to start believing it. Starting your own business gives you a proving ground to show yourself and others that you are valuable, have good ideas, and the capability and experience to make your ideas work. People who are not active can wither away. But a small business gives you opportunities to keep growing and face new challenges.

Personal satisfaction may also come from having new creative opportunities that you didn't have before retirement. You can now decide what you want to do and when you want to do it. There is a general belief that older people go straight from the time-clock to the rocking chair. But going into business can prove to you and *everybody else* what you really can accomplish. Your previous experience and knowledge of businesses in general can give you a better idea than younger people may have as to the type of business to start. You may also have more long-standing business and social contacts in the community, which can prove invaluable in starting a business.

Security is also important. If you are close to retirement age, you may be concerned about being transferred out of your job. Or, you may even face mandatory retirement, or a layoff. Your business can create an estate that you can pass on to your family as a going enterprise in which they can be involved in as managers or employees.

You may also be concerned about how well your pension or retirement plan will cover your financial requirements or desires. You can have the business as a source of income, or to give yourself the "extras" you might otherwise miss. As mentioned earlier, the income from your business can provide you with the chance to maintain or *better* the lifestyle you had before retirement.

Special Considerations for Retired/Semi-retired Entrepreneurs

There are factors to consider for older entrepreneurs. One is obtaining financing. An advantage of your age and experience is the likelihood that you have a well-established credit history - a plus factor when it comes to approval of loans.

On the other hand, if credit has been a problem in the past, you may face difficulties since the lender may be concerned about collecting if you should die or face major medical problems. A lender evaluating your loan request may decide that you will not be physically or mentally capable of managing the business long enough to pay off the debt.

You could consider approaching friends in your age group who are looking for investment opportunities and are willing to back your venture financially. Also, be aware of the possibility that if you back your business with your personal savings and outside loans - and the business does not succeed - you will have that much less to fall back on for your self-support.

If you are already retired, and your major source of income is from Social Security, check the provisions of the laws carefully before you start a business. There is a limit on what you can earn without losing part or all of your Social Security benefits. Your choice will be whether to expand the business so that your earnings make up for any lost benefits, or keep it small enough so that you do not lose benefits. After you reach the age of 70, there are no further earning restrictions and you can get your full Social Security benefits regardless of how much you earn.

Unless you are aware of some disabilities or health problems that are apt to get worse, you should have no more difficulty than a young person in starting a business. If your energy or health present problems, think of keeping your business size small. In addition, get help with your home duties and consider sharing business responsibilities with family members. It will also be important to protect your business with definitive arrangement for succession or liquidation if you should have major health problems or die.

Special Programs for Retired or Semi-retired Entrepreneurs

SCORE is an excellent group of counselors in your age group who can help you make plans for your retirement business. You can get in contact with a SCORE counselor by checking in your telephone directory under United States Government offices for the nearest local SBA branch. These services are free.

Talking with other retirees who are running their own businesses can also help you make plans for your own business and find financing sources. Some of these retirees may also be looking for investment opportunities, so do not pass them by as possible financing sources.

In summary, America is aging. Our older population is growing steadily. Along with this growth, more elderly Americans are becoming entrepreneurs. Medical advancements that allow these people to expect better health well beyond retirement mean that more and more Americans will have the choice to use their retirement years to start their own businesses. They can expect to be healthy enough to start these businesses, make them work, and enjoy the rewards.

Some major benefits for you as a retiree who becomes an entrepreneur include personal satisfaction; making opportunities for work despite your age; providing the income needed to maintain or improve your lifestyle, and providing an estate for your loved ones.

Mothers and Single Parents as Entrepreneurs

At this time, over half of the married women in this country who have preschool children also have jobs. And the number of working mothers is increasing. Along with this, the number of single parent entrepreneurs - who are mostly mothers - is also steadily rising.

In addition to the opportunities and rewards open to entrepreneurs in general, a business provides entrepreneurial single parents special rewards and opportunities in three major areas: freedom, pride and security. Mothers considering going into business usually think of themselves as mothers first and business women second, so the opportunity to bring parenting and work closer together is important.

One very important opportunity a business provides is a flexible schedule and the opportunity to have your child with you during business hours. A business lets you put your ideas and creativity into action and offers you an arena in which to solve problems, test your skills and express yourself. As you succeed at this, your self-confidence and belief in your own abilities grow. Your added income also gives you a way to have a bigger role in supporting your family, and more opportunity to have the things you want. The more useful you can be to others, the more valuable you will feel to yourself. This boosts your self-esteem and self-confidence.

Your business can also shorten your path to personal security. You can create your own opportunities for career advancement, shape your own job and control the environment in which you work . These opportunities essentially eliminate the dangers of being laid off, fired, or not being allowed to advance in your career.

Another part of this security is that you can make a place for yourself in the business world no matter how the job market is. If most of your experience has been in home management, you may find that the regular job market has no room for you. This may also be true if you do not have as much formal education as your competitors in the job market. But your business gives you a place to utilize your experience, and expand it.

Special Problems and Concerns for Entrepreneurial Mothers and Single Parents

Businesses that are home-based are often not taken seriously by lenders or customers. They are not always seen as authentic as other businesses. You will want to think about the pros and cons of moving your business away from your home.

Another aspect in being an entrepreneurial mother may be that your credit history is tied to your husband's. If his credit record is poor, even while yours is spotless, you will need to establish credit in your own name, which can take time. If your marriage is unstable and you intend to go ahead with your business, you will also need to protect the business legally so that if your marriage ends your business will not be divided between you and your husband as community property. An attorney can advise you on these matters.

Aside from the financial support you may get from your husband and family, also think of all your social contacts as possible backers. Do not discount help from people you meet in your children's school or preschool, and other groups you are involved in. Consider increasing your regular business contacts and obtaining advice from consultants on funding.

Be aware of spreading yourself too thin; for example, your family responsibilities may limit the growth of your business. One unique problem for the entrepreneurial mother is the "Super Mom Syndrome". Super Moms are expected to run the home, raise children, and conduct the business single-handedly. To guard against this, make a list of your responsibilities -to yourself, to your family, and to the business. After you have done this, you will need to decide what you can and can't reasonably do. You may want to consider task-sharing with your husband; getting outside help to take care of your home and children while running the business, and setting limits on how big you want the enterprise to become. Single-parent entrepreneurs face essentially the same concerns as other entrepreneurial parents, but without the support of a spouse.

You should consider some of the added risks in making your business succeed if your background in business is weak. You can make up for this by asking the right questions, reading, attending workshops, taking courses and using outside consultants. Many businesses take very little training beyond the skills you use to run your home, so don't downplay the skills you already have.

Use your volunteer contacts and reputation to help establish your credibility, and to "sell" your business plans to financial backers.

If you are an entrepreneurial mother, you also face the concerns common to other female entrepreneurs. Your position as an entrepreneurial mother gives you the chance to be a role model for other women, and for your children.

The picture is somewhat different for a single male parent. Men do not usually run their home or take a major part in child-rearing, so we can assume that the male is more likely to get outside help to care for the home, raise the children, or both. He is more likely to separate home management from business management. He is also more likely to have a personal credit rating and easier access to funds than his female counterpart.

At this time, we are not aware of any regular programs for entrepreneurial parents. However, the programs open to women in general, and some special programs for minority women, are available. It will be helpful to review the sections on special programs for women and minority entrepreneurs.

In summary, entrepreneurial mothers face many of the same opportunities and challenges as other women entrepreneurs, but the situation is different in at least one way. They usually see themselves first as mothers, and only secondly as business women. Their top priority is usually the family.

Entrepreneurial mothers may also have financial concerns beyond what the entrepreneurial woman faces in establishing her personal credit history. Some of those concerns are protecting rights to the business should her marriage end; making her company believable as a real business if it is home-based, and getting initial and ongoing funding for the business. The entrepreneurial mother may have the added support of a spouse who is willing to help with financial backing, and recommend business contacts or relatives who are willing to invest in his mate's business.

Limited education could be a major concern for entrepreneurial parents. It may not be a problem at all if their businesses are quite small, if they are willing to work on any problem areas by using consultants, if they read and ask questions or if they make use of workshops and other classes. Most are surprised to learn that managing their homes involves many of the same skills they will use in their businesses.

Besides the advantages that are common to all entrepreneurs, business gives single-parent entrepreneurs opportunities to control their own schedules; select their ideal workplaces, and get more deeply involved in being parents. It offers a good to outstanding income and the chance to protect their children's security by passing the business on to them, or eventually selling it.

Husband/Wife Teams

Husband/wife teams are a traditional part of American business. The number of these teams has been growing along with the general increase in entrepreneurs. This is a special kind of partnership that combines two talents that move toward a shared goal. Since there is one common objective, they can avoid the conflict that other partners face who have different aims for their lives.

Couple teams (unmarried people) have many of the same advantages and disadvantages as husband/wife teams but are, as a rule, less stable. Legally, they are partnerships and should have a partnership agreement and a contract that spells out ownership responsibilities and a buy-sell agreement that gives clear direction in case they decide to part ways. A lawyer will be needed to help set up this agreement.

Opportunities for Husband/Wife Teams

Couples are able to take advantage of many of the opportunities open to other entrepreneurs - especially those opportunities open to single-parents and entrepreneurial mothers. That includes the chance to work together and use each person's individual skills and experience. This means they can take advantage of their shared and separate experiences so both can play a vital part in the venture's success.

Also, the business gives you the chance to teach your children work and business skills, and personal responsibility. You have a ready-made training ground to teach job skills, business management know-how, responsibility, and other personal values to your children. Your business also protects your children or your spouse's security, as well as your own. It can provide jobs to family members and be passed on to your heirs.

Special Concerns for Husband/Wife Teams

One major concern for married business teams is how the business may change their marriage (or for an unmarried couple how the business can affect that relationship). Couples who have good problem-solving and communications skills seem to do well, and avoid negative impact on their relationships. People who generally get along without conflict still find that the added stress and responsibilities of a business can be hard on their relationship. It is important to recognize the differences between marital and business matters.

Another potential problem area can be the management of relatives working in the business with you. You will have to do advance planning to come up with clear job descriptions, benefits and other responsibilities. Also include a definitive chain of command and succession plans or the business may fold or pass into the wrong hands if for any reason you are unable to continue.

To manage non-relatives, consider profit-sharing or similar plans to increase employee benefits and the opportunities for advancement. It is important for these employees to know that their involvement in your business will not be a dead-end to advancement.

In summary, it can be stated that besides the advantages of business open to other entrepreneurs, a family business gives you and your spouse (or couple partner) the chance to combine your skills and take advantage of both sets of experiences, while working closely together. They also let you plan for your own and your family's financial security. Finally, they provide jobs and a training ground for other family members.

Inventors

Many inventors enter business because they feel they are unable to use their creative talents fully. The realistic picture is this: Only about one in every 100 new products based on big business inventions are successful enough to generate significant profits. Not good odds considering the large investments big firms make in research and development.

Inventors are probably the biggest risk-takers of all entrepreneurs. But when the risk pays off, the financial rewards may be outstanding.

Opportunities and Rewards for Inventors

Perhaps your biggest reward as a self-employed inventor is in personal satisfaction. While many businesses have large research and development budgets, they rarely allow inventors the freedom to control a project from start to finish and put their personal creative touch into the product.

By definition, a patent is an exclusive property right to an invention and is issued by the commissioner of Patents and Trademarks, U.S. Department of Commerce. It gives an inventor the right to exclude others from making, using or selling an invention for a period of 17 years in the United States. After you get an idea for a product or process that you think is functionally sound and economically feasible, put it in writing in a way that provides *legal evidence* of its origin since your claim may be challenged later. Obtain the assistance of a competent patent attorney.

In order to qualify for a patent, the invention must be new and useful. Among other requirements, it should have novelty, which means it should not have been known or used by others in the United States. It should not have been previously patented or described in a publication in this or a foreign country.

In developing a newly patented product, larger businesses may be limited in the types of materials and processes their equipment can handle. This, in turn, may also limit the changes they can make in their production line to accommodate the specifications of a new item. This opens up an opportunity for you to put together a higher quality product on a smaller scale and capture markets that a large company can't compete in. A smaller business may be able to produce your item at less cost, and with higher profits.

As an independent inventor, you'll probably have more control over the quality of your product, and make it more acceptable in the marketplace than if a larger company produces it. You are also open to sell your invention to a larger business once you have developed and patented it. Such a sale can be based on a fixed price, or a price plus a royalty.

In general, the more personal control you have over your work the more satisfied you will be with it. The financial rewards of inventions which succeed can be staggering. There are many kinds of "successful" inventions. Some products may be steady money-makers for years, but their yearly profits will be modest. Others may bring in high profits year after year. "Fad" items may earn high profits for only a short period of time, but make their inventors wealthy in the process. As an inventor, you decide for yourself what kind of success makes most sense to you.

Concerns for Inventors

Not surprisingly, one of the biggest barriers to inventing is obtaining adequate financing. Just what kind of additional costs do you face as an inventor? Besides usual start-up costs, you will need to pay special attention to getting adequate funds to cover:

- Product liability - in case someone is injured or property is damaged using your product.

- Development costs, including equipment and materials, research cost, market research and advertising.

- Consulting fees.

- Legal and licensing costs.

You must have firm belief in your invention to effectively sell your financial backers on the idea. You will also have to do your homework before you present your idea to them. Obtaining a patent requires a patent search in order to find out whether your invention is original before filing the patent application. The total cost of obtaining a patent varies widely. Filing fees are usually less than $100, but the cost of patent searches and legal consulting can be a considerable investment. To protect your ideas, the services of a competent patent attorney is strongly recommended.

Registering a trademark as a name or symbol for your product does not give you the same protection as a patent. It will prevent anyone from legally using your product's symbol or name, but it does not keep others from copying the product itself. Written material, music, or artistic pieces can be copyrighted, which does offer protection similar to a patent.

Like other entrepreneurs, you should check all possible avenues for financing. Be prepared to demonstrate why your invention will succeed, and identify the markets you will offer it to.

Special Programs for Inventors

The Small Business Innovation Research (SBIR) programs fund research and development efforts of a high risk nature that may have excellent commercial potential. Small businesses (under 500 employees) are eligible to participate in the SBIR program, provided the principal inventor spends more than one-half of his time employed by the small business at the time of a financial award and during the conduct of the effort. For information contact the Office of Innovation, Research and Technology or the SBA.

There may also be an inventors' club in your area. Such a group can help you find local financial sources and consultants.

University Innovation Centers (product testing centers usually connected to university business colleges) are set up to test your idea and give you information on how marketable your invention might be; how competitive it seems; whether there are less expensive substitutes; how safe it is, and how much it should cost to produce. Fees for this information are usually nominal. Contact your local branch of the SBA to locate the University Innovation Center nearest you.

There also are invention brokers and invention promotion firms. These companies usually work on a contingent fee basis. That is, their earnings are contingent or depend on the profits your invention generates after they produce, advertise, and sell the product. You may sell them the rights to your product outright, or make other satisfactory arrangements on sharing profits.

Before you consider using any of these firms, check their track record with your local Better Business Bureau, and with the Federal Trade Commission. Request names of clients for references. It costs no more to employ a successful, reputable company than one with a poor record.

As an inventor you face big challenges and risks with an opportunity for significant financial rewards. As desirable as this may be, your rewards in the area of personal satisfaction may be even greater as you see your ideas become products.

Handicapped Entrepreneurs

The number of handicapped entrepreneurs is increasing. This is partly because of medical advances that increase the survival and performance of people afflicted with birth defects, serious illnesses, and injuries. Technology is making it possible for handicapped entrepreneurs to do more of their day-to-day tasks independently. When we consider abilities, most handicapped people can be considered inconvenienced rather than disabled. New tools, including personal computers, electronic devices, and improvements in aids for the elderly, make it possible to concentrate more on abilities than disabilities.

Opportunities for Handicapped Entrepreneurs

As for other entrepreneurs, your needs are just a bit different from everyone else's. Your abilities and disabilities do not exactly match anyone else's, so no one can really say what you can or cannot do. You will have to decide what you want to do, then keep your activities within the scope of your limitations.

One major advantage for you as an entrepreneur is that you have more control over your schedule and workplace than you could in working for others.

You may have disabilities that make it impossible to work outside your home. As an entrepreneur, you create your own work environment in a regular office, shop, or your home. Or, if need be, your room. You have the freedom to decide what makes sense and is workable for you. As an entrepreneur, you have the opportunity to create a job for yourself that your disabilities might make impossible otherwise. This is especially important to you if you are receiving ongoing medical attention that would rule out a traditional job.

Being an entrepreneur also lets you be more independent and enables you to make more choices about your life. Part of the profits from your business can be used to buy the mechanical or electronic aids that let you do more day-to-day tasks on your own, or with less help. Your increased income may make it possible to buy a customized van with wheelchair lift, hand-driving controls or other special equipment. Getting along without help from other people is not as important as being able to decide what you want for yourself and making your own decision on how to get there. Being an entrepreneur can allow you to make these decisions and carry them out.

Succeeding in your own business allows you to put the spotlight on your abilities instead of your disabilities. This is obviously something that can boost your self-esteem and make you feel more valuable to yourself and your family or others around you.

Special Concerns for Handicapped Entrepreneurs

Many of your concerns as a handicapped entrepreneur will be similar to those of other entrepreneurs.

Getting financing is usually a major concern for entrepreneurs. As a handicapped person, you may have to be more creative than others who make business and financial contacts. Especially if it's hard for you to communicate or physically get around to meetings. You may make more extensive use of the telephone and arrange regular telephone meetings with loan officers or other contacts; use fax services or computer communications; or, you can explain your situation and your business plans via letter. It may also be useful to take on a partner or hire someone to do your initial legwork and basic research.

Communication can also be a problem. People are sometimes uncomfortable with your disability because they don't know how you want to be treated. You may not appreciate people who are offering to do things for you that you prefer to do for yourself. Or those who ignore you when you do need a hand. Be very clear about how you want to be treated. This can do wonders in putting people at ease. Also, think about taking a communications or assertiveness course, or joining a recreation class (one especially for people with handicaps, if necessary). You can make business contacts in all of these classes, and learn important communications skills while you build your social network with people you can share your success with and turn to for help, advice and support if the going gets rough.

Another challenge is obtaining adequate financing to customize your workplace so that you can make the most of your abilities. Government subsidies are often available for this purpose, especially if you will be hiring other people who have handicaps. For example, if you are in a wheelchair and plan to open a locksmith shop, this might mean adjusting counter and workbench heights in your workshop, and planning how to reach parts and tools.

Besides making changes, you will also have to adjust your style of operation. The locksmith business would normally involve making housecalls. If you are confined to a wheelchair, you will have to think of ways to cover those housecalls. Or perhaps you will decide to limit your business to in-shop work.

You may decide on a business that can be conducted by telephone or from a stationary position. These can include telephone answering, private postal information and similar types of services. Depending on the nature of your disability, you may also be able to start a business that takes advantage of your home as a formal workspace - like a "Bed and Breakfast" business that turns your home into an inn.

Special Programs for Handicapped Entrepreneurs

If you are a disabled veteran, you may be eligible for special assistance from the Veterans' Administration in locating funding sources. The VA also has programs to help you learn to manage your disabilities in a work setting. Your state's Department of Vocational Rehabilitation or Department of Social and Health Services can offer job-training and support services for handicapped workers, and can refer you to local support groups and general services for handicapped workers. Private vocational rehabilitation counseling firms can also give you advice on local resources., Your local branch of the Small Business Administration has the latest information on federal financing, and offers counseling through the Service Corps of Retired Executives (SCORE). You may also be eligible to apply for SBA loans.

In summary, your career as an entrepreneur offers you greater opportunities for independence, and an income that can make it possible for you to have the mechanical and electronic aids that make you even more independent. Increased independence often brings feelings of increased self-value or self-esteem.

Aside from greater independence, income, and self reliance - you have the advantages of being able to set your own work schedule, work from your home, and custom-make your workplace to fit your needs. Being an entrepreneur gives you a chance to dream big and make those dreams a reality.

Entrepreneurial Immigrants

Like minority entrepreneurs, the number of immigrant business owners is rising. Sometimes immigrants face the same negative attitudes as minority entrepreneurs. But these attitudes can be overcome by fair dealings and hard work. Once you have proven yourself, you can have the same respect and opportunities open to other successful entrepreneurs.

Opportunities and Rewards for Immigrant Entrepreneurs

As an immigrant entrepreneur, you have all the rewards and opportunities open to other entrepreneurs. You may not have had these chances in the country you came from. This makes solid opportunities even more rewarding to you. As an entrepreneur, you create a job for yourself and family members, as well as the security achieved through an outstanding income. Becoming an entrepreneur also gives you the chance to leave a dead-end job, or one you simply do not enjoy.

As with other entrepreneurs, you also receive rewards in personal satisfaction. You can be proud of how your job reflects your skills and planning.

Special Challenges for Immigrant Entrepreneurs

Like minority entrepreneurs, you may sometimes have to work harder for these opportunities than other entrepreneurs do. One problem can be that of *communicating.* A good working knowledge of the English language is essential if you expect to deal with English-speaking customers and suppliers. Most community and junior colleges have low-cost (and sometimes free) English language classes that can be helpful.

Financing is another concern. One barrier you may face in obtaining financing is not having a credit rating in this country. We have discussed this in the section on school-age entrepreneurs.

One problem which holds true for entrepreneurs in general is that you establish your credit rating mostly through borrowing. It usually takes a good credit history to borrow. How do you deal with this? One way is to get a co-signer. This person can be a sponsor, a relative or an organization that signs with you for your loan and guarantees payment.

Another way is to offer collateral. Collateral is something you own that can be sold, traded, or given to the lender to cover the amount of your loan if you fail to make your payments.

A third way is to offer a lender matching funds. This means that you will take a loan for the same amount of money as you have on deposit with the lender.

Finally, your credit history is also built on how well you take care of current expenses such as rent, telephone bills, car payments, credit card payments and other obligations. You also can use the assets in your business as collateral to help establish your credit.

You may look into the kinds of financing open to other entrepreneurs, including programs for minority entrepreneurs and financial help from other immigrant business owners. SCORE counselors can help you plan for your financing. Call your local Small Business Administration branch office, listed in your telephone book under "United States Government Offices".

Special Programs for Immigrant Entrepreneurs

We do not know of any special financial programs for immigrant entrepreneurs at this time. If you are in a large city, your local branch of the SBA may have a special Minority Enterprise department. SCORE counselors also work with these departments.

In summing up, like other entrepreneurs, you will have to work hard to be successful. In some cases you will have to work harder than other entrepreneurs to succeed. But that extra effort can bring you the same respect and opportunities afforded to other successful entrepreneurs. There are two major challenges for immigrant entrepreneurs:

One is financing. SCORE counselors at the Small Business Administration can give you advice on getting financing through the SBA and other agencies.

The other is communications with customers and suppliers. Junior and community colleges provide classes that can help you achieve a good working knowledge of the English language.

Section 4

START-UP DECISIONS THAT
LAY THE FOUNDATION FOR BUSINESS GROWTH

Entrepreneurial Characteristics

It is important to keep in mind as you study this manual that successful entrepreneurs are not carbon copies of each other. As a group, they show some important differences from other groups of people. But as individuals, they can also be very dissimilar from each other.

What is a good business to get into? This question is frequently asked by aspiring entrepreneurs. My answer is, there is no such thing as a "good business" or a "bad business". But there is superior and poor management. A business is only as good or bad as the entrepreneur and his or her management style make it. Often, a business is considered "good" because it is popular or trendy. By the same token, many businesses are viewed as having little glamour or appeal because they have been around for a long time and are not particularly exciting. They do not get write-ups in newspapers, magazines and are not featured on television. However, such "dull" businesses will flourish, even in competitive environments, under competent management. At the same time, a "good" business may not do well under poor management.

All of us are shaped by our backgrounds, past experiences and personalities. These characteristics can be a crucial factor in discovering which types of businesses we are most compatible with and offer the best "fit". It is accordingly advisable to take these factors in consideration before making a firm commitment to any particular business. Markets for products and services, and the needs of individual customers, vary. It takes different styles, backgrounds and ideas to effectively meet these different market characteristics. Your unique style and personality will make you more aware of and sensitive to certain market peculiarities that others might miss.

Unfortunately, it happens too often that people rush into buying or starting a business because they want to be independent. They make decisions too quickly and without being aware that the "fit" is wrong. The result can be a frustrating experience; a business operated in this environment is likely to fail. Of course, you can be successful in a number of different businesses. But you should focus on the search for opportunities where your capabilities and the demands of a business under consideration come together harmoniously. You will find more discussion on this aspect of entrepreneurship in Section 9.

Considerations Affecting Your Future

You are unique. Your experience, personality, the things that have happened to you, and the things you have caused to happen in the past make your situation special.

There is *not* just one kind of personality or temperament that assures success. However, some types of businesses will be better matches for you than others. If you are a go-getter and always like to be on the run, you will do best in an environment where things move quickly and change dramatically daily, monthly or from year to year; such as temporary help services and high-pressure operations like printing or high-technology businesses.

If, however, you are more comfortable with a slower pace and less turmoil, you will do better in manufacturing and some types of retail businesses which may be more suited to that kind of temperament. You can get a feel for various businesses by talking to their owners.

Visualize being in a particular business and ask yourself these questions. What would my "typical" day be like? Are these the kinds of activities I would enjoy, and would the pace agree with me day-in and day-out? Do I have some personal experience in this business? What parts of the business have I enjoyed and been most comfortable with in the past? Can I think of a business that might have more appeal?

In becoming an entrepreneur, the process of investigating, making plans and starting an operation will have a lasting impact on your life. If you are faced with other important changes in your life, it is best to get them behind you before you start your business. Changes include events such as entering, leaving or graduating from a school; marrying or divorcing; buying or selling a house; legal problems; expecting a child; changing work duties in your job; changes in your health and similar occurrences. All of these events you are facing - for better or for worse - could present handicaps.

The desire to start a business is frequently triggered by job dissatisfaction which includes:

- Lack of freedom to make management decisions
- Lack of advancement opportunities
- No chance for ever reaching a desired income
- Lack of control over the choice of work environment
- Inadequate benefits

The timing for quitting your job is extremely important. You will face many questions. How long will it take to open the doors of your business and when will it start showing profits: Immediately? Six months? One year or more? Will you need your job for income while your business develops? Will you have the time and energy to run your business and perform your regular job at the same time? Do you need to make arrangements to work part-time? How long can you continue to hold on to your present job and prepare for your new business?

If you need your current job to carry you through your business start-up, be extremely careful to follow through on your present commitments. You may have to do your planning in the evening and on weekends in order to do what is necessary to start your business and keep your present job. Do not let your outside commitments interfere unnecessarily. If you take time off, be sure to make it up to your employer so that your job responsibilities are covered. This may help you keep the job as long as you need it, without facing an untimely firing. However, it could happen anyway.

Leave your job on friendly terms and do not close any doors behind you. It is only common courtesy (and something you would expect of your *own* future employees) to give your employer ample notice before you quit. Don't burn any bridges! Your employer may be an important connection for you in your new business. You may want to call upon him to furnish references for you.

If you are working in the same type of business you will be entering, you may consider putting out "feelers" for business connections or customers. For example, if you are in sales, you may want to subtly find out if your customers will continue to do business with you when you are on your own. The same would be true if you are an auto mechanic, work for a specialty shop, or have the kind of job where you regularly see customers. Or, you may consider discussing your plans with the suppliers you are currently dealing with. Bear in mind, however, that any of those contacts may become known to your present employer.

At this point, a decision about your next step as an entrepreneur must be made. First, we'll consider four choices that are open to you. Next, we will discuss the process of selecting the type of business best suited for you, and the three ways of entering it. We will also cover techniques of market analysis and finding the right location. We will discuss the three types of business ownership: The sole proprietorship, partnerships and corporations.

Then we will lay out steps for putting together your business plan, which can be important to help you get financing and keep your business on course.

Also discussed will be the capital requirements for your business and how you can go about obtaining the necessary financing.

Finally, we will talk about preparations for the opening of your business.

What to Do Now? A Time for Vital Decisions

There are four choices you can make at this time. You will need to decide which one makes the most sense and is the most logical for you. To further evaluate your likelihood to succed in business, turn to the Self-evaluation tests and discussions in Section 9.

1. If you have already decided to go into business, we want to congratulate you. In the sections that follow, we will lay out ideas on how to make the business you selected a success.

2. You may decide to delay your decision and acquire additional experience and skills. It will be important to recognize just where you need that additional training and where to obtain it. For example, if you are not sure of your accounting knowledge or sales expertise, you may want to take classes in those fields.

3. You may hesitate on what the next step should be because you need more information. In this case you must determine just what you really need to know and where you will get it. Keep in mind, however, that there will *always* be new information to add to what you already have, so be careful not to let information-gathering become a reason to postpone a final decision.

4. You may decide that owning your own business is something you do not want for yourself at this time. Or, you may feel that being in business presents bigger risks than potential rewards. This too, is a realistic decision. It can save you discouragement and money. If you are convinced that being an entrepreneur is not for you, then this becomes the right choice. You will still be a winner by having a clearer idea of what you want to ultimately do with your future. It would be tragic to invest your time, energy and life in something that really is not for you.

No matter what your decision, you now have a good idea of the risks and rewards of entering your own business, because you have looked carefully at what it takes to succeed. It is essential that you make the choice that is right for you. But it is also important to make the choice *now*. Whatever your decision, go for it!

Becoming an entrepreneur is making an investment in time and money. It can be a wise, rewarding investment if it's what you want for yourself, and if you are ready and willing to work for it. You can only reach those rewards by deciding that you really want them, and by doing whatever it takes to reach them. Successful entrepreneurs are not only careful planners, but they put their decisions into action.

Types of Ownership: A Quick-Reference Survey

In this section we will look at three ownership options:

*   The Sole Proprietorship
*   The Partnership
*   The Corporation

The Sole Proprietorship

In a sole proprietorship, you are the *exclusive owner* of a business. Your personal and business funds are not legally separated, although they should be kept apart for bookkeeping purposes.

One advantage of a sole proprietorship is that you have full control in the decision-making process. There are no partners to consult; the line of authority is clear; the implementation of decisions is not slowed down by long deliberations among partners. On the other hand, you also have fewer opportunities to discuss ideas and problems with someone who is equally interested in the success of the business.

In the sole proprietorship, you are the only beneficiary of any business profits and do not have to share them with one or more partners. At the same time, there is nothing to prevent you from changing this business structure at a later date to add partners, or incorporate if it meets your business needs at that time.

A disadvantage for sole proprietorships is that personal financing depends entirely on your funds and credit rating. If you have one or more partners, you obviously have more assets to strengthen the financial position of the enterprise.

Another disadvantage is that your personal and business assets are not legally separate. This means that you are personally responsible for any of your business debts or liabilities.

The Partnership

There are a number of ways to set up partnerships. The actual method you select depends upon the number of partners involved, and their personalities. For example, you may structure a partnership where one partner is "silent". In this agreement, the silent partner is primarily an investor, and only plays a minor role in business management and day-to-day decisions. In other partnerships the owners manage the business operations, and divide management responsibilities.

By law, partners are responsible for each other's business (and in some cases, personal) liabilities. A "general" partnership, is one where every partner is jointly and equally liable for all liabilities of the partnership. A "limited" partnership gives unlimited liability for the business to one who is the general partner, and limits the liability of other partners, who are the limited partners, to the amount they personally invest in the business. If the business folded or had major losses, limited partners would lose only the amount of their personal investments. The general partner could also lose personal assets. For this reason, the person with the lowest net worth is often designated as the general partner.

Two of the main advantages of a partnership are, greater combined financial resources, more diversified management skills and experience which lead to better ideas and decisions.

Partnerships also have some disadvantages. Your decision-making time will usually take longer in a partnership as compared to a sole proprietorship. If you draw the lines clearly for your areas of decision-making responsibility, you may be able to overcome these potential conflicts. You may find it helpful to agree on the kinds of situations in which partners must consult each other. For example, this agreement will establish dollar amount limits at which one partner must consult others before making expenditures on equipment, merchandise, promotions, etc.

In selecting a partner, it is important to make sure that his and your business goals are similar. For example, the amount of time each will be putting into the business or how much of the profits should be personally taken out of the business or re-invested for quicker growth.

If you set your business up as an equal (50-50) partnership, you and your partner will split the tax responsibility for the business. For example, if your business nets $60,000.00, you and your partner will each be responsible for reporting income of $30,000.00 on your personal federal tax returns.

In a partnership of two or more partners it is essential to put all understandings and desires of the partners in writing. This can be accomplished by a Partnership and a Buy and Sell Agreement that spells out procedures and actions that will be taken in the event of:

- Serious disagreements among partners
- Arbitration procedures

- Division of responsibility
- Sale of ownership interests by a partner
- Death of a partner and life insurance policies in connection with it

We do not recommend that the business use one of the partner's personal attorneys to handle these arrangements, or serve as the company's attorney, since there could be a conflict of interest for the attorney if the partners were at odds. Selecting an outside attorney avoids the problem of any preferential treatment of any partner over others.

Keep in mind that partnerships in some ways are like marriages, where partners have common goals and expectations. The negative side of this is that partnerships also have a failure rate about equal to marriages. Personal compatibility is a must. Some points to look at closely are just how long you have known your prospective partner, and what kind and quality of relationship you have been in together: friends, co-workers, friendly competitors, business acquaintances, relatives, etc.

It is important that prospective partners explore their own ideas, working and management styles at great length before forming a partnership. If they are married, their spouses should also have a part in the negotiation at some point, even if they are not going to be part of the actual operation.

The decision of choosing one or more partners is as important as the decision to go into business in the first place. The primary reason in forming a partnership is that the partners complement each other in their experiences and capabilities. For example:

Business	Experience	
	Partner 1	Partner 2
Manufacturing	Salesmanship	Production
Restaurant	Cook	Customer Relations
Retail, Wholesale	Merchandising	Business Management
Hi-Tech	Computer Expertise	Marketing

There should also be a good deal of empathy and personal chemistry between partners - their styles should fit together well. Tension and stress are always present in business, so it is critical that partners have the ability to work smoothly together and keep business interests separate from personal considerations. It is also important to understand and make allowances for the other partner's weaknesses.

The most successful types of partnerships are those in which the partners have known each other for some time, are business-oriented, have been active in the same or a similar kind of business, and have a good understanding of each other and an attitude of give and take.

The Corporation

Incorporating your business gives you some special advantages. One is that it protects your personal assets from business liabilities or losses.

Another advantage is longevity and continuity: The life of the business does not end with your death or that of other shareholder owners. The corporation is a separate legal entity, apart from your own, unlike that of a sole proprietorship or partnership. This stability often makes it easier to get continuing long-term financing from banks or, if a larger business is involved, through sale of stocks.

In many ways, small corporations operate very much like partnerships. The difference lies primarily in the legal structure.

In a larger corporation, the stockholders elect a board of directors who in turn appoint the officers; a president, one or more vice presidents, a treasurer, and secretary. The officers may hire managers, or become managers themselves. In small corporations, the stockholders, directors, and officers are often the same people.

Incorporating also has some disadvantages. One is that the earnings of the corporation can be taxed twice. There are generally two methods available for the shareholder-owner to get money out of the corporation.

- Salaries may be paid to shareholder-owners in the same way as to any other employee. Such salaries are deductible by the corporation and thereby reduce the corporate income tax. One restriction on salaries is that they must be "reasonable" to be deductible. What is considered "reasonable" is a matter of business judgment and should be discussed with your accountant. All salaries received are included in the shareholder-owner's personal income tax return.

- The other method of withdrawing funds is by the corporation declaring dividends. In this case all shareholder-owners receive a pro-rata amount in ratio to their percentage of stock ownership. Corporate dividends are basically funds that are available after the corporation has paid income tax on its earnings. As previously discussed, the dividends are also taxable to the shareholder owners. Under current law, this reflects double taxation on the earnings of the corporation. Within certain limits, it is not always required that dividends be paid. If the corporate earnings are left within the corporation, the funds may be used for any legitimate business purpose, such as buying equipment, expanding the business, etc.

Corporations' activities have some limitations by law. These laws differ slightly from state to state. The activities are spelled out in the corporation's charter. There are sometimes restrictions on "passive" investments, such as real estate. The charter often gives a percentage breakdown on "active" and "passive" investments.

There is also an option to incorporate as an "S" corporation. It offers all the advantages of a regular corporation, such as limited liability and legal protection. However, income and expenses in an "S" corporation are treated as "pass-through" items similar to a partnership. This means in an "S" corporation such items as income, losses, deductions, and credits are passed through to, and taken into account by its shareholder owners in computing their individual income tax liability. With some exceptions, an "S" corporation is not subject to any tax at the corporate level.

In order to qualify for the "S" status, your corporation must have no more than 35 shareholders, no non-resident or alien shareholders, and only one class of stocks. There are also limits on how much "passive" investment is allowed.

If you have considerable personal assets you wish to protect from any business losses, you can incorporate your business, even if you are the sole owner.

Incorporating a business is a complex procedure, and the selection of a competent attorney to handle the details is critical.

Review of Ownership Option Features

Sole Proprietorship	Partnership	Corporation
Full control of business decision-making; clear lines of authority.	Divided control for decision-making; over-lapping authority at times.	More business decision-making channels; clear lines of authority for larger corporations; similar to partnerships - for small corporations.
Easiest formation; usually dissolved when you sell, go out of business or die.	More legal work in formation; possible difficulties with partners.	Most complex formation; continues after death of owner(s).
Undivided profits	Divided profits.	Divided profits; possibility of double taxation.*
Financing more difficult	Easier to finance than sole ownership.	Greatest flexibility of financing.
Combines business and personal assets and liabilities.	May combine business and personal assets and liabilities.	Keeps business and personal financing separate.

*Except for "S" corporations.

How to Conduct Your Search for Your Best Money-Making Opportunity

There are many types of businesses from which to choose, and there is more than one that can be right for you. Your personal likes, dislikes, and capabilities will give you important clues as to what type of business to enter. Reviewing your Personal Inventory in the final section of this manual is one step to guide you toward a good decision. Whether you start a business as a start-up, buy an established business, or acquire a franchise is a decision you can only make after you have decided upon the kind of business that is right for you. In this section, we will discuss the processes in which you can qualify yourself for the type of business that makes sense for you.

For example, if you are the kind of person who prefers to work closely with customers, you will investigate businesses which give you ample opportunities for high customer involvement. These include retail stores, insurance, sales-oriented businesses, or health-care services. The degree of customer contact can vary widely in different service businesses. In general, you will have more direct customer contact in retail and service businesses than in other types of businesses.

Like a mirror, the style of a business reflects its owner. If you are a creative person, you can inject creativity into almost *any* kind of business. For example, in a retail store you can search for unusual types of merchandise that appeal to a specific market. Or you may think of unusual ways to display or demonstrate ordinary merchandise to make it more eye-catching and appealing. In a service business, you can offer a two-hour service while your competitors require two days to complete a job. In manufacturing you can specialize in new products which have little competition. You can start with an established product or product line, and make changes, improvements, and begin to develop related products. You may come up with a product that is so new and different that it will encounter little or no competition.

It is important to continue innovating and improving your product line in order to stay ahead of the competition. Keep in mind that other people will be aware of what you are doing and will start imitating and enlarging on it if you are successful.

For example, if you come up with a hot new design for a woodstove, you may capture the entire market for that product for a while. But you will need to come up with new ideas for improvements as well as other products when the competition begins to move in on your original idea.

There seems to be no limits on how far creativity can take you, whether you are the president of a corporation, or run your own flower stand. In the latter, for example, you can test one location against another to determine which will produce greater sales. Just where you go depends upon your imagination, and how well you can anticipate what will appeal to your customers.

The process of finding and selecting a business that is right for you falls broadly into two parts. First, you will select a major business area that appeals to you such as:

- Manufacturing
- Wholesale/Industrial Supplies
- Retail
- Service

Second, you will narrow your choice to a specific business in that field, such as a diaper delivery service, drapery manufacturing, computer software retailing, and the like.

Here is a brief overview of the major business areas:

Manufacturing generally requires a greater investment than other types of businesses. The capital expenditures for equipment and installation can be considerable. Expansion and profit opportunities are unlimited because manufactured products can be sold from local to international markets.

Wholesale Industrial Supply businesses require little or no capital for equipment. However, funds required for inventories can be a major factor. Goods are usually sold by a sales force and the markets are mostly local and regional.

Retail investment requirements depend upon the size and type of operation. Because of this, these needs can vary widely. Retail businesses are local for the most part. They are among the most popular among start-up entrepreneurs. It is important to begin narrowing down to a specific type of store by identifying what you really enjoy doing and where your experience lies.

Consistent promotion is important in a successful retail business. You must be sales-oriented to attract customers from competitors who may be offering similar products in the same price or quality range. For this reason, it is especially important to do thorough market studies. We will look into this more fully later.

Service businesses are operated to help customers accomplish the things that they can't do or prefer not to do for themselves. These businesses include personal services such as beauty shops, photo studios, health clubs and business services like collection agencies, employment agencies, coffee services, data processing services, repair services, and so forth. Many of these operations can be started with a very small initial investment as compared to other businesses.

In the next step, once you have narrowed your interest to a general business area, you will need to begin looking at specific types of businesses. It is important that you choose a business that is a good match for your needs, skills and financial resources. It can be a mistake, though, to look for a "perfect" match. You may have to compromise to find the business that fits your personal style and financial resources. The surest way not to become an entrepreneur is to wait for that "perfect" match.

One characteristic of successful entrepreneurs is their ability to improvise and be flexible. You may take a traditional business and put your own stamp on it to make it something completely different. For example, you may have a background in traditional child daycare, but really be more interested in working with teenagers or adults. Or you might start providing daycare for elderly people who have special needs or are normally cared for by family members who work during the day and can't afford in-home care.

How well your business fits you is important to your success. Being in a business that is not "you" can work against you and will sooner or later develop problems. Fortunately there are a multitude of good business opportunities around that are compatible with almost any aspiring entrepreneur.

Listing of Business Categories For Idea Starters

A partial listing of business categories follows. Of course, new types of businesses are continually being created as customer needs grow and technologies advance:

Transportation

Airlines, non-certified
Airport, aircraft maintenance
Airport transportation services
Ambulance services
Bus charter, tours
Furniture moving and storage
Garbage and trash collectors
Handicapped transportation services
Irrigation system operations
Limousine services
Marinas
Mobile home transporting
Parcel delivery
School bus companies
Sightseeing tours
Taxicab companies
Travel agencies
Trucking and draying
Trucking, heavy hauling
Warehouses, public and general
Water transportation, sightseeing and
    excursion

Contracting (Home and Industrial)

Alteration/Remodeling supplies and
services
Boiler repair and cleaning
Carpentry
Carpet and rug laying
Concrete and related work
Computer rooms, equipment
Computer rooms, installation
Electrical work
Excavating and foundation work
Fence contractors
Fireproofing contractors
Floor finishing and resurfacing
Floor laying
Furnace repair and cleaning
General contractors
Glass and glazing
Gutters and downspout
Insulation
Linoleum and tile laying

Masonry, stone setting, stone work
Painting, paperhanging and decorating
Patio and deck construction
Plastering
Plumbing
Prefabricated metal building
Residential home builders
Roofing and sheet metal work
Siding
Solar energy equipment
Store front remodeling
Swimming pool and waterproofing
    contractors
Tile
Woodstove sales, supplies and services
Wrecking and demolition

Education

Art schools
Auto driving instruction
Aviation schools
Business, secretarial schools
Data processing schools
Language schools
Modeling schools
Music instruction schools
Real estate schools
Religious libraries
Special libraries
Vocational schools

Manufacturing

Aeronautical accessories
Adhesives/sealants
Advertising displays, signs
Automotive accessories
Blacksmith/cutlery
Boats/boating supplies
Brooms, brushes
Clothing/accessories/outerwear
Cosmetics
Computer software and accessories
Containers; wood, etc.

Cookie, crackers
Cooking equipment, household and
  commercial
Curtain/drapery
Dehydrated fruit, vegetable, soup
Display fixtures/materials
Do-it-yourself kits
Dolls
Engineering instruments
Environmental controls
Electronic equipment
Firearms
Fishing supplies
Flowers, artificial
Furniture; wood, metal, plastic
Games, toys, children's vehicles
Giftware
Hats and caps
Health-care/exercise equipment
Health-care supplies and instruments
Ice cream and frozen desserts
Jewelry-jewelry materials/costume
  jewelry
Kitchen cabinets
Leather goods
Lithographic negatives and plates
Luggage
Metal, fabricated products
Metal, door sash and trim
Metal, prefabricated buildings
Music equipment
Name plates
Optical supplies/instruments
Paint/varnish/paint products
Periodical publishers
Pet foods
Photoengraver
Photographic equipment and supplies
Pickle, sauce, salad dressing
Pottery products
Printers
Printing/Publishing
Sausage and meat products
Scientific instruments
Signs, sign erection, repair
Silk screen printers
Soap/detergents
Sports equipment
Surgical appliances and supplies
Typesetters
Wood pallets
Wood containers

Health Care

Alcohol information and treatment
Animal hospitals and clinics
Dental laboratories
Medical, x-ray laboratories and rentals
Medical equipment, supplies
Nurses registries
Veterinary services

Retail

Aircraft
Antiques
Appliances
Aquariums tropical fish
Art, art supplies
Auto parts
Baked goods
Boats, marine supply
Books
Bridal specialties
Building/remodeling/repair supplies
Candy, nuts, confectionery
Cars
Catering
Chainsaws, electric tools
China, glassware
Cleaning supplies
Clothing/shoes
    Boutiques
    Bridal
    Children's
    Family
    Infants
    Maternity
    Misc. apparel and accessories
    Men's and boys
    Ready to wear
    Sportswear, riding and western apparel
    Uniforms and protective wear
    Women's
Computers, data processing supplies,
  equipment
Computer accessories and software
Convenience foods
Cosmetics, perfume
Dairy products, cheese, ice cream, frozen
  desserts
Delicatessens
Direct sales organizations
Drugs and health-care items
Electric appliances
Entertainment - adult and general
Fireplace equipment
Food - grocery/health/specialty
Fabrics
Floor coverings
Flowers
Freezer, meat lockers
Furniture
Gasoline, car service
Gifts
Greeting cards
Groceries
Gourmet shops
Hardware
Health foods
Hearing aids
Hobby supplies
Home/Office supplies and furnishings
Jewelry
Kitchen cabinets
Lamp, lampshades
Lighting fixtures

Linen
Liquor
Luggage/leather goods
Lumber/paint
Mattress and bedding
Meat, poultry, seafood
Mobile homes
Monuments
Motorcycles
Music
Needlework supplies, knitting supplies
News dealers, newsstands
Overhead door dealers
Nursery, garden supplies
Paint, glass, wallpaper
Party supplies
Pets and pet supplies
Picture frames
Recreational vehicles
Religious goods
Restaurant and fast-food, bars and
    taverns
Salvage, surplus
Sandwiches
Sewing machines, sewing supplies
Snowmobiles, snowmobiling
    equipment/clothing
Sporting goods
    Bicycles
    Bowling equipment
    Fishing tackle
    Golf equipment
    Guns, gunsmithing
    Saddlery
    Ski equipment
    Tennis equipment
Stamps and coins
Stationery, office supplies
Tavern/bar
Telephone equipment
Tires
Trophies and medals
Typewriters
TV/Video/Radio and supplies
Vacuum cleaners
Vending machine operators
Waterbeds and waterbed supplies
Wedding supplies
Wigs, hair goods, hair care products
Windowshades, venetian blinds

Services

Advertising agencies and consulting
Antique repairing and restoring
Appliance repair
Auctioneers and liquidators
Automobile and truck rental and leasing
Automobile repair/restoration/
    painting/muffler
Balloons, novelty and toy
Barber/Beauty shops
Beauty culture schools
Billiard, pool halls
Bowling alleys

Carpet, furniture rentals
Carpet and upholstery cleaning
Car washes
Catering
Cleaning services
    Aircraft
    Automobile, other vehicles
    Building
    Carpet, upholstery
    Chimney
    Cleaning equipment and supplies
    Cleaning equipment rental
    Commercial building
    Hotel, motel
    Home
    General janitorial
Clothing sewing, alterations, wardrobe
    consulting
Coffee/Wakeup services
Collections
Color consulting
Communications consulting
Computer programming, entry, consulting
    repair
Computer software
Computer payroll
Contractors equipment and supplies
    rentals
Copy, duplicating
Cosmetic consulting
Costume rental
Credit reporting
Data processing
Delivery
Detective/protective services
Diaper service
Direct mail advertising
Disinfecting, exterminating
Drafting services
Drapery and curtain cleaning
Educational consulting
Employment/career consulting
Entertainment
Equipment rental, leasing
Executive recruiting
Exterminating
Food, beverage consulting
Foreign trade consulting
Formal wear rental
Fund raising
Funeral parlors
Furniture repair, refinishing
Guard, patrol services
Health clubs, reducing salons
Home health-care and hospice consulting
Home tutoring
Housekeeping and janitorial services
Interior design, interior decoration
Laundries
Lawn mower sharpening
Locksmith
Maid, butler, domestic services
Management consulting, public relations,
Market consulting and research
Marriage and family counseling

Massage parlors
Messengers
Microfilming
Modeling agencies
Musical instruments, repairing
Nurseries, day care
Oil burner services
Party/banquet services
Party equipment
Personnel, labor relations consultants
Pet shops, pet training
Photography, aerial
Photography, commercial
Photography, slide and filmstrip
    production
Photo services and photo finishing
Piano, organ tuning and repair
Pool cleaning
Printing/publishing
Real estate
Reducing salons
Reupholstery, furniture repair
Resume services
Secretarial services
Security services
Sewer, drain cleaning
Shoe repair
Skin care salons
Stenography, reproduction
Swimming pool services
Taxidermy
Tax returns
Telephone answering
Temporary help
Theatrical agencies
Translators
Tool rentals
Tours
TV/radio/VCR repair
Upholstery
Vacuum cleaner repair
Washing machine, dryer repair
Watch, clock, jewelry repair
Welding, welding repair
Window cleaning

Wholesale and Industrial Distributors

Advertising specialties
Appliances
Art goods
Audio visual equipment and supplies
Automobile parts and accessories
Barber/Beauty shop supplies and
    equipment
Burglar alarms
Carpet, floor coverings
China, glassware
Church supplies
Computer, data processing supplies
Data communication equipment and
    systems
Drugs, proprietaries, sundries
Electronic equipment and parts
Exporters
Fireplace equipment
Fire alarm systems
Florist supplies
Furniture, office equipment
Giftware and novelties
Hardware
Home furnishings, housewares
Hospital equipment
Importers
Interior decorator supplies
Janitorial supplies
Jewelry, watch, precious stones
Lamp, lampshades
Manufacturers representatives
Newspaper, magazine distributors
Notions and dry goods
Oil burner sales and service
Opticians' equipment
Piece goods
Photographic equipment and supplies
Physicians' equipment
Plumbing and heating supplies
Rack merchandise distribution
Restaurant supplies, equipment
School supplies
Sporting goods
Stationery supplies
Telephone and intercom systems
Television sets, supplies and parts
Tire wholesalers
Toys, hobby goods and supplies
Video games
Waste paper recycling/confidential paper
    shredding

Some fields that are growing now and look promising for continued expansion in the future are:

Computer-related businesses
Clothing/accessories
Environmental operations
Energy - especially gasoline substitutes and solar energy
Food/shelter
Child and home health care, geriatrics, homemaker helpers
Leisure/entertainment
Security
Self-help (personal improvement, home projects, do-it-yourself
  books and kits)
Telecommunications, fibre optics
Fitness equipment and service
Consulting
Imports and exports of industrial goods

Check the pages of any big city yellow page telephone directory for more ideas. In the yellow pages you can also find sub-specialties listed for areas that interest you. For example, if you are interested in a business dealing with carpeting, check "carpeting" for sub-specialty listings. One telephone book lists the following sub-specialties under carpets:

Carpet Accessories
     Cleaning/Rug Binding Machines
     Cleaning Equipment and Supplies and Wholesaling
     Cleaning Equipment and Supplies
     Dyeing
     Installation
     Layers' Equipment and Supplies
     Rental
     Repair
     Retailing

In summary, by narrowing down your choice to one major classification and several types of businesses, take the following personal factors into consideration:

Your interests
Your experience
Your financial capabilities

Where to Get Valuable Advice at Little or No Cost

Information is the lifeblood of any business. This is as true for established firms as it is for start-ups. Obtaining the right kind of information - from the best available sources - leads to accumulation of new knowledge. These facts will help you overcome obstacles in the start-up phase and progress faster once the business is running.

Start-up and established entrepreneurs are always on the lookout for ideas that relate to the development of new products and services. They want to learn more about better production methods, effective promotions, cost-saving devices and procedures.

The need for new information can also arise when a problem proves difficult to resolve; when you have to make changes due to complaints or pressures from customers, employees or competitors, or when your industry is faced with major changes. Recognizing the need for information, and what it can do for your business, is important. But even more important is the need for motivation to search for it, then apply what you have learned.

In this section we will talk about sources of information and offer suggestions on how to do your investigative work. We have discussed how important it is to recognize your qualifications and personal assets for going into business, but you still have to seek outside information. One of the aims of this manual is to give you the necessary background and recommend methods on how to go about it.

To accomplish this you must become familiar with the information resources available and how to locate them.

Here's a list of some of the best results-producing resources to consider when information is needed:

- Libraries
- Trade Associations (local and national)
- Other people in your business, including competitors
- Banks
- Industry meetings and conventions
- Seminars
- Consultants
- Suppliers
- Chambers of Commerce
- Cassette and video presentations
- Books
- Indexes to articles in newspapers and magazines
- Directories

More specifically, information resources can be classified as follows:

LOCAL
- Successful entrepreneurs and potential competitors
- Business groups and associations
- City hall
- Chambers of Commerce
- Community Development Corporations
- County Offices (Assessor, courthouse information, etc.)
- Libraries (city, county, college or university)
- School vocational or guidance counselors
- Junior and community colleges

- Banks and saving and loan institutions
- The Better Business Bureau
- Publications by city, county and private financial institutions

STATE

- University innovation centers
- Office of the Secretary of State
- Office of state licensing
- State business associations
- Publications

FEDERAL

- Small Business Administration
- General Services Administration
- Federal Trade Commission
- National business groups
- Library of Congress
- Superintendent of Documents
- Government Printing Office, Washington D.C. 20402
- Department of Commerce
- U.S. government book stores

Extremely valuable sources of information listed above, are the Small Business Administration, United States Government book stores, and the Department of Commerce. You will find these agencies listed in your telephone directory under *United States Government*. These organizations will help you obtain all necessary information, or help you obtain referrals to other information sources. These in turn can be contacted by telephone, by letter, or in-person.

There are actually hundreds of information sources. It would only be confusing to list them here with addresses and telephone numbers. For one thing, some of them come and go. Their addresses and telephone numbers, and even their functions change continually. What is more important is that you have a planned approach on gathering useful information.

To get useful information, you must be clear about which specific facts you need each time you make an inquiry. You can start by getting information from one or two of the information sources listed above. Be as clear and precise as you can in asking questions. Vague questions often get unclear answers. The more pointed your questions, the more likely you are to get the right answers.

Try not to spend your valuable time initially with personal visits. Always start with the telephone. Do not hesitate to call long distance if a particular source is located out of town. In the long run, this will save you time and money.

Sometimes it will take more than one call to get to the right place. This can be a frustrating experience, especially if you are calling long distance. But you will find that people will generally go out of their way to help you if you are clear and courteous. When you call, ask if the person or agency has any materials which can be mailed to you. Consider a personal visit only if you need further information after going through these steps.

The best place to begin your search for general information or starter ideas is your local library. The next contact could be the Chamber of Commerce, then your local branch of the Small Business Administration. The people in these organizations can be extremely helpful in either assisting you or referring you to the proper sources. To answer your questions about licenses, zoning regulations and related matters, contact the appropriate city, county and state offices.

A library is often the number one source of information. Librarians can provide a veritable gold mine of facts and figures. They can help you locate books and articles on business in general as well as in your chosen field. Your librarian can also recommend directories that provide the names, addresses and backgrounds of local and national businesses.

The nature of the information you need will determine which sources you should contact first. If your local public library has several branches, use the main facility since it normally offers a wider selection of information. Business librarians are unusually well-qualified to guide your search. If they do not have the information, they can usually refer you to other sources.

Whether you borrow materials from a library or purchase them elsewhere, it is a good idea to make copies of the information that applies most directly to your investigation; bulky materials are too cumbersome to work with continually. Copying saves you from backtracking to the library or other agencies to review material you have already researched. Take detailed notes in situations where you can't reproduce material by copying.

Some other sources of information can be through personal business contacts and successful entrepreneurs. These people have practical business knowledge, and know where to get additional information. You may also be able to get valuable advice from successful entrepreneurs who are in your field but are not direct competitors. One example is a successful operator who is outside of your marketing area.

City hall can give you information on Community Development Corporations, and other local programs that help small businesses with funding. This office can also help refer you to other local offices if you have a question about local programs and regulations.

Another important source of information can be found in your county assessor's tax offices. They can provide you with information on zoning and local land-use regulations and taxes.

If you attend school, vocational and guidance counselors can often be a good starting point. Some schools also have career counseling offices that will have useful information. Junior and community colleges offer business courses, and often have instructors who are glad to share information even if you are not a student.

Accountants, attorneys and business consultants are also good sources of information. Since there would likely be fees involved, do your homework first to avoid paying for information you can obtain *without* cost. The procedure of finding and dealing with consultants is discussed in Section 7.

Business schools and instructors at state universities are often good information sources. These schools usually have their own libraries which are often open for public use.

For a low fee, university innovation centers can help you collect information on testing and marketing a new product or invention.

Information on state financing sources and information about licensing regulations are available at the appropriate state offices.

At the federal level, the Small Business Administration is one of your most useful sources for information. The SBA offers free or low-cost workshops, business checklists and financial worksheets. SBA's Service Corps of Retired Executives (SCORE) can give you direct information and advice on where to find further information. The Small Business Administration is also an excellent source for information on obtaining financing.

The General Services Administration can provide you with an up-to-date listing of local and national business associations.

Local and national business trade associations can provide you with contacts in or outside of your local area.

It is a good idea for you to organize all information you obtain by categories. As you collect more information on each subject from various sources, add it to your subject file. When the information is actually needed, review the entire file. Some people jot down notes on cards as they sort through these materials. Others accomplish the same results by highlighting or underlining important information. You may already have a good idea about a system that will work best for you.

All of your information-gathering should be done with one clear purpose in mind: Stay in touch with changes in your field by collecting general information, but do not accumulate information just for the sake of expanding your files.

Once you have collected and reviewed information, consider how it relates to solving your problem. Keep in mind that new procedures may or may not produce better results than your current ones. New approaches are *not* always better. Examine each piece of new information with a critical eye. If the new information does not give you reasonably precise answers to your questions or solutions to your problems, modify it to fit your situation. Above all, do not be afraid to test and experiment in order to come up with the best solution.

In summary, your ability and knowledge of where to find information is invaluable. It is also important not to be overwhelmed by the number of sources that have useful information. If you can find an answer by using one or two sources, stop right there. It is not necessary or advisable to duplicate your efforts by spending your time checking and rechecking other sources. They are always there in case you really need them.

Three Ways of Entering the World of Business

There are basically two approaches for going into business - starting it from the ground up or buying an existing business. But there is also a third way - the franchise. Although a franchise may either be a new or existing business, the approach to acquiring and operating one is different from other businesses. Therefore, we will treat it as a separate classification.

In this section we will discuss and compare the following three ways of getting into business:

- Starting a completely new company
- Buying an established business
- Acquiring a franchise

The comparison chart and following discussion highlight the advantages and disadvantages of each category.

COMPARISON CHART

Start-up Business	Existing Business	Franchise
1. Founder has control over start-up	Start-up phase has been completed	Joint business venture with franchisor
2. Full control over management decisions and policies. You are completely on your own to make decisions and set policies.	Full control, but already established policies; existing management and back-up - possible history of problems.	Somewhat limited control. Must follow established policies. Management back-up and consulting is provided.
3. Involvement in initial marketing analysis and advertising.	Market characteristics known. Advertising policies in place.	Extensive market analysis completed, advertising methods and policies established.
4. No established customer base or reputation	Established customer base and a good reputation	Name recognition and established reputation
5. New employees to be hired and trained	Trained personnel available	Some choice in personnel selection. Training provided.
6. Profit potential unknown	Current profits and profit history known	Realistic projections for profits available
7. Requires capital to purchase equipment, supplies and inventories	May have all required equipment, supplies and inventories. But may need major repairs or replacements.	Equipment and supplies usually included in cost of franchise. May require ongoing supply purchases from franchisor.

Start-up Business	Existing Business	Franchise
8. Full responsibility for financing; high start-up costs	Possibly owner financed; often lower cost than that of start-up	Frequent franchisor financing; may seem overpriced, but is often worth it
9. Entrepreneur's choice of location	Established location, but can be relocated	Location chosen by franchisor, but choice of sites may be offered
10. Full choice of design and layout	Design established, but can be changed	Fixed design
11. Entrepreneur receives all profits	Entrepreneur receives all profits, but may have to assume previous owner's liabilities	Profits shared with franchisor
12. Expansion planning possible	Expansion may be limited by location	Expansion may be limited by franchisor
13. Highest failure rate	Lower failure rate	Lowest failure rate

Discussion of the Chart

1. A new business gives you maximum opportunity to make independent start-up decisions. If your business experience is limited, you should consider obtaining advice from consultants. New businesses are especially vulnerable to miscalculations in financing, marketing and management approaches.

    Part of gaining experience in business is learning what does *not* work. This process of making mistakes and learning how to correct them is usually less of a threat in an established business than in a new enterprise. In buying an established business, you can safely assume that most start-up mistakes have already been made and overcome.

    A franchise can be either a start-up, or purchase of an existing operation. This can be an advantage, especially if you are inexperienced. However, even franchisors can make mistakes. You can check a franchisor's record of success by visiting other franchisees and talking to them about their experiences.

2. In a new business you have full control over management decisions and policies, even if you share them with one or more partners. With this control comes all the rewards of good management, as well as the risks of making mistakes.

    In taking over an existing business, you have much the same opportunity for making management decisions, but many policies will have already been set. Inherited employees may resist change. So if you plan to retain employees who worked for the previous owner, you may want to make policy changes slowly to give them an opportunity to adjust to your management style.

    Sometimes the business you buy may have been poorly managed by the former owners, and key personnel may be disgruntled or insecure, and in need of careful treatment during the transition period. At the same time, you should not hesitate to replace employees who you feel are not qualified - or who are impeding your policies. If there are no apparent personnel problems, take advantage of the old staff's experience. You may also be able to negotiate to have the owner stay for a limited time as a consultant.

    In a franchise business that has well-established management policies, most basic decisions will be made by the franchisor. This limits your opportunity to be completely independent, and you will have to rely on the franchisor's management skills. One concern that some owners have is that policies are sometimes too general to benefit all franchisees. For example, most franchisors attempt to standardize prices. To illustrate this in a general way, take this example:

    > In an automotive service franchise, the price of a brake installation in a high-income area will usually be the same as in a low-income area. The latter area may be a less attractive market for you because prices are set higher than people are willing or able to pay. In an independent business, you might deal with this problem by advertising to a wider area, raising or lowering prices, or trying other incentive approaches. In a franchise, you may have to consult the franchisor before you can try

any of these strategies. The franchisor will have the final say on your ideas.

3. Before starting your own business, you should conduct a market analysis and begin to plan your advertising strategy according to the information you develop. A very small business may not need a market analysis since you can evaluate your market by observation, and aim promotions for your products and services at the people you think will buy from you.

   In an existing business, many of your marketing and advertising questions will have already been answered. This doesn't mean you should not plan further analyses down the road, but you may be able to do it with less effort and at lower costs. The previous owner is familiar with the profile of the market and the business will already have an established customer base.

   In an established business you will have to pay close attention to market shifts and trends. Be aware that businesses selling fad items may have a lucrative short-term market, but future potential may be limited unless you are continually planning to introduce new products or services.

   It is, however, wrong to assume that all established businesses have adequate marketing and advertising plans in place. Often a business is for sale because it is encountering various problems in the marketing and sales areas. So it pays to take a close look at these difficulties. If you can recognize them and come up with good solutions, you might still consider buying the business, providing you can get it at the right price. In a franchise, the franchisor usually furnishes an elaborate market analysis. Realistically, you should request this information in the initial phase of your negotiations.

4. Your customer base includes your regular and prospective customers. A start-up business obviously has no customers or reputation beyond your own. An existing business will have established customers and, hopefully, a good reputation. Its reputation and customer base also make a difference in evaluating a business. You will have to carefully check and find out if old customers would continue buying products or services from the company when ownership changes. A new franchise, like a start-up business, does not have a customer base, but it should have name recognition and a good reputation. Potential customers will know what to expect from your business based on their experience with other outlets in that franchise.

5. There are also different aspects to personnel management. In a start-up business you have an open choice in the hiring of your employees. If you have one or more partners, you could have some limitations because your partners may have their own ideas on hiring.

   In a business you buy, you have the option to either retain the old staff or hire new employees. Keeping key personnel can save on training costs. However, it is sometimes easier to train new personnel than to retrain employees who have worked for an employer whose management style differs from yours. Employees often have difficulties adjusting to a new owner, so you may have to evaluate each employee individually before you decide to keep or replace that person.

In a franchise, you will generally be responsible for your own employee training. Some franchisors, however, offer not only employee training but will also furnish continued management assistance.

6. Profit potential in a new business is hard to predict. But with the help of a marketing consultant and accountant, you should be able to project future profits with some degree of accuracy.

   Your profit prediction will be easier if you go into a traditional business, since you can base an estimate on the statistics kept for firms similar to yours. If you start a non-traditional business, profits will be more difficult to anticipate.

7. In buying an existing business, you should ask for and review its records, including the profit and loss statement and balance sheets. A thorough inspection of the condition of the premises, machinery and inventory is essential. The availability of this equipment can often be a real advantage over what you would have to pay for it in a start-up situation. Supplies and stock on hand can also be cost-saving factors. It is essential to make sure that the supplies and inventory do not consist mostly of obsolete or unusable items.

   In a franchise, your equipment, starting supplies and inventory are often included in the price. Some franchisors may require you to buy your supplies from them. This can result in paying more for certain items than you would if you had purchased them from independent suppliers. More often, however, your franchisor will be able to keep your supply costs low by using bulk buying power.

8. One of the toughest problems facing a new business is obtaining adequate financing. Existing and franchise businesses often have clear advantages in this area; in both cases, owners may be willing to arrange or provide for favorable financing.

9. Based on market research, the choice of location for a new business is all yours. An existing business, of course, is already situated. A franchise location will be carefully researched and selected by the franchisor, although you may be offered a choice of various sites.

10. In a start-up business you have a wide range of choices for the layout and design of your facility - as budget permits. In an existing business, your choices are limited to remodeling, redesign, or expansion of the facility. In a drop-in traffic franchise, the fixtures and structures are usually uniform - conforming to other sites in the franchise organization.

11. All profits go to the entrepreneur and his partners, if any. When buying an existing business, you may have to assume some of the previous owner's obligations to lenders and suppliers. These payments must be taken into consideration when making cash flow projections. If the seller agrees to pay off his existing obligations, notify all creditors to that effect. Your attorney will advise you on how to go about it.

In a franchise, you will pay an initial franchise fee for the business and usually continue to pay the franchisor commissions on your sales. Plus, supplies for ongoing operations will usually be purchased from the franchisor.

12. In your start-up business, growth planning is completely up to you, and should be included as part of your business plan and choice of location. In buying an existing business, carefully review any expansion plans you may be considering. Find out if the space and facilities are adequate and project the time-frame and costs involved for future expansion. In expansion of a franchise, possibilities may be limited. For example, your carpet-upholstery steam-cleaning franchise may allow you to serve only certain areas of the city so your business does not interfere with other franchised territories. Your franchised fast-food restaurant may also be limited by building size and seating capacity. Any franchise agreement should clearly spell out these limitations.

13. One important consideration is the relative failure rate for the three types of businesses. New firms suffer generally higher failure rates than existing businesses which have already survived the start-up phase. Franchise businesses are built to copy a success formula, and therefore have very low failure rates. Established enterprises are generally less risky than start-up businesses. However, it is important to get as much information as possible about the owners' reasons for selling. When a business has operated under poor management or shows other problems you feel competent to correct, you may consider buying it if you are convinced that you are able to turn things around and make a success of it. After all, the business *has* been able to survive the start-up phase and been operating and supporting the owner. These are positive signs.

Operating Your Business Part or Full-Time

Another decision you will make regarding your start-up is whether it should be a full or part-time business. Each choice offers different advantages and disadvantages, and each will fit your needs differently.

If it is your intention to start your business on a part-time basis before going full-time, it would be a good idea to continue with your current job. It will present less of a financial risk for you while your business develops.

You will also be able to preserve your start-up capital and re-invest your profits into the business for quicker growth. If your choice is to permanently conduct your business as a part-time operation, it will give you more time for other responsibilities such as raising children, and for outside interests. It can also be ideal for people who do not have the time or energy, to be involved full-time.

Experience has shown that most successful part-time businesses will invariably develop into full-time operations.

In a full-time business, you should be prepared to work long hours, at least initially, until it begins to show profits. You will, consequently, experience faster growth and larger profits than in a part-time operation.

Your Business and its Location

Now that you have made the decision to start a business, you will begin to put your ideas to the test to see how realistic they are. Just renting a place, hanging out your shingle and waiting for business to come in is a sure way to set yourself up for disaster.

The next logical step after choosing the right type of business is to conduct a market analysis to discover just how it fits into the marketplace. This step is important *regardless* of the kind of business you are going to end up in. The following chart will give you an overview of market or trading areas for different types of businesses.

Overview of Market Areas For
Various Types of Small Businesses

Trading or Market Area	Manufacturing	Wholesale Industrial	Retail	Service
Neighborhood or entire town			X	X
State	X	X		X
Regional (several states)	X	X		X
National	X	X		
Export	X			

There obviously are exceptions, but the chart illustrates that manufacturing businesses are most often aimed toward regional, national, or international markets. Retail and service businesses go after markets closer to their base of operation.

No matter what type of business you have under consideration, you must determine what the demands for its products or services are. The investigative process requires close examination of two factors: Customer needs and demands for particular products or services, and the competition from other businesses which already meet those needs. The following basic example can be applied to many types of businesses:

If you plan to open a grocery store in a residential neighborhood, you must first determine how many people live close enough to your store to become customers. You should find out how many similar stores there are in the area and how they are doing. Determine whether they are solid, successful businesses, or are barely getting by. Knowing the answers to these questions will make your decision to locate in this neighborhood easier.

Evaluating Business Locations

Commercial Sites

While some entrepreneurs start their businesses from their homes, the majority will locate in commercial locations such as downtown, in shopping centers, strip centers, industrial parks or business-zoned residential areas.

The major advantage in situating a small business in a commercial location as compared to operating from your home is that it will be accepted by customers and suppliers more readily as a regular type of business. Your location, its appearance, the ease of reaching it, and the convenience of shopping, give people a feeling of stability and permanence about you and your business.

If you have a retail or other kind of drop-in business, you should probably be in an area close to other businesses to get the benefit of additional customer traffic. This will generally result in higher sales and profits.

Other considerations for locating in a commercial site are financial factors. If you have adequate financing for your start-up and continuing overhead expenses, your business will generate sales more quickly than if its location were in your home.

Below is a list of advantages and disadvantages for commercial business sites:

Advantages:

- Higher credibility - confidence-inspiring business-like appearance.

- Higher visibility and better location which generates additional customer traffic.

- More separation of your home-life and business.

- Fewer interruptions from family members.

Disadvantages:

- Higher overhead costs.

- Less availability to family members, if needed.

- Possible problems with access for handicapped entrepreneurs.

Yet it is interesting to note that many successful businesses have been started in entrepreneurs' homes and eventually moved to commercial locations. After reviewing additional information on home-based businesses, you will be in a better position to determine which way would be best for you.

The Pros and Cons of a Home-Based Business

We will first examine the advantages and disadvantages of operating a business from your home.

The number of home-based businesses is growing along with the increasing number of two-income families in the United States. These families work together to produce the income needed to support them. That often means parents can choose between being full-time employees and part-time parents, or having more time with the children and a lower income when one parent stays home. It can be an attractive alternative for parents who want to run a start-up business in their home and solve their child care problem at the same time.

What types of business can you operate from your home? Residential zoning will prohibit some types of businesses - especially high-traffic, hazardous or noisy operations. Crafts, specialty, mail-order and many service enterprises are often suitable. Bed and Board operations (modern-day inns operated in your home) are increasingly popular home businesses.

The most appropriate home businesses are ones that do not generate high customer traffic to survive and thrive.

Along with the increase in the number of two-income families, the affordability of personal computers has helped make some home businesses more practical. Computers can often handle the bookkeeping and payroll needs for a small business, as well as word processing, correspondence, and accessing information from other computers. Small computers can be equipped to make connections over telephone lines to communicate with other computers. These modems allow self-employed people to do work for larger companies via home computers. They are often called Telecommuters. While computers are useful and cost-effective, they are usually *not* essential to the operation of a small business.

Another reason why home-based businesses are attracting start-up entrepreneurs is that expenses for rent and furnishings can be cut. Utilities, telephone, wardrobe and other items are also reduced. Many a business that started in an entrepreneur's home developed into a successful enterprise. It's a good way to start if you operate on a shoestring.

One of the major disadvantages of a home-based business is establishing your credibility. It is important that your business appears to be professional and well-organized, particularly when you are dealing with drop-in customers. It can disrupt your home-life and your business if customers have to walk through your home to reach your shop or office. This can make them feel they are stepping into your personal life, and that can be uncomfortable. Also, if your home is not well organized or untidy, your customers may not be favorably impressed about your business management. Running your business from your garage, a building, or a room on your property that has a separate entrance is a better choice. You can convert your attached or free-standing garage to give it a business-like appearance. You can consider a portion of remodeling costs as a business expense when the premises are used exclusively for that purpose. Be sure to carefully check IRS regulations regarding this deduction.

Another disadvantage is being isolated from regular business contacts. It is easy to develop "cabin fever". A good way to guard against this is by staying active in local and national business groups; to read newsletters from business associations and organizations, and to maintain regular contacts with other local entrepreneurs. If you are home-bound, make use of your telephone, computer, and other media to stay in touch. Many home businesses use telephone answering machines or answering services to maintain communications between the business and its customers and suppliers.

An SBA publication observes that it may be tempting to "keep the money in the family" by employing family members. It is likely that the interrelationships will be about as harmonious as the members of the household are with each other on a personal basis. Keep this in mind.

Home-based business people also report that the family "pecking order" can be an issue. A family member who is generally considered head of the household may not be the right person for a position requiring supervision and training by another family member. Ruffled feathers can easily lead to lack of objectivity, poor decision-making, and an unproductive work environment.

Potential drawbacks to hiring family members need to be examined and balanced against potential assets such as convenience; frequent communication about business matters; the opportunity to provide young people with job training, etc. A family member is likely to bring a spirit of teamwork to the job and a willingness to deal wholeheartedly with crisis situations. The result of hiring family members can be, like so many other aspects of running a business, a full-time balancing act between conflicting ideas and opinions.

It is also important to guard against excessive time demands of family members during business hours. Decide ahead of time how much attention you will normally give them during business hours, and what kind of emergencies would justify an exception. For example, you may decide to set aside certain hours when your children can be with you in the work area, and when they will have to be away from your activities and watched by someone else.

Before you start your home-based business, check into the zoning laws with your city or county authorities. Some business activities blend well in a family or residential neighborhood. But other activities are not suitable since they may generate noise, pollution or heavy traffic. It is advisable to consult with an attorney before committing time and money to your project. One wrong step can be costly.

Another workplace issue is how you divide your home-space and your work-space. Tax laws are very specific about how you use the space you claim as shop, office, or merchandise storage space. For example, the Internal Revenue Service will not allow you to deduct part of your home expense as an office if you also use that area for non-business purposes (like using your office as a den during non-business hours).

Here's a quick look at the pros and cons of a home business:

Advantages:

- Lower start-up and ongoing expenses for overhead (including office space and furnishings, utilities, telephone, and wardrobe).

- No commuting costs (gas, parking, automobile expenses, and travel time).

- Special use of telecommuting for mobility-disabled entrepreneurs.

- More flexibility in your schedule, and opportunities to be with children during normal working hours.

Disadvantages:

- Lower credibility than a commercial business location.

- Isolation from the business community.

- Interruptions by family members.

- Difficulties in keeping work and personal space separate.

Major Business Categories and Site Considerations

Start-up businesses can broadly be divided into four major groupings:

- Manufacturing
- Wholesale and Industrial distribution
- Retail
- Services

Manufacturing

If you are planning to manufacture a product line, for example, ceramic pottery, you should conduct your investigation along the following lines: First, you should be confident that your products are unique - that they are sufficiently different from competitive products on the market. It is essential to get to know these competing product lines. Your market investigation should include interviews with retailers and wholesalers. Based on their experience, you will learn about the sales potential of *your* products. A cost study of your manufacturing process should reveal whether you can produce these products at costs that will enable you to sell them profitably. Of course, if you plan to enter a business field you are already fully familiar with, your market analysis will be much simpler.

If you decide to start a manufacturing operation, you should be thinking in terms of a *product line*, rather than offering a single item. A product line consists of a number of related products. For an example, it could be a line of scuba equipment and accessories, tanks, regulators, wet and dry suits, fins, face masks and so on.

Why is it so important to have a full line, rather than one specialty item? Suppose you have designed and developed a revolutionary new fireplace insert. You have determined that it is unique, and distributors and retailers are anxious to sell it. Your fireplace insert becomes a great success. There is a good possibility that competitors will imitate your ideas and, in some cases, with added improvements and at *lower* prices.

The most effective way to overcome competition is to innovate and produce improved and new versions of your products. Another strategy is to wholesale related items to your dealers; containers for indoor wood storage and other utensils are related to woodstoves, so would fit this strategy.

The first step in deciding on the viability of a new product or product line is to talk with the people who will sell them. This includes retailers, industrial supply companies, distributors, etc. They will give you a "feel" for the market. Also contact manufacturing trade associations for additional data. Find out which ones are involved with products like yours. Don't be afraid to talk with competitive manufacturers. You will find most of them willing to give you information about that market. By pulling together and analyzing the various bits of information, you will gain good insight into your industry and, in the long-run, avoid costly mistakes and save time and money.

The first prerequisite for success is to offer the types of products and services that meet your customers' needs. That's why it is important to learn as much as you can about your market and competition. This will be discussed in greater detail in the section about *Building Sales and Profits*.

In choosing a location for your manufacturing business, consider the following guidelines:

- Whenever possible, allow room for future expansion; consider taking an option for additional space.

- Choose a location that is relatively convenient for your employees. It should be accessible by car or public transportation. Many out-of-the-way plants have difficulties in retaining employees due to this fact.

- If your operation has heavy electrical power requirements, make sure these services are available since the linework needed to bring additional electric service to a business can be costly.

- Check the availability of services by freight, express and parcel delivery companies. You do not want to find yourself in a position of having to pick up and deliver materials.

  If the facility is above or below the ground floor, investigate the condition and load capacity of the freight elevator. This will be especially important if the weight of your equipment and materials are excessive.

Wholesaling and Industrial Supply

This is a broad field. Wholesalers traditionally buy merchandise from manufacturers and sell them to retailers. We also include in this category businesses selling to other businesses and organizations, such as industrial suppliers, telephone equipment companies, computer and data processing suppliers, janitorial supplies, etc.

Wholesaling is basically a warehousing and sales-oriented operation. Depending on the products and merchandise you are handling, your market area can range from local to national distribution.

Most wholesalers serving a particular industry carry the same kind of merchandise at the same price levels. Very few offer "exclusive" items. In view of that sameness among wholesalers, success hinges largely on these factors:

- Having an efficient warehouse operation and inventory control
- Providing outstanding service to customers
- Superior salesmanship

Unless you are fully familiar with a specific type of wholesale or industrial supply business you will need to research the market conditions in your area for this type of business. Investigate your competitors, and determine how well their businesses are doing. Your bank may be able to supply you with Dun and Bradstreet data on the scope, size and sales volume of their businesses. This information can help you assess your potential to succeed in this business. It can also be helpful to visit prospective customers to find out what they think of their present suppliers, and whether there is room for one more.

Wholesaling requires little specialized equipment except for storage and material handling like storage racks and forklifts.

Your choice of a wholesaling business site will be much like that for locating a manufacturing plant. In addition, it is advantageous to find a facility with high ceilings for your warehouse area. This will enable you to store more goods per square foot by using storage racks, resulting in savings in rent and utilities.

Retail

After you choose the kind of store you are going to open, the next consideration is site selection. Of all businesses, retail depends more than any other on the right location in order to succeed. In fact, it often has been said that the three most important factors in the success of a retail business are location, location and location. The importance of location cannot be overemphasized.

Everything else being equal, a store with good visibility and offering easy parking will attract more traffic than one in an inconvenient and hard-to-reach location.

There are other considerations important to success. You will need to determine how many customers or families it will take to support your store. This obviously varies with the type of store it is. A grocery store owner can make a living by drawing business from people living within a few blocks. A sporting goods store may need a customer base from a wider area - often covering smaller towns or several zip codes in a larger city.

Everyone buys groceries, but markets for specialty items are spread over larger areas since not everyone will have an interest in golf or ski equipment. Your trading area is the geographic area which will provide a sufficient number of customers and a sales volume to make your business profitable. This area may be a neighborhood; a small town; an area covered by one to several zip codes, or even an entire city. These demographics are particularly important if you are a specialty retailer, like an upscale dress shop, a pet store or a gourmet deli, to mention a few.

The demographics in a trading area include key facts such as average incomes and age levels; educational backgrounds; ethnic makeup, and occupational characteristics. This information enables you to plan a store that will appeal to the residents of the area. Keep the obvious in mind: Expensive merchandise or services will not sell in a low-income area, while low-priced goods do not do well in high-income areas.

You can begin the process of choosing a location by driving around your town or in the areas you are considering. Become familiar with the various neighborhoods, shopping centers, and downtown shopping districts. After you begin to narrow down your choices, examine the remaining areas more closely.

Next, contact the U.S. Department of Commerce and obtain the Bureau of Census reports on areas and population. They are broken down into small sections (SMA's or "Standard Metropolitan Statistical Areas"). These will give you information on the various sections of your community, or your town in general. Reports include information on income; ages; occupations; living situations (apartments and homes); movement in and out of the area, and related data.

You can use this information to help you target your customers. For example, if you are considering opening a clothing store, part of your decision whether to sell off-the-rack clothing or more expensive specialty items will depend upon the income of residents in your targeted area.

You can also contact the post office in your trading area to find out how many homes and apartments there are in each zip code. If your store's trading area does not cover a complete zip code, the post office has statistics and maps for smaller sections, called carrier routes, within each zip. This will give you a good idea of how many households there are to draw business from. You can obtain further information through discussions with your local banker and other merchants in the area. You may also gain valuable information by observing how busy your competitors are during certain hours and days of the week. Shoppers can also be interviewed briefly. This gives you additional input on the characteristics of your potential customers.

The next step is to determine how many customers you can reasonably expect to patronize your store. Customer traffic volume studies for automobiles and pedestrians are often a good indication of how active a shopping area is. There are companies that furnish this information. You can also conduct these surveys by yourself. The kind of information that is usually collected in a traffic count is:

• The number of pedestrians and/or automobiles passing the site during business hours at regular (usually half-hour) intervals. This is often broken down by age ranges, sex, or other obvious characteristics.

• The number and percentage of pedestrians who patronize competitive businesses. The total number of pedestrians passing the site is divided by the number who enter. This gives the percentage of people who visit that store. For example, at one store, 1,000 people pass and 157 enter during one day. That is 15.7% of the pedestrian traffic.

• The number and percentage of pedestrians who enter the business and make a purchase. This can be determined by counting the ones leaving with packages.

By themselves, these figures don't mean too much. However, if you know the dollar amount of an average purchase for that type of business, you can make some estimates of monthly and annual sales volume.

For example, an average of 2,000 pedestrians pass a certain store each day. 200 people, or 10 percent, enter. And 50 people make purchases. These 50 represent 2.5 percent of the people who walked by or 25 percent of the people who went in. Estimating that the average purchase for this store is $30.00, the sales would be $1,500.00 per day (50 x $30.00) or about $450,000 per year (based on 300 business days).

Many business areas, from neighborhood strip centers (businesses clustered on the same street) to shopping malls, have anchor stores. These stores are large retailers (including department stores, supermarkets or large drugstores) which attract high customer volume through reputation and heavy advertising. They generally have a large loyal customer base. Smaller stores often do well being located near these high-volume stores.

Specialty stores can be located almost anywhere. These shops do not require high visibility since customers look for them. Typically, specialty stores depend more on publicity and advertising than on casual drop-in business. They usually carry medium to high-priced merchandise. Shoppers are willing to go out of their way to visit them. Generally, a location that offers free or merchant-paid parking is preferable to one with street parking only.

A word about competition. Some competitors do quite well by being located close to each other; for example, clusters of furniture stores or car dealers. Smaller stores in shopping centers often attract traffic for each other. They encourage customers to comparison-shop, but because of high customer traffic, present no real competitive problems.

Another aspect in finding the right location is the rental factor. You may be faced with a choice of paying high rent in a prime area, or paying low rent in a less desirable location. If you can estimate which location will lead to higher profits (an estimate you can make with the help of your accountant) then the decision where to locate should be much easier.

Services

Service businesses can be attractive to new entrepreneurs because they are relatively easy to start and generally require smaller initial investments. The major service groupings are personal services; such as photo studios; health clubs; rental services, etc., business services such as advertising agencies and others. And repair services such as automobile; welding; musical instrument repair, etc.

Much of what we have discussed in the retail category also applies to service businesses. One exception to this is location. A service business does not need to be in a high customer traffic location. Since service businesses are more personal in nature, customers are willing to travel a bit more to patronize them. Whenever services are performed on the customers' premises, that is, in their homes or businesses, your business location may be relatively unimportant. However, if your business is more retail-oriented (like a photo studio or a dry cleaner), its appearance should resemble more to that of a retail store.

The key to a successful service business is *service*. This means doing a good quality job at a reasonable price and performing it to the customer's complete satisfaction. It also requires being prompt and guaranteeing your work. Almost anyone following these guidelines can be assured of success. Not surprisingly, service businesses generate the greatest number of complaints with regard to workmanship, unfair and "extra" charges, broken promises, and failure to complete jobs on time. An entrepreneur who is truly service-minded and has the ability to get things done will find an excellent opportunity to do well regardless of competition.

Additional Guidelines for Renting or Leasing a Business Location

By the time you begin to look for a location, you should know how much money to allocate for rental expense. If you have a business plan, it will show as a budget item. To be on the safe side, allow for an additional 10 percent if you find an *exceptional* location. Be aware, however, that the terms of the rent or lease can be more important than the price per square foot. Utilities, janitor service, garbage disposal, taxes, repairs, etc., are all items that affect the cost of the basic rent, depending on who pays for what; and they are negotiable.

There is usually a percentage lease in good retail locations. You pay a certain percentage of your sales in addition to a fixed lease payment. The length of the lease, and options for lease renewal, are also very important. Another item to closely consider is the cost of getting the premises ready for your occupancy according to your requirements. Also, who is to pay for it: You? The owner? Or on a shared basis? If you weigh each of these items carefully, you will be able to calculate your *real* lease cost.

Based on the type of business you plan to enter, you should have a general idea of what is important in a location. As previously discussed, driving around various areas will help you narrow down the most desirable areas, and the ones that meet your requirements.

Most, but not all, vacancies will have signs posted either by realtors or owners. If you want to check on a vacancy listed by a realtor, do not attempt to contact the owner directly. The fact that a property is listed usually indicates that the owner prefers not to deal personally with prospective tenants. It is better to work through the realtor since he is often in a position to get you a better deal than you could secure on your own. The realtor will also have information on other locations that may not be identified by posted signs.

Pay close attention to the zoning, building and fire codes of the locations you are interested in. Make certain there are no present violations, or likely future conflicts with your business operations. The same applies to electrical and plumbing codes. It is highly recommended that you personally check these items out with the proper authorities. This is not a task to delegate to someone else since it can cost you dearly if you later find yourself in violation.

Some other important questions are:

- Are the premises and foundation in good condition, or will they need major repairs?

- What is the estimated cost for renovation?

- Are utilities and equipment adequate?

- Will there be major repairs required now or in the near future?

- Will you, the owner, or the utility company be responsible for any repairs?

- Does the owner seem willing to deal with your needs promptly, as they come up?

Talk with other lessees about the owner's attitude in such matters to determine what kind of person or company you are dealing with. It is advisable not to lease the first location that appeals to you. Shop around and compare. Don't be afraid to tell the realtor that you can get a better deal elsewhere, if that happens to be the case. Remember that everything is negotiable. Offer less than you expect to pay, and be prepared to compromise.

One more important location factor: Be sure that your site, the zoning and other codes will allow for expansion. Many businesses need to expand even before the first lease term ends. This can put businesses that do not have room to expand on-site in a financial bind since it may mean moving or renting additional space, both of which are time consuming and costly.

Before you enter into serious discussions for a lease with the property owner or realtor, be prepared for some bargaining. Bear in mind that the people you are dealing with have more experience than you in negotiating a lease. Make a list of the amenities you want the owner to provide, such as improved lighting, plumbing, painting, free parking and other improvements. Be flexible in trade-offs or shared expenses. You can offer to do some of these things at your expense for a reduction in rent or free rent for a certain period of time. Once you have reached a general understanding on the lease terms and special arrangements, request a letter summarizing the details. Do *not* sign a lease without your attorney's approval.

A relatively new development in providing space for new enterprises are the Small Business Incubators. They are sponsored individually or jointly by public agencies (federal, state, local or universities) with the participation of private enterprises. In an Incubator, several small businesses share a receptionist, copying facilities, consultants and pay initially low rent which gradually increases as the firm's ability to pay grows. The National Business Incubation Association will provide further information on the program and offer referrals to local contacts. Check it out at the library or with the SBA.

Buying an Established Business

Some of the major advantages in buying an established business are:

- The business has already gone through a successful start-up phase.

- It has proven management policies and trained personnel.

- It has an established market, a reputation and a customer base.

- It has a known history of earnings.

- It has equipment, inventory and supplies on hand.

- Financing for the business may be available from the owner.

- The purchase price is often less than that required to start a similar business as a start-up.

- The facility is in current use and can often be taken over without any additional expenditures.

- The success rate of an established business is higher than that for most start-ups. Over 80 percent of established companies are still in business five years after the purchase, compared to less than 20 percent for start-up businesses.

Where and How Do You Find An Established Business to Buy?

The first step is to decide what types of businesses you would like to be involved in. Review the *How To Conduct Your Search for Your Best Money-Making Opportunity* in this section, to determine the type of business that especially interests you.

Next, watch the Business Opportunities column in your local newspaper's classified ads. Call and talk with the advertisers to see what they have to offer. If you are looking for a larger, more substantial business, the Wall Street Journal may be an excellent source. Also, check with your lawyer, banker, realtor, trade association contacts, and friends for any information they may have on businesses that are for sale. Contact one or two reputable business brokerage firms.

Once you have found a business that sounds interesting to you - and the asking price falls within an acceptable price range - you can begin with your investigation.

The first step is to review the financial aspects. Ask for annual statements for the last five years, the income tax returns of the owner and the company, if it is a corporation. If the business is less than five years old, proceed with extreme caution in your analysis since such businesses have higher failure rates. Also, request monthly or quarterly statements, if available. A quick examination of these documents can tell you whether it is worthwhile to move on to serious negotiations. Unless you are an accountant, get the help of a qualified CPA to help you assess the firm's financial health. Do not use an accountant recommended by your business broker since self-interest could get in the way of an objective opinion. An accountant will be able to identify many of the positive and negative aspects of the business, and advise you on what kind of questions to ask to clarify doubtful points.

Obviously you want to buy a business showing good profits. But some businesses may show losses. This in itself should not deter you from investigating further. Perhaps you have the capability to turn the situation around and make the business profitable. A loss situation should, however, influence the price you are willing to pay. If you decide that it is worthwhile to continue your investigation, proceed along the following lines:

Make a thorough personal inspection of the premises, paying particularly close attention to the condition of the fixtures, equipment, inventory and supplies. Also determine whether supplies and inventory are in usable condition.

If the firm is a retail store, or a business that depends on customer traffic, analyze the location according to the outlines previously discussed. Here are some questions to ask yourself: Is the space adequate for the business as it is now? Would it be sufficient for any expansion you anticipate? Is adjoining space available?

Investigate the customer base and get answers to the following questions about the business:

- Who are their customers?
- Where are those customers located?
- How many current customers are there?
- Are purchases seasonal or year-round?
- What are the key customer characteristics?
- Is customer loyalty closely tied to the present owner?
- Would customers stop doing business with a new owner?
- Will customers be concerned about who owns the business?

These questions are important regardless of the type of business involved.

It is also important to ask the owner *why* he is selling the business. Although he may or may not give you all of the real reasons, the answers you do get can be revealing. Indicate that you would like to check with his bank, suppliers and major accounts (if the business is industrial). Get his permission first, since the owner may not desire any premature disclosure about a sale. You should also request a copy of the rental or lease agreement, to make sure it allows you to continue operating on an unrestricted basis at that location.

By this time you should have a fairly good idea what the business is like - its current status, its potentials and drawbacks. You will develop a sense of whether the business is growing, static, or losing ground in sales, profit and market share. Make projections of how it will be doing in one or two years under *your* management.

Next, investigate the operational style closely. How well has the business been managed? How have the owners worked with their employees? Were the managers included in the planning, operational and decision-making process? Are they involved in the long-range and day-to-day decisions?

If you are permitted to talk with a manager or some of the employees, you may get an accurate picture of how well you may be able to work with them, and if their loyalty to the previous owner may present problems.

Question the owners on how they look at their business, how they see its strengths and weaknesses. Then make a judgment on how well you might deal with these aspects.

Based on your investigations, observations and gut-feelings, you will make the final decision on whether you will make an offer. If an offer is made, you will need to make three determinations:

- The value of the business

    There are a number of ways to arrive at the value of a business. The most commonly used formulas are:

    a. Return on investment
    b. Discounted cash flow or discounted future earnings
    c. Replacement cost
    d. Price/earning estimate of value
    e. Comparable sales approach (sales prices of similar businesses)
    f. Combinations of any of the above.

- The maximum you are willing to pay.

    You must establish reasons to support the maximum price you are willing to pay by considering the following:

    a. Value as determined by one or a combination of the above formulas
    b. Capital available for investment
    c. Capital available for "working capital"
    d. Availability of credit and loans on acceptable terms

- The offer and terms

    In making an offer for a business the following points should be considered:

a. The price and the terms should be most favorable to you as the buyer.

b. Establish the difference in value between an all cash offer and one with part cash and the remainder on contract.

c. Be aware of the difference in total cash outlay for contracts of varying lengths and interest rates.

d. Make sure your initial offer provides substantial negotiating room both in price and terms.

It is beyond the scope of this manual to go into the technical details of each negotiating area. The best advice we can offer is this: Use the services of a competent accountant and attorney to help you negotiate and consummate the purchase. Business brokers can also sometimes be helpful in negotiating, but they *do* represent the interests of the seller. Keep your banker informed about the progress of your negotiations, and listen carefully to your consultants' advice and observations.

None of your consultants can or should make the final decision for you. They are there to advise you, offer opinions, make recommendations, and help you negotiate. However when the chips are down the decision is all yours - you have the final say on the wisdom of going ahead with a deal or walking away from it.

If you decide to buy, your attorney will draw up a Letter of Intent which is presented to the owners. If this letter is accepted, your and the owner's attorney will prepare all other documents necessary to finalize your purchase. After all papers have been signed and money has changed hands, you will receive the keys and you are in business. Review Section 8 on How to Sell Your Business at a Profit. It will give you insight into the sellers' points-of-view which should be helpful in how you should deal with them advantageously.

Acquiring a Franchise

You may enter a franchise as a start-up business, or buy an existing franchise. The franchise approach relieves you of some of the work you would have to do if you started or bought an independent business since many of these steps are taken care of for you.

One significant difference between being a franchisee and an independent entrepreneur is this: As a franchisee, the rules and regulations that govern the way you must operate the business are set by the franchisor. If you feel strongly about being independent in business, approach the idea of becoming a franchisee with care. If you like to take risks and believe you can do better on your own, you will not be a happy and successful franchisee. But if you have previously worked in a structured environment in a large organization, and feel comfortable adhering to guidelines, a franchise may be the best way for you to go.

The price of franchise operations usually consists of the initial franchise fee and continuing royalties based on sales volume. In addition, you must provide working capital and funds for equipment and improvements. Most franchisors will help you obtain the necessary financing for these outlays. Here are some of the major advantages of buying a franchise rather than an established business:

- Clear, outlined start-up steps.
- Established management policies.
- Management training, consulting, and sometimes employee training.
- Marketing consulting and a completed extensive market analysis.
- Local and national advertising.
- An established reputation and name recognition.
- A track record of success.
- Standard equipment and supplies that are often (but not always) low-cost because of the franchisor's bulk purchasing power.
- Franchisor financing.
- Completed location analysis.
- Facility design.
- Comparatively high success rate.

How do you go about selecting a franchise? Much the same way as you would select an established business. You begin by identifying your own likes, dislikes, and interests. The U.S. Department of Commerce's *Franchising Opportunities Handbook* is a good resource. It provides a thumbnail sketch of information on franchises across the country. It lists the following information on U.S. franchises:

- Location of the franchise headquarters.
- Description of the franchise operation.
- Number of franchises.
- The year it was established.
- Equity capital needed to buy a franchise.
- Financial assistance.
- Training.
- Management assistance.

There are many other books and publications dealing with franchise operations available. Check with your library or in bookstores.

Just as in buying an established business, it is up to you to carefully check the background of the franchisors you are dealing with. You should be interested in learning more about:

- Company's profile.
- Financial statements.
- Officers' backgrounds.
- Terms and conditions of franchise agreement.
- Training provided for you and employees.
- Advertising procedures.
- Volume discounts.
- Accounting procedures.
- Exclusivity of territory you purchase.
- References from other franchisees.
- Reliability.

You should still go through the same qualifying procedure as you would in checking out a start-up business. But it won't be necessary to perform a market study - and site selection will not be required; these are almost always provided by the franchisor and reviewed by you.

Before you sign closing agreements, you, your accountant and attorney should review the franchisor's disclosure statement. The franchisor is required by law to file this financial statement with the Federal Trade Commission at least 10-days before the deal closes. The statement will give you an idea of the franchisor's current finances, predicted earnings per franchise, franchise terms, and the track record of franchise successes.

The Business Plan

In this section, we will first discuss the importance of a formal business plan. Then we'll go through the steps of actually setting one up. This plan can be essentially for start-up or existing businesses since it is one of the most important tools for obtaining financing. As you go through this section, keep in mind that the information is applicable to both existing *and* start-up businesses.

Importance of Your Business Plan

Setting up a formal business plan is important for three major reasons. The first is that most lenders and investors require it. The business plan provides an overview of where you expect your business to go in the future. It also introduces your ideas and outlines how you plan to use the loan proceeds. It affords a basis for lenders to evaluate your start-up ideas or the needs of your established business before they consider your request for funds.

First a word about writing a business plan. The best way is to present it in a straight-forward manner. Use short words and sentences, active modern language. Avoid stilted outmoded expressions. It has been estimated that as many as half of all business plans are rejected on writing alone.

Organization of the plan plays an important role. Do not make the reader dig through the entire text before he knows what your objective is. If writing a plan seems intimidating to you and you feel you are not fully qualified in writing it yourself, hire a professional to do the job. The cost will more than pay for itself. But make sure that the ideas presented are your own.

A second reason for preparing a business plan is that it will, like a road map, show where your business has been and in which direction you expect it to go. This will also help you to compare your actual performance with your plan and manage your resources accordingly.

Finally, a well developed business plan helps you look carefully at your business - the way an outsider might see it. This objective view enables you to step back and observe its strong and weak points more clearly. By reviewing your plan from time to time, you can determine whether you are reaching your targets or if certain corrections are called for.

Organizing Your Business Plan

As mentioned, it is essential that the ideas presented in your business plan are your own or those of you and your partners. Putting it together can initially be a nearly overwhelming undertaking. But like any big project, it will seem more manageable when you break it down into small components and deal with each part one at a time. There isn't a single best way to organize a business plan, but here are some ideas on how you can approach it:

- Begin by listing your objectives and how the money will be used. For example, to open a store or a service business; to move to another location; to add additional services; to increase your operation's sales volume by 50 percent in a two year period, or for the acquisition of new equipment.

- Explain why your objectives are important and give reasons for having these objectives. For example, buying a specialized piece of equipment may be desirable because it will lower your production costs and/or raise the quality of your products, giving you advantages over your competitors. Another objective may be the development of new markets.

- Description of your personal and business background. If you are already in business, give an overview of the industry and your business history. If you are a start-up entrepreneur, also fully describe your past business-related activities. Evaluate the competition you are facing.

- Estimate the amount of the loan or line of credit needed and propose a re-payment schedule.

- Get your accountant's ideas on how to present your figures, explaining how the amount requested will accomplish your stated objectives.

- Before you actually begin writing the plan, review its outline personally with prospective lenders, investors, or banks to determine what their requirements are in order to properly evaluate it.

- Your plan should look as professional as possible in terms of physical appearance; it represents your business. The first part should deal with the plan itself. The balance will consist of supporting documents such as actual or pro-forma statements, brochures of your products, etc. It should be bound in a folder. Although there are no set rules, most plans run between 30 and 100 pages. How clearly you put down your ideas is much more important than length of the document.

- Prospective lenders and investors are most interested in the nature of the business; the amount of money required; how it is going to be used; the terms; your management team; sales and profit projections and the uniqueness of your products or services. Venture capitalists who usually take an equity position in a company have five requirements before they consider a proposal seriously:

1. Superior Management*
2. Superior Management*
3. Superior Management*
4. Uniqueness of Products and/or Services
5. A well-formulated Marketing Plan

*It *is* that important!

Next, a generalized outline of the essential elements contained in effective business plans. Please note that we are not presenting an actual example of a business plan. This could influence the writer of a plan to follow it too closely, and might suppress the use of original ideas.

Each plan is different in that each situation is unique. The substance of the business plan must be tailored to each circumstance.

BUSINESS PLAN

Name of Company

Address

Telephone Number

by

Your Name,
President

This page is optional. Here you may enter a statement to the effect that the business plan is your property, and that it is not to be used without your permission. Here are two ways to make that statement:

This business plan is for the proprietary use of
_____ and _____
(Your company)   (Your name)

Those receiving this plan agree to use it only with the authority
of _____.
                (Your name)

                                    or

This business plan is for the proprietary use of the XYZ
Corporation and its president (your name). Those receiving this
plan agree to use it only with the authority of (your name).

TABLE OF CONTENTS

A.   Introduction
B.   Description of the products/services offered
C.   Your Market
     · Size and potential
     · Competition
     · Economic factors affecting
       – Advertising
       – Sales methods
D.   Product/Service Cost and Pricing
E.   Operations
     · Facility/Equipment
     · Expansion schedule and plans
F.   Finances
     · Historical statements
       – Income
       – Balance
       – Cash flow
     · Projections ("pro forma" statements)
       – Income
       – Balance
       – Cash flow
G.   Management Organization
     · Background and experience of principals
     · Table of organization
H.   Financial Proposal
     · Funds requested, and use
     · Repayment time
     · Collateral
I.   Attachments
     · Advertising copy
     · Personnel resumes

Depending on your situation, you can add to or delete from these headings.

A. Introduction

Your introduction is a summary of your business plan. It is a quick overview and summary of your business, its activities and your needs for financing. It should cover:

- Name and location of your business (existing or prospective).

- Type of products and services offered.

- Type of ownership.

- Amount of financing required and use of funds.

- Repayment terms desired.

- Guarantees or collateral for the loan or funds, if applicable.

Introduction to Northeast Biostructure's
Business Plan

Northeast Biostructure, a corporation chartered in the state of Maine, has recently received patent rights to produce Bio-joint 3, a surgical cement for use in human bone-joint replacement and some orthopedic surgery procedures. Bio-joint 3 can be used in place of surgical pins to bond healing bones. Bio-joint 3 is not x-ray opaque, so it will not interfere with post-surgery diagnostic x-rays.

Bio-joint 3 surgical cement has been in veterinary testing for five years and has now been approved for human use.

Use of this cement will add from 5% to 15% to the cost of usual bone-setting surgery. However, it will eliminate need for bone-pin removal procedures and the added cost and discomfort of those procedures, since the cement requires no invasive removal. This is estimated to result in a total cost savings of between 15% and 25% over usual procedures.

Northeast Biostructure was started by Mr. Terry Jones in 19__ as a sole proprietorship. It was incorporated in the state of Maine in 19__. Mr. Jones is the majority stockholder of the corporation, with Mr. Keith Smith and Ms. Jane Galloway being minority stockholders.

The company has been involved in the research and development of various medical products and manufactured a line of medical specialty products. (See attachments)

The corporation is now seeking funds in the amount of $980,000 with terms and a re-payment schedule shown in an attachment hereto.

The money will be used to purchase new and modify existing production equipment for the manufacture of Bio-joint 3. Our market research and interviews with medical experts in this field have elicited favorable comments. The product has received wide publicity in several medical journals (see attachments) and many inquiries from physicians expressing intense interest and requests for information. Our marketing plan provides for personal contacts with physicians and an intense selling effort to medical supply houses.

Assuming a loan approval is received and commitment for the funds by February 15, 19___, we should be able to commence production by September of this year. It is our projection that we will achieve a 50% market share within two years of its introduction in the New England area and a 15% - 20% market share, nationally, within five years.

The loans can be secured by a second mortgage on our manufacturing facilities and personal guarantees by the stockholders.

We are looking forward to a personal meeting with you and your staff at your earliest convenience to discuss this matter in greater detail.

Sincerely,

Terry Jones
President

B. Description of the products and services offered.

Following the introduction, you will next describe in greater detail the nature of your business and the application of funds. Avoid, however, going into minute details. This can sometimes lose the attention of your reader and your financing. It could also place your project in a vulnerable position, especially if your idea is original. It is very unlikely that a lender would misappropriate your idea, but it is not necessary to expose any more than necessary at this point.

Examples:

This electronic sensor/alarm attaches automatically to any bathtub or washbasin, and sounds an alarm if water is over 105° (or any other set temperature). This is a warning device that can guard against burns, and is especially important in homes with young children or the frail elderly. Customers are expected to be middle-aged, married, with middle-class incomes.

Or, describe what the product or service does, and how well it performs.

"Care" provides a full range of day care services and care-taker respite services (including counseling, health-care, exercise, and special interest groups) for adults with Alzheimer's disease. People who are taking care of these people in their homes will be able to carry on their regular work and home schedules with the help of this service, at a cost considerably lower than that charged in nursing homes.

C. Your market.

This section will define your market, your competition, and your marketing strategies. Begin by talking about the market's size and potential for growth. If you have not included an "Application and Primary Prospects" section, you will need to point out now just who will use your products or services and the channels of distribution.

Estimate the total number of possible customers and users for your product or service. For example, one product, a protective car seat for children aged one to four. The number of children in this age range is expected to increase by 20 percent within five years. Over 90 percent of the customers for the product are expected to be college educated mothers up to 32 years of age. To estimate the market size for this product, divide the total market size, that is, the number of children (information available in census reports) in this age bracket by the number of manufacturers for child automobile safety seats. For the purpose of the estimates, we assume that the competitors are equally strong and attract the same number of customers.

Next, describe your competitors. In order to evaluate your position in the market, most lenders will want to know more about them -

- Who they are, their number and locations.
- Their sales volumes.
- Their marketing sales techniques and channels of distribution.
- Their advertising programs.

Explain why you expect customers to prefer your products or services over those of your competitors. Think of other selling points which may favorably influence lenders. For example: If your business serves the local market and a major employer has announced the opening of a new facility, show how the influx of this labor force will benefit you and how you will go about attracting those newcomers.

D. Product/service cost and pricing.

In this section you will elaborate on costs and mark-ups of your products or services and show anticipated profits. It is also important to compare your costs and pricing to those of competitive products or services. If your products or services are higher priced, explain why this is so and how you expect to sell them profitably against the competition.

E. Operations.

Here you will describe your current or planned facility, its location, and equipment. Then you will talk about future plans for expansion and describe anticipated changes in your facility. For example, your plan may call for additional floor space if your volume is expected to increase over the next few years. Explain the reasons for these expectations, the estimated cost, and the advantages and disadvantages of making the changes now or later. In some cases you will also discuss how the business will operate during the move or construction period; whether it will be necessary to shut it down or if it can be conducted from temporary quarters.

F. Finances.

As a start-up entrepreneur, you will show your business' projected earnings. For an established existing business, you will also need to elaborate on the business' financial history. Your accountant can help organize this information. You will include balance sheets, profit and loss and cash flow statements for at least five years, if available. In a new enterprise, you will include Pro Forma profit and loss statements, balance sheets and cash flow statements. A Pro Forma statement is an estimated or projected statement showing what the Balance Sheet, the Profit and Loss statement, or what the cash flow statement will look like after the acquisition by a new owner, or after new funds have been received and put to work.

When you make your projections, you will show the expected increase in sales, expenses, and profits, taking inflationary factors into account. The next chart shows a projected Profit and Loss statement.

PRO FORMA PROFIT AND LOSS STATEMENT
Diaper Express

		Yr. of 19-1	%	19-2	%	19-3-5*
(A)	Total sales	370,000.00	100.00	419,507.00	100.00	
	Cost of sales					
	Laundry	120,500.00	32.57	137,000.00	32.66	
	Laundry supplies/ diapers	9,500.00	2.57	10,500.00	2.50	
	Pickup and delivery	22,000.00	5.95	23,500.00	5.60	
(B)	Total:	152,000.00	41.09	171,000.00	40.76	
	Expenses					
	Employee wages/ payroll	48,000.00	12.97	51,300.00	12.23	
	Supplies	750.00	.20	770.00	.18	
	Maintenance and repair	2,750.00	.74	2,790.00	.67	
	Van maintenance	2,500.00	.67	2,810.00	.67	
	Advertising	10,000.00	2.70	11,500.00	2.74	
	Accounting/legal	5,250.00	1.43	5,350.00	1.28	
	Rent	12,000.00	3.24	16,000.00	3.81	
	Utilities	6,000.00	1.62	9,500.00	2.26	
	Phone	1,400.00	.38	1,450.00	.35	
	Insurance	2,500.00	.68	2,700.00	.64	
	Taxes	4,500.00	1.22	4,650.00	1.11	
	Interest	4,000.00	1.08	700.00	.16	
	Depreciation	5,000.00	1.35	700.00	.16	
(C)	Total Expense	104,650.00	28.28	110,220.00	26.26	
(D)	Net Profit [D=A-B-C]	113,350.00	36.63	138,287.00	32.98	

Prepared by Arthur B. Simon, C.P.A. April 1, 19__

*Note that a full projection would show figures for each year of a five year period. For simplicity, this example has been limited to show only the first two years of a five year period.

PRO FORMA BALANCE SHEET AFTER
FINANCING
Silver Spurs Riding Academy
As of December 31, 19__

Assets:

Current:
    Cash   13,500.00
    Receivables   1,500.00
    Inventory/livestock   85,000.00
    Prepayments   2,000.00   102,000.00

Noncurrent:
    Leasehold improvements   25,500.00
    Furniture/fixtures   500.00
    Equipment   12,000.00
    (Depreciation)   (8,000.00)   30,000.00
    Total Assets: 132,000.00

Liabilities:

Current:
    Accounts payable   8,900.00
    Notes payable (current)   8,700.00
    Accrued taxes   1,400.00   19,000.00

Noncurrent:
    Notes payable (deferred)   67,000.00   67,000.00
    Total liabilities: 86,000.00

Net Worth:
    Owner Investment   27,000.00
    Retained Earnings   19,000.00
    Net Worth: 46,000.00   46,000.00

Total Liability and Net Worth: 132,000.00

If you seek financing to buy a business that has been losing money, point out the problem areas. Then discuss your plans for turning the business around. Give sufficient details - or specific examples - to show how your plan will work.

G. Management and Organization

This section will deal with the backgrounds of your management people, key personnel, and shows how the company is organized.

Prospective lenders and investors will want to know all about you and your key people. They expect to see a detailed background on each individual including the current or proposed compensation and benefit schedules. The information on you and your partners, if any, should be more elaborate than that provided on a standard resume. Explain what you have done in the past, your accomplishments, your goals and your business philosophy.

The clearest way to show these areas of responsibility is in the form of a Table of Organization. It illustrates how your present or proposed company is structured and who reports to whom.

<h3 style="text-align:center">Table of Organization
for a
Manufacturing Business</h3>

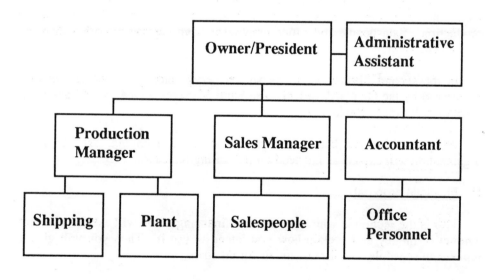

Illustration 1

Table of Organization
for a
Retail Business

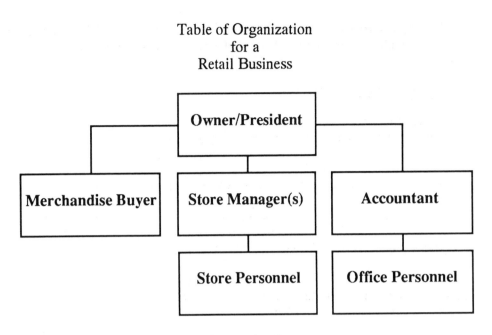

Illustration 2

In both examples, the Owner/President has ultimate authority over all personnel. The Administrative Assistant (see Illustration 1) does not have any direct authority over other personnel, and is supervised by the Owner/President. Also, the Production Manager has authority over shipping in addition to production. Salespeople and office employees have supervisors other than the Owner/President.

In the second illustration, all personnel except those in sales are directly supervised by the Owner/President. The Store Manager serves as the immediate supervisor for these employees.

As your business becomes bigger and more complex, the table of organization will expand as the need for delegating increases.

H. Financial proposal

This is the section in which you request financing. You will ask for a certain amount of money and explain how you intend to use it. Then you will give a repayment schedule, and list collaterals for the loan.

Some proposals are lengthy, others may be brief. The length is not important as long as you cover all important points.

For example:

Clayton Industries is asking for a loan of $50,000 for re-tooling and repair work at its Hagerstown, Maryland plant. These funds will be divided between re-tooling the XY-2w3009 Injector (serial number A-2W-1513), at $43,000 and overhauling the Cumcron Lifter (1982 model, serial number C7705), estimated at $7,000. We are asking for a five year loan term and propose to liquidate the loan in 60 monthly payments of $1,062.36 per month at a 10 percent interest rate.

You may also include a funds usage and sources statement. This shows where the loan you are requesting fits into your total financing package. For example:

Sources of Financing

Personal	$ 45,000.00
Investor (Friend)	25,000.00
Requested Loan	40,000.00
	$110,000.00

Usage

Purchase of business	$ 50,000.00
Additional Equipment	15,000.00
Re-tooling	20,000.00
Working Capital/Reserve	25,000.00
	$110,000.00

Notice that the top column shows what types of funding this business intends to use and the bottom column how the total funds will be used.

I.   Attachments

This section is a collection of supporting documents referred to in your plan. You might also include marketing surveys, advertising plans, drafts, and other materials and pertinent data including samples of products, if applicable, your resume and those of your partners and key personnel, will also be helpful. Also add any evidence of accomplishments, awards, publicity, etc. that point to your skill and competence as a business person.

Getting Ready to Do Business

In this section we will go over some of the details involved in getting ready to take over a business you have just purchased, or in opening the doors of a start-up operation. The following list does not necessarily indicate the sequence to be followed, but rather gives you guidelines to the more important steps involved.

• Set the opening date of your business as soon as the following occurrences have taken place: Your financing is in place; you have rented the premises; you know when your fixtures, equipment, merchandise and supplies will be available to you.

• Obtain all the governmental permits and papers required to operate a business. This includes federal, state, city and county licenses and permits. Regulations and requirements vary with each business and for each city, county and state. Your best approach is to contact the following organizations and agencies for complete information:

<u>Federal</u>
- U.S. Department of Labor
- Federal Regulatory agencies (if your business falls under their jurisdictions)

<u>State</u>
- Secretary of State, or Department of Commerce and Development
- Department of Revenue
- Department of Labor and Industry
- Department of Licensing

<u>County</u>
- Tax Assessor's Office

<u>City</u>
- Department of Licenses
- City Regulatory Agencies (if your business is affected by them)

Your business may also require special permits. They are required for food handling; dispensing alcoholic beverages; carrying toxic chemicals; health-care; building, remodelling and others.

There may be other agencies which require permits; some may have special reporting requirements for firms located in certain designated areas; and others call for permits for various types of operations. By contacting the agencies listed above, you will become aware of what is needed, and how to meet all requirements.

Telephoning or mailing requests for information to these organizations will save you time-consuming personal contacts. Your accountant, who continually deals with these agencies, can assist you with any paperwork.

- It is essential that you cover yourself and the business with adequate insurance *before* you open for business. Here are the major categories you will be concerned with initially:

    - Liability
    - Fire
    - Casualty
    - Automobile

More about insurance later.

- Establish your bookkeeping system and have it in place. This is especially important since you'll begin incurring some expenses long before you actually open your doors. A good bookkeeping system is one of the keys to success in business. Ask your accountant to help you set it up.

- Arrange for the utilities to be connected. These include power, water, gas and telephone. Contact the telephone company *early* regarding deadlines for placing an advertisement in the yellow pages.

- Order necessary equipment, supplies, and office stationery (including letterheads, envelopes, business cards, invoices, and statements).

- Make arrangements for re-sale merchandise to be delivered in time to stock and display properly.

- Order and install advertising signs. Also don't forget about internal informational signs (exit, restrooms, goods on aisle, department locations, etc.)

- Arrange for announcements and advertising. If you buy an existing business, send an announcement or letter to all customers. You may consider sending a joint announcement with the previous owner. In a start-up business it is important to let your prospective customers know you are open for business. See the section of *Operating Your Growing Business* for more discussion on advertising.

  One word of caution: Do not advertise until you are in complete operation and ready to serve customers. Nothing is more harmful to a new business than to have customers come in expectantly, only to find disarray, insufficient merchandise and displays and untrained salesclerks.

- Employees should be hired and trained as early as possible to acquaint them with your business. This assures a running start on opening day. If you have acquired an established business, chances are you will take over the old staff, even if you plan to make changes later.

Section 5

ANSWERING SERIOUS QUESTIONS
ABOUT MONEY

Sources of Money and How to Tap Into Them

Initial Capital Requirements and Financing

One of the most challenging problems facing the start-up entrepreneur is securing adequate financing. Now we will begin to discuss in greater detail the steps involved in starting and operating a business. Our first topic covers ways of obtaining the necessary funds.

Capital requirements vary considerably with each business. The cost of acquiring equipment for a manufacturing business will obviously be higher than that for a home-based computer payroll service, or a small retail store.

Unless you plan to go into a very small business which needs little start-up capital, you may need the help of an accountant, plus the guidance of future suppliers and other qualified people to determine your initial capital requirements.

When purchasing an existing business or franchise, the seller will often provide partial or full financing.

Financial requirements to buy an existing business are often lower than those in a similar start-up situation. The price for a franchise or an existing business usually includes equipment, furnishings, supplies and inventory. Service-type operations need less start-up capital, while businesses with special equipment or major inventories (like manufacturing or retail) will require more capital. The following Capital Requirements Chart offers a general idea on how to arrive at start-up and continuing expenses. The column on the left shows some of the major one-time expenditures which apply to most businesses.

The column on the right lists the recurring expenses that arise once the business is operating under your control. Some expenses in the right column are designated as "occasional" because they occur infrequently. These include remodeling, consulting or major promotional costs. Enter your estimated figures in the applicable blank spaces after each item, and add other items which apply to your situation. The total of the right column represents the monthly expenses. Because there are always unexpected outlays, it is advisable to add from 5 to 15 percent for cost overruns to the totals in both columns.

Estimated capital requirements are essential in preparing your proposal for financing, and for setting up a budget. Total "A" is the amount of money required before you are open for business. Total "B" represents the anticipated monthly expenses once the business is in operation. The break-even point is reached when your sales equal "B". The business will show profits once the sales exceed "B".

ESTIMATED CAPITAL REQUIREMENTS CHART

For Start-up and Continuing Monthly Expenses

One-time Start-up Costs "A"		Continuing Monthly Expenses "B"	
Market Analysis/Consulting	_____	(Occasional)	_____
Advertising for Opening	_____	Advertising	_____
Accounting (Initial)	_____	Accounting	_____
Insurance	_____	Insurance	_____
Lease Deposit	_____	Lease	_____
Legal Consultations	_____	Legal	_____
Incorporation Costs	_____	(Not applicable)	
Dues/Subscriptions	_____	Dues/Subscriptions	_____
Licenses/Permits	_____	(Occassional)	_____
Deposits for Utilities/ Telephone	_____	Utilities/Telephone	_____
Decorating and Remodeling	_____	(Occasional)	_____
Furnishings/Fixtures	_____	(Occasional)	_____
Installation of the above	_____	(Occassional)	_____
Production/Office Equipment and Installation	_____	(Occasional)	_____
Equipment Maintenance Contracts	_____	Equipment Maintenance	_____
General Supplies	_____	General Supplies	_____
Salaries and Wages Before Opening	_____	Salaries and Wages Your Salary	_____
Start-up Inventory	_____	Inventory Purchases	_____
Cash Reserve/Operating Capital*	_____	Additional Expenses	_____
Additional Expenditures	_____		_____
	_____		_____
	_____		_____
Other Costs	_____	Other Expenses	_____
	_____		_____
	_____		_____
			_____
Total	_____	Total	_____
Cost overruns (5%-15%) of Total	_____	Overruns (5%-15%) of Total	_____
Total "A"	_____	Total "B"	_____

* For the period of time it takes for the business to break even and begin to show profit.

PERSONAL FINANCIAL STATEMENT

Assets		Liabilities	
Cash in Banks	_____	Note Payables	
Notes Receivable	_____	Banks	_____
Contracts Receivable	_____	Others	_____
Accounts Receivable	_____	Accounts Payable	_____
Stocks and Bonds	_____	Loans against Life Insurance	_____
Cash Value Life Insurance	_____	Notes and Contracts	_____
	_____	Other Installment Payments	_____
	_____		_____
	_____		_____
Total Current Assets	_____	Total Current Liabilities	_____

Real Estate		Real Estate	
Residence	_____	Residence	_____
Other Real Estate	_____	Other Real Estate	_____
Automobiles	_____		_____
Personal Property	_____		_____
_____	_____	Total Liabilities	_____
_____	_____	Net Worth	_____
		Total Liabilities and Net Worth	
Total Assets	_____		_____

Sources of Income (per year)			
Salary	_____	Real Estate Income	_____
Bonus and Commissions	_____	Other	_____
Dividends	_____	Total Gross Income	_____

You can lower some of the capital requirements for your business simply by keeping expenses as low as possible. To accomplish this, obtain several competitive price quotes for supplies, fixtures, labor, and other costs. This will save money without affecting the end result. Avoiding unnecessary frills and going out for bids is one way to reduce cash drain. It will often be more economical and beneficial to cash flow to rent or lease equipment instead of buying it. Confer with your accountant on these buy vs. lease decisions.

In most start-up businesses, the sales volume in the first few months of operation will probably not be adequate to cover your expenses and loan repayments. This means that you will have to allocate additional funds to make up for the difference between incoming and outgoing monies until you reach a break-even point. These additional funds should be taken into consideration when you estimate your initial cash requirements.

The Estimated Capital Requirements Chart can serve as a valuable guide in the process of obtaining adequate financing for your enterprise. Keep in mind the importance of allowing for your living expenses for the time it takes for your business to start paying you a salary. Depending on the type of business you are in, it could be a year before you reach this point - the averages being three to seven months.

In order to gain a clearer picture of your financial status, we recommend that you also complete a Personal Financial Statement *before* you approach a lender. It will give you better insight on how much money you can raise from your own assets such as cash, securities, real estate contracts, notes receivable, and others. This will answer one of the first questions a lender will ask you.

It is not necessary to take this statement to the bank since most lenders will provide you with their own form. After reviewing your financial statement, the lender will determine your credit-worthiness and the amount and terms of the loan they can offer you.

In addition to your personal financial statement, the lending institution will generally require copies of your personal income tax returns for the prior three years.

Now that your capital requirement needs have been calculated, it's time to identify the best sources for loans. Here are a few suggestions on where to look for sources for funds whether you are a start-up entrepreneur or operate an established business. You may consider sounding out friends, relatives, business and social contacts about their willingness and ability to guarantee your loan repayment, or to invest in your business. It is especially important that you inform them of the risk they will be taking should your business fail and you are unable to repay them. Also bear in mind that in this event you may lose their friendship and goodwill, along with your own investment.

Another method of raising money is to place a second mortgage on your home. This is like getting a loan with your equity as the collateral. A major concern is that if you default on the mortgage for any reason, you could lose your home along with your equity. You may also be able to borrow on the cash value of your life insurance, or try for a personal loan from a credit union.

In summary - your self-financing can come from:

- Your savings and cash on-hand.

- A loan based on the cash value of your life insurance policy.

- A personal loan from your trade or credit union.

- A second mortgage on your home.

- Loan guarantees from relatives, friends, social or business contacts.

A survey conducted by Venture Magazine shows the following breakdown on where most business start-up capital comes from:

- Personal Savings.   54%

- Bank Loans.   14%

- Loans from relatives and friends.   11%

- Cash flow.   9%

- Private Placement.   5%

- Venture Capital.   4%

- Other.   3%

If you decide to go for a bank loan, it's a good idea to get acquainted with a banker or loan officer long before you submit your application. It is important to include that person in the early planning stages of your business, as well as keeping her or him informed of your progress and plans once your business has been started. The more you involve your banker and keep in touch, the more confidence you will establish in your ideas and your ability to build a successful company. This confidence will make your contact more likely to go out of his way for you when special needs arise in the future.

The next step is to prepare your business plan, as previously discussed. This should include a financial proposal. This plan is not absolutely necessary in every case. For example, it will probably not be needed for very small businesses or start-ups that do not require major financing.

In reviewing your loan application, the bank will take a hard look at these three areas:

- Your credit record.

- Your experience in the business field you are entering.

- Your ability to repay the loan.

To give yourself the best chance of obtaining bank financing, you will first need to convince the banker or loan officer that your business ideas are sound, that your plans are realistic and that you know how to implement them.

You will also have to demonstrate the extent of your own financial commitment to your enterprise and how the proceeds from the loan will be used.

You will be required to document the collaterals or the guarantees from others to reassure the bank that it can recover some or all of the loan should you fail to do so.

In the event your application is turned down by one or several lenders, you may consider changing your business plans to make your loan request acceptable. You may also consider applying for an SBA guaranteed loan. In this case, the bank makes the loan and the SBA agrees to repay up to 90 percent of the loss in the event of default. These SBA guaranteed loans are available through most banks.

The SBA also makes *direct* loans to certain categories of applicants. General credit requirements, the amount of loans available, maturity, interest rates and fees are discussed later in this section under SBA Loan Facts. Contact your nearest SBA office to determine whether you qualify. Small Business Investment Companies (SBIC) and Minority Enterprise Small Business Investment Companies (MESIC) also participate in the SBA loan programs.

If your business is located in a rural area, you may also be eligible for financing through the Farmers Home Administration.

Here's a recap of outside financing options:

- Loans through banks and some savings and loan associations.

- Loans guaranteed by The Small Business Administration.

- Loans through Small Business Investment Companies, Minority Enterprise Small Business Investment Companies, and the Farmers Home Administration.

- Financing through Venture Capital firms (applicable only for minimum requirements from $25,000 to $1,000,000).

- Loans from other finance company sources.

- State-sponsored Venture Capital (inquire if available in your state).

- Some localities have investment clubs made up of active and former chief executives looking for investments.

Another strategy in obtaining financing is to take in one or more partners. The combined financial resources and strength will often attract easier financing. We have already discussed the pros and cons of partnerships and corporations.

In summary, you can improve your odds for getting regular financing by taking the following steps:

- Get to know your banker and stay in regular touch with her *before* you need a loan.

- Acquaint your banker or loan officer with a workable, well-planned business concept. In most cases via a formal business plan.

- Show that you are willing and able to invest your own funds in the business.

- Prepare a comprehensive plan for using the loan funds.

- Provide proof through your credit history and reputation that you can and will follow through on your commitments and repay the loan.

Money Management

The positive flow of money is the lifeblood of any business. The successful entrepreneur must understand the relationship between money coming into the business from -

- Sales

- Loans

- Additional sources

And money going out for -

- Purchases

- Expenses

- Loan payments

- Equipment (fixed assets)

Credit and collection policies play an important part in the financial health of your business, as does proper documentation of all transactions; your record-keeping.

Dealing With Lenders

Most of the information in this handbook on financing applies to established businesses and start-up operations. The following information *can* be helpful to established firms.

There are *five steps* in obtaining a loan or setting the stage for a future loan from a bank or other type of lender:

- Select a banker or other suitable lender.

- Establish a working relationship with the loan officer.

- Be prepared with facts and figures.

- Request a loan for a *specific* purpose.

- Pay off the loan as scheduled, and continue to communicate with the lender.

Your choice of a particular bank or lender depends on the needs of your business and on your own preferences. You may prefer to deal with a small bank where you might reasonably expect to receive more personalized service. Or, you may be able to find a larger bank with more resources that can also extend a personal touch. Do not hesitate to search for a new bank if you don't feel comfortable with your present connection.

Another important factor in the choice is your relationship with the lender or loan officer. You may find one acceptable to you through referrals or by comparison shopping. These individuals often have the authority to make decisions on commercial loans up to pre-determined maximum amounts.

The key to building an effective relationship with your lender and loan officer is to communicate frequently in person or by telephone. According to a Venture Magazine survey, entrepreneurs who contact their loan officers on a weekly basis have higher average loan balances, higher average lines of credit, and receive more business referrals than those who call or visit their loan officers less frequently. Many entrepreneurs make it a practice to establish good communications and strong ties with more than one bank.

Good communications with lenders involve:

- Sharing your plans, ideas and requirements clearly and enthusiastically.

- Laying out the strengths and weaknesses of your business honestly.

- Listening carefully to advice, and asking questions to avoid any misunderstandings.

- Keeping them aware of changes in your business.

For larger loans, you will usually be expected to give the lender a copy of your formal business plan, discussed previously. This plan includes your loan proposal that tells the lender -

- How much capital you need to borrow.

- What the capital will be used for and why it's important. For example, to upgrade machinery which will expand a product line, or to purchase additional stock before a peak buying season.

Your company's financial statement provides the best evidence on how your business has performed in the past. Your lender will be especially interested in -

- Balance sheets.

- Profit and loss statements.

- Personal financial statements.

- Cash flow statements.

- Pro forma statements.

These statements are discussed in greater detail under Business Plans. Understanding these basic financial statements will help you in your planning and decision-making.

Your lender may also be interested in your personal and business credit history. These records can be obtained from generally available credit information sources. They show the amount and type of loans you have had in the past, and how promptly you met your obligations. You will usually be asked to complete a personal financial statement. The factors upon which lending decisions are being made include:

- Your reputation for honesty and reliability and the lender's sense of how well you understand and can present your financial position and plans.

- The financial health of your business.

- Your ability to repay the loan.

- How the general economy may affect your business.

- What collateral the business or you personally can provide to secure the loan.

Year-to-year increases in profits and net worth are positive signs and favorable for obtaining loan approvals. But loan officers will also look for negative factors such as:

- Deterioration in the firm's cash position.

- Slowdown in accounts receivable collections.

- Rapid rise in current debts.

- Declining gross-profit margins.

- Increasing sales with declining profits or operational losses.

- Significant increases in overhead.

Short-term Loans

They may be used to cover 30 to 90-day accounts receivable, seasonal inventories, or other short-term requirements. These loans are usually repaid at the time when short-term projects are completed. For example, you may obtain a loan to build an inventory of back-to-school supplies. Your lender will expect repayment when the merchandise is sold, usually in 90-days.

Loans can be either secured or unsecured. A secured loan requires you to back your repayment promise with collateral. Collaterals are assets that you or your business possess that the lender can liquidate should you default on the loan.

Collaterals include real property such as automobiles; tools and equipment; real estate; accounts receivable, business inventories, savings accounts; life insurance; stocks and bonds, etc.

You may also secure loans if other firms or individuals are willing to back them with their collaterals. A guarantor may sign your note to give you the benefit of his credit rating. He agrees to make the note good if you are unable to do so. Another option is to have a "co-maker" sign the note with you. Here, you and the co-maker are equally responsible for repayment.

An unsecured loan does not require collateral. With this type of loan, the lender bases approval of the loan on your past record of regular repayments.

Aside from outright loans for short-term purposes, you may also be able to use supplier or "trade" credit. We will discuss this further in the section on credit. The most obvious advantage to this type of financing is that it does not require the same steps needed to obtain regular loans, and in many cases has lower or no interest charges.

There are two other short-term financing methods available which should be used only in exceptional circumstances - if at all. Should a sudden or critical need for funds develop unexpectedly and there isn't sufficient time to secure a loan through conventional channels on short notice, funds can be obtained from consumer finance companies or with personal credit cards. This approach should, however, be considered only as a temporary measure and the funds obtained from these sources should be re-paid promptly.

Intermediate and Long-Term Loans

These loans run over one year in maturity and are also known as "term" loans. Like short-term loans, they can also be obtained from banks and, sometimes, savings and loan associations. Since these loans are usually larger than most short-term loans, they may be harder to obtain. Also, the risk to a lender is greater due to the longer term. A lender looking at these loans must make a more in-depth judgment about the long-term prospects and growth pattern of your business and industry.

For longer "term" loans for companies with substantial assets such as equipment and real estate, commercial finance companies will often make loans at lower interest rates than those available at banks. If you are unable to obtain a long-term loan through a conventional lending institution, you may consider obtaining an SBA guaranteed loan.

If you need a loan to expand your plant or hire additional personnel, you may be able to get funds from business and loan development corporations. These semi-public organizations make long-term loans for construction purposes and to help create jobs. Contact your regional SBA office to help you locate one nearest you.

SBA Loan Facts

GUARANTY LOANS: SBA's lending is almost entirely based on the SBA guaranteed bank loan program, in which a bank makes the loan and the SBA agrees to repay up to 90 percent of the loss in case of default. All banks are eligible to participate. This is SBA's best means of helping small firms obtain long-term financing for business needs such as working capital; machinery; equipment; furniture and fixtures; leasehold improvements; building acquisition or construction, and in some circumstances debt consolidation.

DIRECT LOANS: If private lenders will not provide financing either on their own or with SBA's guaranty, then you may under some circumstances qualify for a direct government loan. At present, direct loans are available to only three categories of applicants: (1) Handicapped people, (2) Veterans who are 30 percent disabled or who served in the Vietnam era, (3) Firms operating in areas of high unemployment. If you believe you qualify and cannot get bank financing, call the SBA for further details. Direct funds are scarce, however, and there may be waiting lists. Also, financing your business through commercial institutions (with or without an SBA guaranty) is a better way of building your company's credit standing.

To apply for a direct loan, submit an outline of your business plan, financial statements, and rejection letters from at least two banks (one if you live in a town of less than 200,000 population). Please note, however, that *rejection letters are not needed for a bank/SBA guaranty loan.*

GENERAL CREDIT REQUIREMENTS: SBA uses much the same credit criteria as any private lender. Their three primary tests of creditworthiness are:

- Cash Flow: Applicants must show that they can meet business expenses, owner's draw, and all payments from the earnings of the business. This is usually demonstrated with a cash flow projection.

- Management: Applicants must show ability to operate the business successfully. For a new business, applicants must have significant management experience as well as experience in the type of business they propose to enter.

- Equity: Applicants must have enough of their own capital at stake in the business:

  - For a New Business (or when buying a business), applicants should have approximately one dollar of cash or business assets for each two dollars of loan.

- For an Established Firm, the pro forma (after the loan) ratio of total debt to net worth should be approximately 4:1 or better.

NOTE: Pledging of non-business assets to secure the loan, while it may be required for collateral, is not an acceptable substitute for business equity. Equity is the owner's net investment in the business.

AMOUNTS: SBA may guarantee up to 90 percent or $750,000 of an eligible bank loan or 75% on larger loans. Direct loans, when available, are limited to $150,000.

MATURITY: The maximum is 25 years. Working capital loans are usually limited to seven years.

INTEREST RATES:

- Guaranty Loans:

  - For SBA Guaranteed bank loans with maturities of less than 7 years, the maximum rate is 2-1/4 percent over New York prime.

  - Guaranteed loans with maturities of 7 years or longer may have rates up to 2-3/4 percent over New York prime.

  - At the bank's option, the note may have a variable rate which is adjusted monthly, up or down, following the New York prime. In recent years, nearly all SBA guaranty loans have had variable interest rates.

  - The SBA encourages participating banks to provide guaranty financing at less than the maximum rates cited above.

- Direct Loans: Have a fixed rate for the life of the note. The direct rate is near market rate for commercial loans. Handicapped assistance loans are 3 percent.

FEES: A fee of 2 percent of the guaranteed portion of the loan is payable upon loan closing. The fee may be financed (i.e., built into the loan amount).

COLLATERAL: SBA's collateral policy is in two parts:

- Lack of collateral will not generally keep SBA from making an otherwise qualified loan. On the other hand, abundant collateral will not convince them to make a loan which does not meet their credit criteria.

- When a loan is approved, the SBA expects all available company assets to be offered as collateral.

ELIGIBILITY: Most small businesses are eligible to apply. *However, the laws under which SBA operates forbids them to make loans:*

- If the applicant company is too large (see size standards, below).

- If the funds are otherwise available on reasonable terms.

- If the loan is to pay off creditors who are inadequately secured.

- If the loan is for speculation or investment; for example, purchase of rental property.

- If the applicant is a newspaper, magazine, book publisher, movie theater, or non-profit enterprise (except sheltered workshops).

SIZE STANDARDS: The upper size limit for SBA eligibility varies by specific industry. The complete size standards are therefore rather lengthy, but the general guidelines are:

- Retail or Service Businesses - Annual sales less than $3.5 million.

- Wholesalers - Fewer than 100 employees.

- Manufacturing - Fewer than 500 employees.

- General Contractors - Average annual receipts less than $17 million over the past three years.

- Specialty Contractors - Average annual receipts less than $7 million over the past three years.

- Farms - Annual sales less than $500,000.

APPLYING FOR A LOAN - STEP-BY-STEP PROCEDURE:

If after reading the preceding information, you believe you qualify and wish to apply for an SBA loan, follow this step-by-step procedure:

For Established Businesses:

- Prepare a current balance sheet listing all assets and all liabilities of the business. Do not include personal items.

- Have an earnings (profit and loss) statement for the previous full year and for the current period to the date of the balance sheet. Also a projection of earnings if needed to show repayment ability.

- Prepare a current personal financial statement of the owner, each partner or each stockholder owning 20 percent or more of the business.

- List collateral to be offered as security for the loan, with your estimate of the present market value of each item.

- State amount and uses of loan.

- Take this material to your banker. Ask for a direct bank loan. If declined, ask the bank to make the loan under SBA's Loan Guaranty Plan. If the bank is interested in an SBA guaranty loan, ask the banker to contact SBA for discussion of your application. In most cases, SBA will deal directly with the bank.

- To speed matters, make your financial information available when you write your bank or SBA.

For New Businesses:

- Describe in detail the type of business established.

- Describe experience and management capabilities.

- Prepare an estimate of how much you have to invest in the business and how much you will need to borrow.

- Prepare a current financial statement (balance sheet) listing all personal assets and all liabilities.

- Prepare a month by month detailed projection of earnings for the first year the business will operate.

- List collateral to be offered as security for the loan, with your estimate of the present market value of each item.

- Take this material to your banker. Ask for a direct bank loan. If declined, ask the bank to make the loan under SBA's Loan Guaranty Plan. If the bank is interested in an SBA guaranty loan, ask the banker to contact SBA for discussion of your application. In most cases, SBA will deal directly with the bank.

- To speed matters, make your financial information available when you write or visit your bank or SBA.

Please keep in mind that SBA policies and regulations change from time to time. It is advisable to review the current requirements whenever you apply.

Other Loan Programs

If your business is not eligible or fails to qualify for an SBA loan, other government programs may be available to you. Three such programs are the Farmers Home Administration (FHA), the Department of Housing and Urban Development (HUD), and the Minority Small Business Enterprise Program. The Small Business Administration can provide you with information on other programs that may be of help. It can also give you advice on changes necessary in your business or your management style in order to qualify for loans. You can locate the nearest Small Business Administration Branch Office by checking your local telephone directory, listed under United States Government Offices.

In all of your dealings with lenders, it is important to keep in mind that they are in business to make a profit from your success. The more information you share with them, the quicker they will make their decision on your application.

If the purpose of the loan is considered to be too high-risk for your business, at this time, the potential lender may advise you what kind of changes are necessary to qualify.

Loan Approval

When your loan application is approved, you will schedule a meeting with the lender to discuss the terms of the loan. All terms are binding only after you sign all the necessary papers. Or if you deal through the SBA, terms are binding when the loan is authorized. Until that point the terms are negotiable.

Loan terms include the amount of the loan, the repayment schedule and interest rates, and sometimes limitations. Limitations are "positive" and "negative" promises or covenants. Positive covenants are commitments you make, such as supplying the lender with regular financial reports, following a set schedule of payments, or making certain changes in managing the business. Negative covenants are those things that you as a borrower agree not to do. This can include agreements not to take on additional fixed assets, not to increase owners compensation, etc. Lenders require these restrictions in order to protect their investments. The restrictions are aimed at keeping your business healthy by limiting debt, protecting profits, and keeping growth within planned limits.

Lenders should be willing to supply you with a copy of these suggested limitations before the loan closing. It is advisable to consult with your accountant and attorney before you agree to any limitation. Once you sign the note closing the loan, you and your business will be legally bound by the agreed-upon limitations.

Equity Financing

A third type of funding is "equity" capital. Equity capital is not a loan, and does not have to be repaid like a loan. This capital is generated by selling part of the equity in your business. This means giving up part of your ownership, some management control and a share of your profits. Individuals or venture capital firms may also buy into your business. Minimum loans from venture capital firms often start at $250,000. These firms avoid high risk enterprises because a business must succeed for them to recover their investment and make a profit. They are mostly interested in businesses with good long-term growth potential. Usually these firms will also set certain conditions or restrictions on how you must operate your business.

To obtain venture-capital financing, you will need to make a detailed report on your business and its financial projection for growth. These reports often require outside specialists to be properly prepared. If a venture capital firm decides to invest in your business, it will present an offer spelling out what type and amount of financing they will provide, and their role in your business, (controls, shareholder rights, etc.).

If you consider equity or venture capital financing for your business, consult your accountant and attorney since these investors are, in effect, buying a part of your business. So professional advice is *essential.* The Guide to Venture Capital Sources, available in book stores or the local library, has listings of these firms.

In summary, banks will usually be your first choice for short-term loans. The SBA can serve as the lender of last resort, if you are unable to obtain loan funds elsewhere. Some other funding options are available through equity or venture capital, trade credit, or personal loans.

The key to successful borrowing is to plan ahead so the groundwork has been laid long before a need arises. This advance planning allows you more freedom to negotiate favorable loan terms for your business.

Setting Up Controls

The objective of a good record keeping system is to provide you with a better understanding of how your business is functioning. It can give you valuable clues on what needs to be done to help you reduce expenses; increase employee productivity; keep tabs on equipment performance, inventory levels and the like. By keeping accurate records and knowing how to use the data, you will be able to make the right decisions which ultimately lead to greater profits. Certain records are required by law, by city, county, state and federal agencies and are subject to regular and occasional audits. Even if you are not knowledgeable in accounting, you must stay actively involved in all phases of record keeping, making sure that records are up-to-date, properly documented and filed for easy access.

A short course in accounting can help you learn to "read" and interpret the numbers so that you can understand what is going on in your business. Accurate records also serve as the basic sources for calculating local, state and federal taxes. Whether you do your own record keeping or employ a part or full-time bookkeeper, discuss these records frequently with your outside accountant. He can assist you in interpreting the meaning of the figures and advise you where to look for any corrective actions.

Here is a list of some basic records:

Financial Records

- General journal
- Purchase journal
- Sales journal
- Cash receipts journal
- Cash disbursement journal
- Payroll journal
- Accounts receivable ledgers
- Accounts payable ledgers
- Loan records

Informational Records

- Inventory records
- List of customers
- Sales records by -
  - Salespeople
  - Merchandise or products
  - Labor sales

The Small Business Administration lists financial records needed by most small businesses on a daily, weekly, and monthly basis as follows:

DAILY

- Cash-on-hand.
- Bank balance (keep business and personal funds separate).
- Daily summary of sales and cash receipts.
- A record of all monies paid out by cash or check.

WEEKLY

- Accounts receivable (take action on slow payers).
- Accounts payable (take advantage of discounts).
- Payroll (records should include name and address of employee, social security number, number of exemptions, date ending the pay period, hours worked, rate-of-pay, total wages, deductions, net pay, check number).
- Taxes and reports to state and federal government (sales, withholding, social security, etc.).

MONTHLY

It is important -

- That all journal entries are classified according to like elements (these should be generally accepted and standardized for both income and expense) and posted to general ledger.

- That a profit and loss statement for the month is available within a reasonable time, usually 10 to 15-days following the close of the month. This shows income of the business for the month; the expense incurred in obtaining the income, and the profit or loss resulting. From this, take action to eliminate loss, adjust mark-up, reduce overhead expense, pilferage, incorrect tax reporting, incorrect buying procedures, failure to take advantage of cash discounts.

- That a balance sheet accompanies the profit and loss statement. This shows assets (what the business has), liabilities (what the business owes), and the investment of the owner.

- The bank statement is reconciled. That is, the owner's books are in agreement with the bank's record of the cash balance.

- The petty cash account is in balance. The actual cash in the petty cash box plus the total of the paid-out slips that have not been charged to expense total the amount set aside as petty cash.

- That all federal tax deposits, withheld income and FICA taxes (Form 501) and state taxes are made.

- That accounts receivable are aged, i.e., 30, 60, 90-days, etc., past due. Work all bad and slow accounts.

- That inventory control is worked to remove obsolete stock and order new stock. What moves slowly, reduce. What moves fast, increase.

The SBA also poses some interesting questions on how adequate records can decrease the chances of failure and increase the likelihood of staying in business and earning larger profits.

These can best be answered by keeping a simple but adequate system of records.

- How much business (cash and credit) am I doing? How much is *tied up* in receivables?

- How are my collections? What are my losses from credit sales? Who owes me money? Who is delinquent? Should I continue to extend credit to delinquent accounts? How soon can I anticipate realizing a return on my accounts receivable?

- How much cash do I have on hand and in the bank? Does this amount agree with what records tell me I should have. Or is there a shortage? How much is my investment in merchandise? How often do I turn over my inventory? Have I allowed my inventory to become obsolete?

- How much merchandise did I take out of the business for personal or family use which affects my gross profit calculations?

- How much do I owe my suppliers and other creditors? Have I received all of my outstanding credits for returned merchandise?

- How much gross profit (margin) did I earn?

- What were my expenses, including those not requiring cash outlays?

- What is my payroll? Do I have adequate payroll records to meet the requirements of workers' compensation, wage hour laws, social security, unemployment insurance and withholding taxes?

- What is my capital? That is, of my total assets, how much would be left for me after I pay my creditors in full?

- Are my sales, expenses, profits, and capital showing improvement or did I do better last year? How do I stand as compared with two periods ago? Is my position about the same, improving, or deteriorating?

- On what lines of goods or in what departments am I making a profit, breaking even, or losing money?

- Am I taking full advantage of cash discounts for prompt payments? How do my discounts taken compare with discounts lost?

- How do the financial facts of my business compare with those of similar businesses?

Different businesses have varying needs for information. The sheer number of possible records can be overwhelming. However, a record is only important if its contents help the owner make better decisions. Have your accountant work with you to set up a record keeping system that meets the needs of your particular business.

Following is a discussion of records most valuable for decision-making. These records can be produced manually, on bookkeeping machines or on a computer.

Sales Records

By breaking down your sales into various categories: Departments; types of products and services; territories; sales representatives and other criteria, an alert owner can draw a number of conclusions on what products or services sell best. Records can also be set up to show which territories and sales representatives show the best performances.

A women's specialty store, for example, could benefit from the following analysis:

Dollar Amount and Percentages of Sales

	Current Year				Prior Year			
	March		Jan. - March		March		Jan. - March	
Apparel	$14,000	(70%)	$41,250	(71%)	$13,500	(70%)	$30,750	(65%)
Shoes	5,000	(25%)	14,000	(24%)	4,500	(24%)	13,000	(28%)
Accessories	1,000	(5%)	2,700	(5%)	1,200	(6%)	3,250	(7%)
Total	$20,000		$57,950		$19,200		$47,000	

An analysis of the percentage figures indicates that sales in apparel and shoes are relatively stable and on the increase, while accessories show a decline. Based on this information the store owner can make decisions regarding merchandise selection, pricing, advertising, etc.

Other factors to consider are departmental profits. It is possible to show lower sales in one department, yet produce *higher profits* due to higher mark-ups or lower departmental expenses.

	Dept. A		Dept. B		Dept. C	
	Amount	%	Amount	%	Amount	%
Sales	$10,000	100%	$10,000	100%	$10,000	100%
Cost of Sales	6,000	60%	7,000	70%	8,000	80%
Gross Profit	4,000	40%	3,000	30%	2,000	20%
Overhead Cost	2,000	20%	2,000	20%	2,000	20%
Net Profit	$ 2,000	20%	$ 1,000	10%	0	0

The above chart indicates that Dept. B must sell twice as many products as Dept. A to generate the same Net Profit. It also indicates that Dept. C should be reviewed to see if costs or overhead can be reduced.

A similar kind of chart can accomplish the same objectives in manufacturing and service businesses. By comparing the sales and cost figures of labor and materials over a period of time, you will gain an in-depth understanding as to which way your business is moving and how to improve your profits.

Bookkeeping and Accounting Records

Cash Disbursement Journal

It records all cash payments the company makes to suppliers, delivery companies, petty cash - including cash advances to employees. In short, all monies paid out in the form of cash.

Cash Receipts Journal

This journal will record all cash sales and cash payments from customers who originally purchased on credit. This journal can also provide the names and addresses of your cash customers which can be very valuable in your direct mail promotions.

Both the cash disbursement and receipt journals are also the basis for your monthly cash flow statement, showing the cash-on-hand to meet current and expected requirements.

General Journal

It can be used to record some or all of a business' activities. Some companies utilize it to show only those transactions that do not fit into any of the other journals. In a very small business it can serve for all of the transactions, but they must be sorted later in preparing the statements.

Purchase Journal

The principal application is to record all purchases made on credit. It shows what has been purchased, the amount, any discounts, and the due date for payment. It shows how much is owed on merchandise at any given time and enables you to arrange the payment schedules.

Accounts Receivable and Accounts Payable Ledgers

They are essentially the mirror image to each other. The accounts receivable ledger lists the amounts of money that is owed to you by each customer. It should also provide information regarding each customer's credit terms and limits, and other pertinent information concerning the account. The payable ledger, similarly, keeps track of what you owe to each of your suppliers. Both ledgers will reveal quickly the total amounts owed to and by you. This information can be a valuable planning tool.

The names and addresses on your receivable ledger can be extracted to set up a mailing list for promotional purposes. You also can create an aging schedule which quickly reveals the names and amounts of delinquent accounts.

For example, a high number of invoices owed for over 90-days can mean that your billings are not reaching customers promptly, or that payment reminder notices are not being sent. It may indicate that too much credit is being extended to certain customers. Another possibility is that your collection procedures are not working properly. Your accountant can be helpful in using information from your accounts receivable records to pinpoint likely causes of difficulties in collecting payments.

Payroll and Individual Earning Records

The payroll journal is the summary of all the individual earning records. At the end of each pay period - weekly, semi-monthly or monthly, all pertinent information for each employee is posted to the payroll journal. This includes the gross wages, hours worked and overtime - if applicable, and deductions for social security, withholding taxes, health and insurance plans, vacations and sick leaves, advances, etc.

Each employee should also have a separate file containing the employment application, job description, withholding information, performance evaluation, promotions, commendations or disciplinary actions.

Inventory Records

Inventory records give you a firm control over the goods for sale on an item-by-item basis. They will tell you what is selling and what is not. By taking periodic physical inventories, you can keep your records accurate and discover any shrinkages based on errors or theft.

Many companies also keep inventory records on major supply items such as replacement machinery parts for equipment, tools, computer supplies, etc.

Financial Statements

Financial statements are summaries of your records. They show trends in your business and can answer important questions relating to marketing, sales and efficiency.

Three of the most important statements are:

- The balance sheet
- The profit and loss statement
- The cash flow statement

The balance sheet basically shows the net worth of your company. Examples of a balance sheet and a profit and loss statement are shown at the end of Section 5. Cash flow statements are discussed under Managing Cash Flow in this section. Information conveyed in a balance sheet can be expressed in this formula:

Net worth = Assets - Liabilities

The assets consist of everything the company owns, such as -

- Cash
- Inventories
- Equipment
- Accounts receivable
- Supplies
- Others

Liabilities are entries of items the company owes, such as -

- Loans
- Contracts
- Accounts payable
- Other short and long-term obligations

The difference between the assets and liabilities is the book value or the net worth of the company. This figure does not necessarily present the amount at which a company can be bought or sold. Other factors such as goodwill, replacement values, etc., will enter into the picture.

The profit and loss statement shows the amount of money a company has made or lost over a certain period of time (month, quarter or year). An example of a profit and loss statement is provided.

Information conveyed in a profit and loss statement is presented in this formula:

Profit or loss = Sales - cost-of-sales - expenses

Sales describes the total revenue from all goods and/or services. Cost-of-sales is the amount you have paid for goods and/or labor to produce what you sold. The expenses are the costs of doing business. That is, the overhead (rent, supplies, salaries, commissions, advertising, insurance, interest on loans, etc).

The cash flow statement, often called funds and resources statement, shows how much money is available to the business to take care of its obligations. It can be expressed by this formula:

Available funds = Receipts - payments

Receipts come from sales, collections on accounts receivable and any other income.

Payments are outgoing cash for obligations such as materials, merchandise, labor, services, salaries, loans and overhead items.

These three statements are important in several ways. They organize information to simplify the identification of financial problem areas and opportunities within your business. They make it possible to rectify shortcomings or put further emphasis on already strong areas. The statements organize information to show strong and weak areas within your business. They are important to planning, obtaining loans, or selling your business.

In summary, your business records are important for a number of reasons. They are necessary for day-to-day operations including collecting accounts receivable, and short and long-range planning purposes. In addition, they are used to assess future trends and profit potential. This information is particularly important for obtaining loans or in selling your business. It is also necessary for tax reporting. To be most useful, records must be *accurate and up-to-date.*

Your accountant can advise you on setting up a record keeping system and help prepare and interpret your business' financial statements. You may decide to keep the books yourself, or hire full or part-time bookkeeping help.

Credit and Collections

In this section we will discuss both the credit extended to you by other businesses, and the credit you grant to your customers, plus collection procedures.

Credit extended to your business

A business with a good credit history, built on timely payments of obligations (paying its invoices and loan payments promptly) will enjoy better relationships with suppliers and banks. Such a firm can obtain goods and services without credit delays. Its bank will often extend a "line of credit" allowing the company to borrow against an agreed dollar limit without having to formally apply for it on each occasion.

A business may also occasionally find it convenient to make credit card purchases. However, these should be kept to a minimum since interest rates on credit card balances are much higher than for a similar balance taken out as a short-term bank loan.

Most suppliers will allow their credit-worthy customers a period of 30-days (in some cases up to 90-days) from the day of delivery of their goods and services to the time payment is due.

The most common type of trade credit is the "open account" where you order from a supplier and receive an invoice for each delivery, plus a monthly statement. The statement shows the terms of sale. That is, when the account must be paid in full; when payment must be received for cash discounts; the amount of the cash discounts and the interest on past due accounts. For example, if the terms call for 2/10 net 30, that means the buyer can take a 2 percent discount if the invoice is paid within 10-days. Net payment is expected within 30-days.

Another type of trade credit, "wholesale financing", is provided with the agreement that you will repay the supplier as items are sold. This type of credit is frequently used with more expensive inventory items such as major appliances, automobiles, furniture, or heavy equipment. In effect, it allows you to borrow from your supplier at no interest, thus reducing your cash requirements.

Where no credit is offered, suppliers require cash before delivery of merchandise or services. This is abbreviated as CBD - cash-before-delivery. Suppliers requiring cash at the time of delivery operate under COD or cash-on-delivery terms.

"Seasonal dating" follows the same formula as ordinary or monthly dating, although the payment maturity period is longer with seasonal terms. This practice is used most frequently with seasonal merchandise such as toys, apparel and similar merchandise. You should take advantage of any discounts offered for early payment whenever possible. It can sometimes be cost-effective to take a bank loan to make a payment rather than miss these discounts. Trade credit is a privilege your business earns and keeps by making its payments on an agreed-to basis. A supplier will evaluate your business' credit standing in much the same way as you evaluate your customers' creditworthiness.

Suppliers may also rely on reports made on your business by credit bureaus, national research firms such as Dun & Bradstreet, banks and other sources.

Some suppliers work on an account consignment agreement with their bank to finance their accounts receivable. These are balances due from their customers who have purchased on credit. The bank takes these accounts receivable in place of a cash deposit and gives them credit for a certain percentage of that amount until all invoices are paid. In some cases, their customers will be required to send their payments directly to the bank.

In summary, credit can be an important tool for expanding your business or providing for regular or unusual expenses. Trade credit can help keep your inventory costs from tying up vital working capital.

By all means, *compare* credit costs and benefits to decide where credit fits into your business plans and how credit can be used most advantageously by your business.

Credit extended to your customers

Many of the items discussed above are also relevant to credit you extend to your customers. The difference is simply that you are now in the creditor's shoes.

A written credit policy is not necessary for all businesses. However, a formal policy can help customers and employees understand your firm's ground rules. Extending credit to your customers can stimulate sales and add to your profits. But extending credit also increases your company's needs for operating capital since giving credit is really no different from making loans to customers.

Whether your business offers credit will depend upon:

- How much operating capital you can make available for these short-term "customer loans".

- How profitable these credit sales are to your business.

- What types of credit terms are available to customers from your competitors.

Once you decide that offering credit will result in increased sales and profits, proceed to establish a credit policy. Some policies require that customers pay a deposit before receiving goods or services. This approach reduces your exposure to losses.

Some policies set dollar limits on total credit that can be extended per sale without approval by a manager.

Your policy will depend in part on an estimate of the maximum cash amount your business can allocate for customer credit without jeopardizing cash flow. It should also spell out billing procedures, including collections on past due accounts. Some companies have strictly enforced collection policies, while others are more flexible and consider individual circumstances.

Your credit policy should outline procedures for screening and the granting of credit. You can use a standard application form or design one of your own. Consult your attorney to make certain your application asks all needed questions, and does not contain or imply illegal discrimination on the basis of age, sex, race, marital status or religion. It is advisable to indicate that credit limits and down payments depend on applicants' credit histories.

Generally, be aware of the following pitfalls and opportunities in setting a credit policy:

• New start-up companies are often too generous in granting credit since they are anxious to build sales. This can be dangerous as it may deplete capital faster than planned and could result in a tight cash position.

• Sometimes customers have temporary cash problems. The answer is to work out a realistic re-payment schedule on the old balance. This new schedule could be interest-bearing. Put these arrangements in writing. You can also insist that new purchases be put on a COD basis until the past-due portion is paid.

Ask your outside salespeople for frequent reports on slow-paying accounts. They are in constant contact with these customers and should be in a position to report on what is happening. Whether to use salespeople as "collectors" is a question that should be resolved in each individual case. It depends on the type of relationship that exists between your salesperson and the customer.

You should designate a qualified person who is authorized to approve or reject customer credit.

Aside from the credit your business offers directly, you may also accept certain credit cards. Credit card firms charge a percentage commission on sales, but they also take full responsibility for collections. This means that your business will not be penalized should these customers fail to pay. Sales slips for these credit sales are deposited in the bank in much the same way as checks are deposited.

The test of a realistic credit policy is, does it succeed in holding credit losses to a minimum? Acceptable average credit losses differ by type of business. These data are published in various trade and government publications. If your losses rise above published averages, your credit policies should be re-examined for serious flaws. If your losses fall far below the average for your type of business, your policy may be too strict, and you could be losing profitable business by discouraging potential customers.

Your business should also have established policies for accepting checks. For the convenience of your customers, policies should be clearly spelled out and your employees fully familiar with them.

Your policy should include:

- A dollar limit on the size of checks you will accept.

- Type of identification required.

- Limits on the amount of change a customer can receive, if any, on checks made out for more than the purchase price.

- Types of checks which will or will not be accepted.

Identification most often required is a valid local driver's license or other standard identification with the bearer's signature and photograph. Other identification should show the customer's signature, and come from a recognizable issuer such as a major credit firm. Checks should be signed in the presence of your employee. Whatever identification is used, employees should carefully compare the signatures on identification with the signature of the customer endorsing the check. Any photograph should be verified as the likeness of your customer.

There are many types of checks. *Personal checks* are made out on an individual's checking account and signed by that person. Two pieces of identification should always be required. If there is *any* doubt about the legitimacy of a check, it should only be accepted after bank verification is obtained. Checks are normally made out for the exact amount of purchase, although some companies do allow a customer to write a check for a higher dollar amount than the purchase and give change for the difference.

Government checks (including payroll, social security, income tax, welfare, etc.) are sometimes stolen or forged. They should be accepted according to the same guidelines that apply to personal checks.

Payroll checks issued by local businesses should only be accepted if the customer is known. They are usually machine-produced. Payroll checks that are handprinted, rubberstamped or typewritten should be verified through the issuing bank. Some businesses make it a general policy not to accept payroll checks.

Cashier's checks are made out by the bank to your customer. These checks are not drawn from customer accounts, but are bought from and guaranteed for payment by the bank. These checks do not require customer identification if they are made out to your business.

Traveler's checks show a pre-printed amount, and are signed at the time they are issued. They should be signed a second time when used, and the endorser signature must match. Identification is not usually required for these checks since they are guaranteed for payment by the issuer.

Private money orders are usually bought in order to send money by mail. It is often difficult to determine whether these money orders are authentic. They are not generally accepted for regular purchases.

Two-party checks are personal checks signed over by the first endorser to a second endorser. Two party checks are difficult to verify and are generally accepted only under extraordinary circumstances.

"Blank" checks which do not have pre-printed information such as the issuer's name, address, and account number, should always be verified through their respective banks, since they can be easily forged. In general, these checks are high risk, and you may consider adopting a policy against accepting them.

Checks from out of town or out of state may also present problems, because they are difficult to verify. They may be treated in the same way as personal checks, or you may set a general policy and circumstances for honoring them.

In accepting *any* check, identification and signatures should be carefully checked. If a check cannot be cleared through the issuing bank (or a check verification firm), it should not be accepted. The only exceptions to this are with traveler's or cashier's checks which are both guaranteed for payment by the issuer.

Checks should be carefully examined to see that the following items are included and are accurate:

- Preprinted name, address and telephone number of the customer.

- Preprinted name and location of the issuing bank.

- Current date.

- The same numerical and written amounts on the check.

- Account holder's signature, executed at the time of the purchase.

Bad checks are usually for moderate amounts; $20 to $40. The objective is no doubt to draw as little attention as possible. Still, only a small percentage of checks will be bad, and your policies and your employees' watchfulness can keep losses to a minimum.

Whatever your general check cashing policies are, your check verification and authorizing procedures should be quick, and not embarrassing or offensive to your customers.

One word of caution: Be on guard against certain types of new customers who make small purchases and establish a satisfactory credit relationship by paying promptly. Then suddenly they will make an uncharacteristically large purchase. Having already gained your confidence, they will put this exceptionally large purchase on their open account. Next, one of two things can happen: They may create a dispute over the quality of the product or service they purchased and refuse to pay. Or, they may disappear without paying or leaving a trace.

There is a history of individuals - small time operators or even organized crime groups - that use this technique to victimize legitimate businesses. This is not to say you must be suspicious every time a new customer comes in with a big order, but caution should be exercised by proceeding carefully when buying patterns abruptly change.

Here are some general guidelines for guarding against potential credit losses:

- Proceed with caution if a credit applicant has no record at your credit bureau.

- Investigate if there is a change in management or ownership in a company you have done business with before, but were never introduced to the new people.

- Be wary if credit references furnished to you have post office boxes as addresses and answering services as telephone numbers.

- Be alert in the case of a customer who is new in town. Or a company unlisted in the telephone book and other directories.

- Be suspicious when a new customer who has recently established credit with you uses you as a credit reference elsewhere.

Collection Procedures

The key to good credit policy is to take steps that prevent difficulties before they happen. Bad receivables are not completely avoidable if your company grants credit to its customers, but they can be kept low by careful planning.

The first step in collections is to insure that invoices are accurate and mailed out on time. Two of the most common excuses for non-payment are that billings are in error, or that invoices have not been received. Errors in billing can also lead to lost good will of otherwise loyal customers.

If it's the usual trade practice in your industry, offer a discount for early payment. Discounts for the timely payment of invoices are often very effective, but they eat into your profits and should only be used to follow customary practices in your industry, or to reach a particular goal.

Having a clearly laid out, common sense credit policy will also limit bad receivables. Your credit policies will dictate the maximum dollar amounts for credit that can be extended to customers. You may also have extra safeguards for new customers, such as requiring a deposit before release of goods or complete performance of services.

Temporarily holding up orders for customers with past-due accounts is one effective collection tool.

Your invoices should also clearly describe any extra charges that would be charged in the event of late payment. You may also set a time limit for reporting damage to merchandise or inadequate service. Some purchase orders also include a statement to the effect that the customer agrees to pay legal costs resulting from any collection efforts you have to resort to. Consult your attorney before finalizing such a statement.

Letters concerning non-payment should be matter-of-fact, never threatening or impolite. They should tell your customer what you intend to do, and any alternatives your company is willing to offer, such as accepting an interest-bearing note.

The following is a sample letter sent to a customer after 60-days of non-payment.

Company Letterhead

Mr. Thomas Mercury
7115 - Second Avenue
Moose Jaw Bend, Idaho   83841

Dear Mr. Thomas:

Enclosed is our second notice requesting payment for the balance of your account.

If you are having difficulty with payment, please contact me by telephone before January 10, 19__ so we can discuss special arrangements for payment.

If I do not hear from you or receive payment on the balance of your account by January 21, 19__, I will regretfully turn your account over to a collection agency.

Sincerely,

Larry Duncan
Customer Credit Representative
(   )555-7170, Ext. 5

LD:aa

Enclosure

Books and publications on collection procedures are available through local libraries. They contain numerous sample letters and information on telephone collection techniques. In general, these letters progress from gentle reminders for payment to increasingly forceful letters which outline the consequences of nonpayment.

In some cases, a telephone call will achieve good results. Telephone collection procedures are more effective in business-to-business than in business-to-consumer environments. Telephone conversations with delinquent customers can often uncover the underlying reasons for non-payment, such as dissatisfaction with a product or service. In these cases the problem must be resolved before collection will be possible.

Occasionally, even your best efforts may fail to result in payment. In these cases, you may still be able to recover by turning the account over to a collection agency. By prior agreement, these agencies keep a substantial amount of the money they collect, so you should make every reasonable effort to collect before turning over an account. Often, a letter from your attorney can be highly effective in getting an immediate response.

Managing Cash Flow

Cash flow statements reveal how your incoming funds are being used and show the amount of cash your business has on hand on a month-to-month basis.

Managing your cash flow takes careful planning, follow-through, and a good sense of timing. Even very profitable businesses can find themselves in trouble if this area is not meticulously managed. Cash, as we refer to it in this section, represents funds in the company checking account in addition to actual cash.

Cash flow is the process of expending current available cash for resale merchandise and/or materials; labor and overhead to manufacture products or services, which when sold will generate sufficient cash to continue or expand this cycle. That process is shown in this chart:

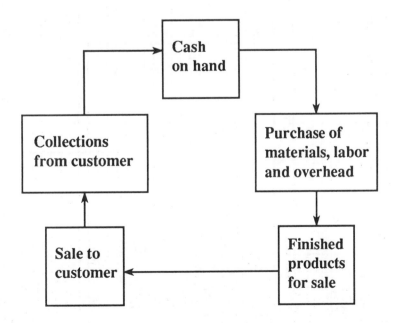

The following SBA Cash Flow Projections illustrate this in further detail.

MONTHLY CASH FLOW PROJECTION

NAME OF BUSINESS _____ ADDRESS _____ OWNER _____ TYPE OF BUSINESS _____ PREPARED BY _____ DATE _____

Values shown are the "Estimate" figures for each month. (Pre-Start-up and Month 1 show Actual = 5000 for Cash on Hand.)

Line item	Pre-Start-up	1	2	3	4	5	6	7	8	9	10	11	12	TOTAL Cols 1–12
1. CASH ON HAND (Beginning of month)	5000	5000	1350	700	50	900	1250	1600	1950	2100	1750	2100	2950	
2. CASH RECEIPTS														
(a) Cash Sales		1000	2000	6000	7500	7500	7500	7500	7500	8000	8000	8500	8500	
(b) Collections from Credit Accounts														
(c) Loan or Other Cash injection (Specify)			4000											
3. TOTAL CASH RECEIPTS (2a + 2b + 2c = 3)		1000	6000	6000	7500	7500	7500	7500	7500	8000	8000	8500	8500	
4. TOTAL CASH AVAILABLE (Before cash out) (1 + 3)	5000	6000	7350	6700	7550	8400	8750	9100	9450	10100	9750	10600	11450	
5. CASH PAID OUT														
(a) Purchases (Merchandise)		1000	3000	3000	3000	3000	3000	3000	3200	3200	3500	3500	4000	
(b) Gross Wages (excludes withdrawals)		1000	1000	1000	1000	1000	1000	1000	1000	1000	1000	1000	1000	
(c) Payroll Expenses (Taxes, etc.)		200	200	200	200	200	200	200	200	200	200	200	200	
(d) Outside Services														
(e) Supplies (Office and operating)		50	50	50	50	50	50	50	50	50	50	50	50	
(f) Repairs and Maintenance														
(g) Advertising		400	400	400	400	400	400	400	400	400	400	400	400	
(h) Car, Delivery, and Travel		300	300	300	300	300	300	300	300	300	300	300	300	
(i) Accounting and Legal		150	150	150	150	150	150	150	150	150	150	150	150	
(j) Rent		300	300	300	300	300	300	300	300	300	300	300	300	
(k) Telephone		50	50	50	50	50	50	50	50	50	50	50	50	
(l) Utilities		100	100	100	100	100	100	100	100	100	100	100	100	
(m) Insurance		100	100	100	100	100	100	100	100	100	100	100	100	
(n) Taxes (Real estate, etc.)														
(o) Interest														
(p) Other Expenses (Specify each)														
(q) Miscellaneous (Unspecified)														
(r) Subtotal		3650	5650	5650	5650	5650	5650	5650	5850	5850	6150	6150	6650	
(s) Loan Principal Payment					500	500	500	500	500	500	500	500	500	
(t) Capital Purchases (Specify)										900				
(u) Other Start-up Costs														
(v) Reserve and/or Escrow (Specify)														
(w) Owner's Withdrawal		1000	1000	1000	1000	1000	1000	1000	1000	1000	1000	1000	1000	
6. TOTAL CASH PAID OUT (Total 5a thru 5w)		4650	6650	6650	6650	7150	7150	7150	7350	8250	7650	7650	8150	
7. CASH POSITION (End of month) (4 minus 6)	1350	1350	700	50	900	1250	1600	1950	2100	1850	2100	2950	3300	
ESSENTIAL OPERATING DATA (Non-cash flow information)														
A. Sales Volume (Dollars)														
B. Accounts Receivable (End of month)														
C. Bad Debt (End of month)														
D. Inventory on Hand (End of month)														
E. Accounts Payable (End of month)														
F. Depreciation														

FORM 1100

To keep this Cash Flow Projection current and useful, fill in the actual figures and revise future estimates accordingly.

This Monthly Cash Flow Projection will tell you at a glance in which direction your money is moving. If Cash Receipts (3) are greater than your expenditures (6), then the cash balance has increased during that month. But if the Cash Receipts (3) are smaller than the Cash Paid Out (6), you will experience a decrease in your cash balance.

In order to project the direction your business is going, it is necessary to prepare a monthly cash flow projection that covers a twelve-month period. For a cash flow projection to be beneficial, it will be necessary to record the actual expenditures alongside your estimates for each month. After two or three months of operation, the projection should be compared with the actual figures. If it is obvious that some projected figures are in error, corrections should be made in the projections for the remainder of the year.

These figures *do not,* however, present your monthly profits or losses in the business. For a complete picture on the financial status of your business, a regular financial statement, prepared by someone fully qualified, will be required. Only a financial statement will provide this information by considering other factors such as depreciation and inventories. By observing the changes in this statement on a month-to-month basis, you will learn to operate more cost-effectively. It can serve as an "early warning" system that indicates when to reduce expenditures or increase sales efforts in order to keep the cash flow positive.

You may ask yourself this question: If your business is showing profits every month, how can a cash shortage develop? It can happen where profits are insufficient or too much cash is invested in expansion, inventory, customer credit, or other expenditures.

Cash flow statements show how much cash your business has on-hand each month, and are used to predict your cash flow in the future. It can serve as an early warning signal to keep your cash reserves from becoming too low to meet regular and unexpected expenditures.

Here are some practical examples on how to analyze cash flow:

Cash Flow Chart

Gilpin High Country Tours

January 19__

	Cash in	Pay Outs	Balance
Beginning of month balance	12,200.00		12,200.00
Receipts	21,000.00		
Other Income	250.00		
Total Income	33,450.00		

Cash Disbursements:

1.	Employee Payroll	4,500.00
2.	Supplies	175.00
3.	Maintenance/Repair	75.00
4.	Van Maint./Operations	450.00
5.	Catering	525.00
6.	Advertising	175.00
7.	Accounting/Legal	200.00
8.	Rent	500.00
9.	Utilities	240.00
10.	Telephone	105.00
11.	Insurance	370.00
12.	Taxes	745.00
13.	Loan Repayment	2,000.00
	Total Disbursements	10,060.00

End of Month Balance: 33,450.00 — 10,060.00   = 23,390.00

In this example, Gilpin High Country Tours' cash on hand increased by $11,190.00 during January (23,390.00. - 12,200.00)

The next chart shows cash on hand in February. In this month, a loan for $20,000.00 is taken to buy a new van. The loan proceeds will increase the cash receipts for February. The vehicle is purchased in March and results in additional cash disbursements for van maintenance, operating expenses, insurance, taxes, and hiring of an additional employee. Sales in March do not increase significantly as an immediate result of purchase of the van. From March onward the business will have the added outlays for repayment of the loan for the van, the cost of additional supplies and the salary of the new employee. These additional expenses should be offset by increased sales or Gilpin will eventually face a cash flow crisis, with its cash balance declining from month to month.

Cash Flow Projection

Gilpin High Country Tours

February 19__

	Cash in	Cash Out	Balance
Beginning of month balance	23,390.00		23,390.00
Receipts	26,500.00		
Other Income (Loan)	20,000.00		
Total Income	69,890.00		
Total Disbursements (Items 1 to 13, see page 5-34)		15,000.00	
End of Month Balance:	69,890.00	- 15,000.00	= 54,890.00

March 19__

Beginning of month	54,890.00		
Receipts	25,600.00		
Other Income			
Total Income	80,490.00		
Total Disbursements (Items 1 to 13, see page 5-34)		17,000.00	
Disbursements			
Van purchase		23,500.00	
New employee		1,200.00	
Misc. Expense		5,000.00	
		46,700.00	
End of Month Balance:	80,490.00	- 46,700.00	= 33,790.00

Next is an example of a quarterly cash flow chart for the Peabody Comic Book Exchange.

Quarterly Cash Flow Projection
Peabody Comic Book Exchange

	Cash in	Cash Out	Balance
Jan. 1 balance	1,000.00		1,000.00
Receipts	450.00		
Loan obtained	750.00		
Total	2,200.00		
Disbursements		900.00	
Additional Inventory			
Purchase		750.00	
Cash End of Month			
and in bank	2,200.00	- 1,650.00	= 550.00
April 1 balance	550.00		
Receipts	1,200.00		
Total	1,750.00		
Disbursements		900.00	
Cash End of Month			
and in bank	1,750.00	- 900.00	= 850.00
July 1 balance	850.00		
Receipts	1,200.00		
Total	2,050.00		
Disbursements		900.00	
Cash End of Month			
and in bank	2,050.00	- 900.00	= 1,150.00
October 1 balance	1,150.00		
Receipts	1,200.00		
Total	2,350.00		
Disbursements		900.00	
Loan Repayment		300.00	
Total Disbursements			
Cash End of Month			
and in bank	2,350.00	- 1,200.00	= 1,150.00
New Year Jan. 1 balance	1,150.00		
Receipts	1,300.00		
Total	2,450.00		
Disbursements		900.00	
Loan Repayment		290.00	
Total Disbursements			
Cash End of Month and in bank	2,450.00	- 1,190.00	= 1,260.00

This extended cash flow projection shows how the company's current earnings and plans for borrowing will cover expected expenses for attending a January Comic Book Collectors' convention. By purchasing the inventory in May, Peabody will be able to take advantage of lower unit prices and a wider selection. This careful planning also gives the company owner an idea of how much cash on hand there will be for additional inventory and special display materials for this convention.

The main purpose for the cash flow projection is to predict when your cash on hand will be needed most and avoid any cash shortage at these times. Borrowing can help you cover some of these expenses, but borrowing should be occasional and carefully planned so that loan repayments do not come due at the same time your company has other large cash commitments.

If you see your cash balance decreasing from month to month - or you expect high cash outlays for a certain time - you should:

- Examine your other financial statements and consult your accountant about ways to handle this problem.

- Consider postponing payments that are not due.

- Consider ways to generate more cash, such as a special sale or a short-term loan.

- Consider ways to reduce expenses.

- Determine if rapid growth is depleting your cash reserve and review your expansion plans accordingly.

This kind of a financial review will keep your business from borrowing unnecessarily; overextending itself with too many loans or growth commitments, or having insufficient cash to pay for unexpected expenses.

Protecting Your Business with Insurance

It is important to carefully examine the type of insurance you require. Coverage needed by most businesses fall in these major categories:

- Property
  - Fire, smoke, water
  - Floods
  - Windstorms
  - Other natural disasters
  - Customers' property at your premises

- Automobile
  - Cars
  - Trucks
  - Trailers
  - Other road using vehicles

- Casualty
  - Liability
  - Business interruption
  - Employee health and disability

- Life
  - Owners
  - Officers
  - Key personnel
  - Partnership

After some general comments, we will look at some of these types of insurance requirements. Insurance planning is an area where the services of a competent insurance agent is invaluable.

First, it is important to identify the types of losses a business may face. It is much less costly to insure for potential losses than to cover those losses from business funds should they occur. Many companies have been put out of business by failing to carry adequate insurance coverage.

Once you have decided on areas of vulnerability, you should proceed to talk to insurance agents or brokers. The process of choosing one who is right for your business is similar to selecting any other consultant. This is discussed in the section on consultants, later in the manual. Be aware that most insurance agents represent only one company, while brokers can handle any number of insurers. There are advantages and disadvantages in dealing with either agents or brokers. The variations in coverages and premiums can be significant. Your final selection of the right representative will depend on a combination of factors such as quality of coverage, costs, and how you think you will get along with him or her. Whenever possible, use one insurance agent or broker to cover all of your insurance requirements. This protects your business from any duplication in the coverage or leaving a potential exposure uninsured.

It is important to compare the cost of coverage to the cost and consequences of possible loss. This keeps you from over or under-insuring and paying for premiums without getting adequate coverage should a loss occur. Using coverage with high deductibles can reduce the cost of premiums. Many package policies that offer coverage for an array of exposures are very economical compared to individual policies.

After you have purchased the policies, it is important to periodically review them to see that they are still adequate to meet the needs of a changing business. These reviews are frequently overlooked by entrepreneurs once their original policies have been purchased.

Your agent or broker can suggest coverage necessary or desirable for your particular business. The following is a general overview of the more common types of insurance coverages.

Liability insurance covers bodily injuries, and sometimes libel or slander to people outside of your business. This coverage pays court costs and legal fees if suits are brought against your company. It also covers damage to property that results from your business operations or by the actions of your employees. Most policies require your business to report even minor incidents that may eventually result in claims. Consult your broker for advice on dollar limits for coverage.

Property insurance covers disasters like fire, floods, windstorms, water damage, etc. Fire insurance is usually offered as the basic disaster coverage, and other coverage can be added at relatively low cost. You can and should carry insurance sufficient to cover customers' property being held on your premises, where applicable. An exception would be if customers are able to provide evidence that they have insured their property on your premises. It is also important to insure your premises if your lease requires you to do so.

You may need additional protection beyond fire/disaster insurance to cover loss of documents, deeds, cash, securities, and business records.

Automobile insurance covers property damage, liability and injuries. If your business has more than one insured vehicle, you may be able to save premium dollars by getting fleet rates. Again, accepting high deductibles is another way of reducing your expense for insurance coverage.

Employee insurance programs cover areas such as life, health, disability insurance, and Worker's Compensation. Worker's Compensation insurance is required and administered by most states and is paid as a percentage of your payroll, based on the degree of potential hazards for each particular job. This is usually required by law to be paid to a state compensation fund, but some states permit coverage through private workers' compensation programs. Most businesses are eligible for group life, health, disability, and retirement income at much lower rates than for individual policies.

Key personnel or business life insurance provides a way to financially stabilize your business if you or a key employee dies. The most cost-effective way to achieve this coverage is to obtain term life insurance policies. For sole proprietorships, this insurance provides finances to continue the business after your death. For partnerships or corporations, it will furnish the funds necessary to buy out the deceased partner's share. This protection also provides the funds necessary to fill the deceased key employee's position in the business.

This coverage can enable your survivors to liquidate your business, or your share in it, if they need immediate cash.

In all cases you should make certain that your policy does not conflict with your will, and that legally binding plans have been made for the takeover or liquidation of your business upon your death.

Consult your lawyer before committing to any particular plan.

Business interruption insurance covers expenses incurred if your place of business is destroyed or heavily damaged by fire or natural disaster. This insurance reimburses you for rent, salaries, and other major expense items, including the extra expenses incurred for moving and returning to your location for the period it takes to complete repairs.

Crime coverage includes burglary, robbery, theft, vandalism, and other crimes, including the actions of dishonest employees. There are plans to deal with individual types of crime, such as burglary, as well as comprehensive plans which deal with more than one category.

In summary, before you select an insurance agent or broker, list all the potential risks inherent in your business that should be considered for insurance coverage. Your agent or broker will help you identify the types of coverages that are essential, and those which are optional. He will also suggest how to combine risks in packages for greater economy.

It is necessary to re-evaluate your polices periodically to see that your business is not over or under-insured. The premiums for identical coverage from one company to another can vary widely, so it will pay to comparison-shop. An insurance broker's advice can be very helpful in setting up and monitoring your insurance needs since your requirements will constantly change.

Balance Sheet
December 31, 19___

Current Assets:
Cash	$2,320	
Accounts Receivable	1,460	
Inventory	9,320	
Prepaid Expenses	300	
Total Current Expenses		$13,400

Fixed Assets:
Delivery Equipment	15,000	
Furniture & Fixtures	4,600	
Total Fixed Assets		19,600
Total Assets		$33,000

Liabilities

Accounts Payable	$6,430	
Notes Payable	2,320	
Payroll Tax Payable	150	
Sales Tax Payable	1,900	
Total Liabilities		$10,800

Capital:
Owner's Equity		22,200
Total Liabilities & Capital		$33,000

Profit and Loss Statement
October 1 - December 31, 19___

	Dollars		Percent
Net Sales	$68,116		100.0
Cost of Goods Sold	47,696		70.0
Gross Profit on Sales		$20,420	30.0
Expenses			
Wages	$6,948		10.0
Delivery Expense	954		1.4
Bad Debts Allowance	409		0.6
Communications	204		0.3
Depreciation Allowance	409		0.6
Insurance	613		0.9
Taxes & Licenses	1,021		1.5
Advertising	1,566		2.3
Interest	409		0.6
Other Charges	749		1.1
Total Expenses		$13,282	19.5
Net Profit		$ 7,138	10.5
Other Income		886	1.3
Total Net Income		$ 8,024	11.8

(Adapted from SBA-Introduction to Recordkeeping.)

Section 6

BUILDING SALES AND PROFITS

Pricing for Profits

Your goal in pricing is to *maximize profits*. This is done by setting prices at levels that are competitive and acceptable to customers. There are a number of factors which influence profits. These include direct and indirect costs of your product or service; your overhead expenses; your sales volume, and competitive price levels. Each of these factors must be taken into consideration to establish a realistic pricing structure.

Having a good understanding of current market prices and pricing formulas will ensure that your prices will -

- Be competitive
- Cover all direct and indirect costs of your products and services.
- Maximize your profits.

There are three prime factors that have an important bearing on the determination of the prices:

- *Overhead.* Overhead costs are the expenses of running your business, exclusive of re-sale items, production materials and saleable labor costs. These include administrative and management salaries; office/shop supplies; rent and utilities; accounting; marketing; advertising; sales; interest, payments, etc.

- *Cost of production labor.* These are hourly wages plus any benefits such as vacations; sick pay; retirement or insurance.

- *Cost of re-sale merchandise and materials.* Merchandise is purchased and re-sold without change or modification. Materials usually become parts of a manufacturing process or a service-type operation.

There are a number of workable pricing formulas to choose from. One way to categorize them is by types of industries. In some businesses, the pricing levels are well established, in others, they are flexible.

Industries with Well-Established Price Levels

First, we'll take a closer look at businesses in industries with well-established price levels. Customers of such businesses are aware of what prices generally are and fully expect to pay within that range.

The basic formula for pricing is:

Selling price = item or service cost + overhead + profit

Customer expectations, along with industry standards, allow for very little flexibility in the setting of prices in these businesses. Here, it will be necessary to pay close attention to cost factors and sales volume in order to achieve and maintain profitable levels.

Your profit will increase if you -

* Reduce your expenses in your overhead, sales and production departments and purchasing costs.

* Increase your sales volume. By doing so, the increase in overhead will grow at a slower rate than that of the sales volume.

Profits with Low Overhead

Sales	$100,000	(100%)	$150,000	(100%)
Cost of Sales*	60,000	(60%)	90,000	(60%)
Overhead**	30,000	(30%)	35,000	(23.3%)
Profit	$ 10,000	(10%)	$ 25,000	(16.7%)

Profits with Higher Overhead

Sales	$100,000	(100%)	$150,000	(100%)
Cost of Sales*	65,000	(65%)	100,000	(66.7%)
Overhead**	32,000	(32%)	40,000	(26.7%)
Profit	$ 3,000	(3%)	$ 10,000	(6.6%)

You also must be aware of the fact that when sales drop, the overhead will stay the same or decrease only slightly. For example:

Sales	$100,000	(100%)	$80,000	(100%)
Cost of Sales*	60,000	(60%)	48,000	(60%)
Overhead**	30,000	(30%)	28,000	(36%)
Profit	$ 10,000	(10%)	$ 4,000	(4%)

*For merchandise and/or labor.   **All other expenses.

To keep the profit at desired levels, such as 10 percent in our example, you would have to raise your prices to compensate for it. This, however, is not always possible.

Profitability in pricing can be best described by setting prices high enough to maximize the profits and keeping them at levels your customers are willing to pay.

To illustrate how mark-ups and sales volume affect your profits, refer to the following chart. Assuming that the direct cost of manufacturing or the purchase of a re-sale item is $5.00 per unit, and the selling price is in the $7.00 to $9.00 range, you calculate your profit as follows:

	Number of units sold	Your selling price	Your cost	Gross profit per unit	Total Profit
(A)	10,000	$9.00	$5.00	$4.00	$40,000.00
	10,000	8.00	5.00	3.00	30,000.00
	10,000	7.00	5.00	2.00	20,000.00
	15,000	9.00	5.00	4.00	60,000.00
(B)	15,000	8.00	5.00	3.00	45,000.00
	15,000	7.00	5.00	2.00	30,000.00
	20,000	9.00	5.00	4.00	80,000.00
	20,000	8.00	5.00	3.00	60,000.00
	20,000	7.00	5.00	2.00	40,000.00

For the purpose of this example, we do not take the overhead cost allocated to this product into consideration. If you believe you can sell 15,000 units above in a moderately competitive market, and price it at $8.00 per unit, your profit will be $45,000.00 (B). But if you price it at $9.00 per unit and sell only 10,000 units, your gross profit will decrease to $40,000.00. (A)

Prevailing market prices and price formulas are useful guides that can help your business move toward profits on all items and services, rather than profits on some items and losses on others. Up-to-date knowledge of market conditions is necessary because the "right" price depends in part upon current market conditions. It has to be competitive, cover your costs *and* generate profits.

There are a number of ways to control cost factors. One is to buy your merchandise and materials at the most advantageous prices and terms available. Buy in bulk or off-season, if these steps can reduce costs. Take advantage of any available trade and cash discounts. Consider using lower quality, less expensive materials or merchandise *if they do not affect customer acceptance.*

Control of labor cost is important. Some costs can be reduced by better production scheduling or streamlining flow of work through the shop or plant. An idle machine or unproductive employees will increase costs. Good supervision and on-going training will reduce costs, and can raise employee productivity and reduce losses incurred by slowdowns or mistakes. It also reduces employee turnover and the need to invest time and money in training or re-training.

Pay close attention to overhead costs. Your business can keep these expenses to a minimum by analyzing each expense item. First, determine whether an expense can be reduced without undermining its original usefulness. This applies on everything you buy - from paper clips to travel expenses. Low rent, for example, will save on overhead costs as long as the location of the business does not have a negative effect on customers or internal operations.

Maintain your desired profits by keeping your prices in close proximity to those of your competitors and by using some of the above suggestions.

Industries with Flexible Pricing Practices

Now we'll look at businesses with flexible pricing. Some industries do not have firmly established price levels. Customers of these businesses will comparison shop and ask for competitive quotations. You can arrive at prices by using the formula previously mentioned:

Selling Price = Item or service cost + overhead + profit

Be careful not to price yourself out of business. Competitors in these types of businesses may often move in quickly to undercut your prices. Be flexible in the event this happens. You may have to reduce prices to meet the competition. However, keep in mind that the price cut will come directly off of your profit.

In some businesses, products and services are often purchased on a competitive bid basis. This is particularly true when dealing with governmental agencies and larger companies.

If you have an efficient operation, your bids can be profitable, if accepted. Also be aware that if all of your bids *are* successful, your prices may be too low. If a bidder makes a mistake in calculations, anticipated profits can be quickly eaten up and often result in losses.

Costs generally fall into three categories.

- Production labor.
- Materials and resale merchandise.
- Overhead.

Production labor is the cost of direct labor in the manufacture of products. It also includes labor expended in services performed such as repair work, modifications of products, food preparation, printing, construction work, etc.

Materials that are part of a finished product or used in repair services are resale items. This can include steel, lumber, paints, plastics, machine parts, chemicals, circuit boards, etc. Merchandise bought from wholesalers and manufacturers are also re-sale items.

Overhead expenses are costs that are fairly constant, regardless of the volume you produce or sell. Overhead items can be either "fixed" or "variable". Fixed overhead items include:

- Rent
- Insurance

- Utilities
- Depreciation
- Interest on loans
- Salaries for personnel, other than production workers
- Owners' salaries
- Others

Overhead items are variable. They depend on the volume of business being done, and upon management decisions. They include:

- Advertising
- Marketing
- Supplies
- Transportation
- Maintenance and repair
- Sales expenses
- Salaries for sales personnel
- Shipping
- Others

Before you price products or services, you will have to precisely determine your costs. Manufacturing and service businesses use similar approaches. Retailing and wholesaling use different methods.

Costing and Pricing in Manufacturing and Service Businesses.

The most significant cost item in these types of businesses is production labor, followed by material costs. In most service businesses, however, labor is the most predominant cost factor.

Production labor costs are usually based on hourly rates. Added to this are employee benefits such as insurance, social security, vacation and sick pay, profit sharing and pension plans, etc. These benefits can add from 20 percent to 35 percent to the hourly wage rates. Benefits are pro-rated on an hourly basis and added to production labor costs. This results in the total cost for each hour worked. Since not all of an individual's time is being spent productively, you must make an allowance for non-productive time. Non-productive time can be the result of equipment breakdowns; faulty or misunderstood instructions; lack of motivation or just plain loafing; poor scheduling and many other factors. Time lost due to these causes can increase production time and costs by 15 to 50 percent and must be added to the cost of the product. Often a seemingly profitable operation begins to show losses, when the costs of rejects or time losses are not taken into consideration.

Many businesses which fail to take the above-described factors into account lose money without being able to pinpoint the reason. Every manufacturing operation will experience a certain amount of time losses and reject problems. A good manager will establish acceptable limits for these. If losses exceed these limits, a thorough investigation should be conducted to determine the causes and ways to correct them.

Particular attention must be paid to the percentage of rejects and work to be done over. These costs must be included in your production costs and added to the total cost of the product.

Your overhead also plays a role in determining your hourly labor production costs. There are a number of ways to calculate the hourly overhead costs. We'll illustrate some of these approaches in the examples that follow.

To arrive at the overhead cost for each hour worked, begin by finding your total monthly overhead cost (from your actual or projected Profit and Loss Statement). Divide this figure by the total number of production employees for each hour worked.

Total Monthly Overhead	$15,000.00
12 Production Employees, each working 174 hours per month for a total of	2,088 hours
Overhead cost per hour worked = $\frac{15,000}{2,088}$	$7.18 per hour

In this example, the total monthly overhead is $15,000.00. This figure is taken from averaging monthly profit and loss statements or future projections. Twelve production employees worked during the month, being paid for 2,088 hours (174 hours per month x 12). The total overhead is divided by total production labor hours to give the overhead cost per hour worked.

One way to determine the net cost of your product is to add material costs to production labor costs and overhead costs. Rejects and time losses are not considered in this approach. Here's an example.

We will assume that the cost of the materials in your product is $25.00. Direct Labor is $12.00 per hour. The item requires five hours to manufacture. The pricing calculation is as follows for 100 percent productivity and for 75 percent productivity:

	100% Productivity	75% Productivity
Material cost	$25.00	$25.00
Production labor (five hours direct labor)	60.00	80.00
Overhead (five hours @ 7.18 per hour)	35.90	35.90
Net cost	$120.90	$140.90

These calculations show a net cost for the product at two different levels of productivity. To arrive at a sales price, you will add a percentage of profit to the net cost. Your profit will usually fall between 10 to 35 percent of net cost, although it can be higher if your market will support it. In our example, we will add a 20 percent profit.

	100% Productivity	75% Productivity
Net cost	$120.90	$140.90
Targeted profit (20% of new cost)	24.18	28.18
Selling price	$145.08	$169.08

The percentage of profit margin you set is somewhat arbitrary. It should be big enough to give you a cushion for unexpected losses. It must also be kept small enough to keep your selling prices within an acceptable market range.

Machine hour pricing. This method is often used when the equipment cost is substantial. For example, a machine hour on a particular piece of equipment may sell for $50.00 per hour. The hourly machine cost approach is somewhat more complicated to calculate. It takes into consideration the cost of the equipment; its useful life; the annual depreciation; repairs; power requirements and maintenance based on the number of hours or percentage of time it is used.

Assuming the hourly cost of a piece of equipment, based on an eight-hour day and five year usefulness, is $50.00 per hour and it is being operated less than a full day on the average, the hourly cost could increase to $60.00 or more. To this figure, you will add the cost of the labor required to operate the machine and the proportionate share of the hourly overhead cost. Finally, by adding the mark-up or profit, you will arrive at a figure that represents your hourly sales price on this piece of equipment.

The X-times labor approach. "X" is an arbitrary factor by which the hourly labor cost (without employee benefits) is multiplied to arrive at the selling price. For example, if the hourly rate is $8.00 and "X" is three, all labor performed by the employee will be billed at $24.00 (eight times three) per hour.

No matter which method you use - and there are many others - it is advisable to have your accountant help you work out a formula best suited for your business.

Retailing and Wholesaling. Many of the cost factors mentioned under manufacturing also apply to retail and wholesale costing. The major difference being that retailing and wholesaling do not involve production labor costs.

In retailing or wholesaling, you will buy someone else's manufactured product, mark it up, add overhead costs and desired profit to arrive at your selling price. Both of these types of businesses have well-established price levels which leads to less flexibility in pricing.

Basic cost factors for these businesses are the cost of the merchandise and the overhead. Merchandise bought for resale will obviously vary except for "name brands" which generally are quite uniform.

Your overhead costs will depend on the type of business you are in. They can be expressed as a percentage of your total sales volume. For most businesses, overhead will fall somewhere within 20 to 35 percent of the sales volume. It will depend upon the size of your business, the location, type of merchandise offered, and other factors.

For example:

Total yearly sales		$210,000.00
Less cost of merchandise (assuming that it is 67% of selling price or has a 50% markup)	$140,000.00	
Less overhead (at 25% of sales)	52,500.00	192,500.00
Profit		$ 17,500.00
Profit as a percent of total sales	$\dfrac{17,500.00}{210,000.00}$ or	8.3%

This pricing method enables you to set a "price floor" or a minimum price level - the amount you must charge to recover costs and obtain a certain amount of profit. A maximum price is the highest price the market will bear. Where you set your prices will depend upon the needs of your business, the characteristics of your products or services and your sense of the market. In some cases, your price floor may be higher than your competitors', or too high for the market to accept. In these cases, four major alternatives are available:

- Reduce costs for material, labor, or overhead.

- Differentiate your product from your competitors by emphasizing non-price factors such as product performance, service, delivery, financing, and other features.

- Accept a lower profit margin.

- Discontinue offering unprofitable products and sell them out at or below cost.

In establishing prices, it is generally better to err on the high side than setting them too low. It is much easier, in terms of customer acceptance, to reduce rather than raise a price. If you offer a product that you cannot sell at a profit, special sales at or below cost will at least make it possible to recover some of your investment. There may be reasons for continuing with a product that is unprofitable or has a very limited market. But it should be done only to complement a product line or offering it as a "loss leader" to attract buyers for higher mark-up items. Items that do not show profits or other enhancements to sales of other products should be dropped as soon as the maximum possible amount of their costs can be recovered.

All of your pricing should be cost-oriented, always taking the desired profit into account. Being able to make the best use of pricing formulas demands accurate estimates of direct costs, overhead, and expected sales volume. Your sales plan should include projections for profits that you can periodically compare to the actual sales and profits. This information will help in formulating prices.

A few final words on pricing: Once you have established the minimum price for your product or service, compare it with prices charged by competitors. Pay special attention to make your price as attractive as possible. Price tags or markers should be clearly displayed and easy to read.

In a retail business, consider odd-ending prices. Most customers know that a $5.99 item is simply a $6.00 item in disguise. But many studies suggest that the odd-ending prices are more attractive and generate more sales.

When putting on a sale, consider using the same price for similar, but not identical items (i.e., displays of apparel, kitchen utensils, records, etc.), or combining items at a reduced 2-for-1 price.

Loss-leaders are items offered at or below cost in order to attract customers. Loss-leaders and one-cent sales (where a second item is sold for one cent above the price of the first item) should be used very sparingly. They can be very effective strategies to build up a customer base and boost sales for higher mark-up items, but can become counter-productive if repeated too often.

Prices and estimates for services should be clearly explained and available to the customer in writing in an easily understandable form. Customers' questions on pricing should be answered as clearly as possible. However, it is important to point out such benefits as guarantees, post-purchase servicing, etc., rather than only discussing price.

In summary, we have presented some approaches to costing for manufacturing and service businesses, and a similar approach that applies to retail and wholesale businesses. They are by no means the only ones. There are a number of pricing and costing formulas that can be used to set prices, but they all relate basically to direct and indirect costs.

All costing approaches require careful planning, attention to cost factors, and an awareness of prices being offered by competitors. Your accountant can help you design the costing approach that will be most useful for your particular business.

Pricing Checklist

(Information based on a publication of the Small Business Administration.)

This checklist has been designed for the benefit of small retailers, but has useful application for many other types of businesses. These questions should help you think of various aspects in pricing. You should be able to easily relate them to your business:

	Yes	No
• *Is the relative price of this item important to your market (Price consciousness of customers)?*	[]	[]

The importance of price depends on the specific product and the specific individual. Some shoppers are very price-conscious, others want convenience and knowledgeable sales personnel. Because of these variations, you need to learn about your customers' desires in relation to different products. Having sales personnel seek feedback from shoppers is a good starting point.

	Yes	No
• *Are prices based on estimates of the number of units that customers will demand at various levels?*	[]	[]

Demand-oriented pricing such as this is superior to cost-oriented pricing. In the cost approach, a predetermined amount is added to the cost of the merchandise, whereas the demand approach considers what consumers are willing to pay.

	Yes	No
• *Do you know what competitors are doing price-wise?*	[]	[]
• *Do you regularly review competitor's ads and other promotions to obtain information on their prices?*	[]	[]
• *Are you prepared to comparison-shop your competitors in person, by mail, telephone?*	[]	[]
• *Should your overall strategy be to sell at prevailing market price levels?*	[]	[]

The other alternatives are an above-the-market strategy or a below-the-market strategy.

	Yes	No
• *Should competitors' temporary price reductions ever be matched?*	[]	[]
• *Can private-brand merchandise be obtained in order to avoid direct price competition?*	[]	[]
• *Is your tentative price compatible with established company policies?*	[]	[]

Yes No

Policies are written guidelines indicating appropriate methods or actions in different situations. If established with care, they can save you time in decision-making and provide for consistent treatment of shoppers. Specific policy areas that you should consider are as follows:

- *Will an occasional one-price promotion, under which the same price is charged for similar items, be extended to other items in a department?*   [ ]   [ ]

- *Should any leader offerings (selected products with low, less profitable prices) be used?*   [ ]   [ ]

- *Have the characteristics of an effective leader offering been considered?*   [ ]   [ ]

Ordinarily, a leader offering needs the following characteristics to accomplish its purpose of generating shopper traffic: Used by most people; bought frequently; very familiar regular price, and not a large expenditure for consumers.

- *Would periodic special sales, combining reduced prices and heavier advertising, be consistent with your company's image?*   [ ]   [ ]

- *Do certain items have greater appeal than others when they are part of a special sale?*   [ ]   [ ]

- *Has the impact of various sale items on profits been considered?*

Sale prices may mean little or no profit on these items. Still, the special sale may contribute to total profits by bringing in shoppers who may also buy some regular-price (and profitable) merchandise and by attracting new customers. Also, you should avoid featuring items that require a large amount of labor, which in turn would reduce or erase profits. For instance, according to this criterion, shirts would be a better special sale item than men's suits which often require free alterations.

- *Did you get a "good deal" on the wholesale price of this merchandise?*   [ ]   [ ]

- *Is this item at the peak of its popularity?*   [ ]   [ ]

- *Are handling and selling costs relatively high due to the product being bulky, having a low turnover rate, and/or requiring much personal selling, installation, or alterations?*   [ ]   [ ]

Yes No

- *Are relatively large levels of reductions expected due to markdowns, spoilage, breakage, or theft?*   []   []

  With respect to the preceding four questions, "Yes" answers suggest the possibility of or need for larger-than-normal initial mark-ups. For example, fashionable clothing often carries a higher mark-up than basic clothing such as underwear because the particular fashion may suddenly lose its appeal to consumers.

- *Will customer services such as delivery, alternations, gift wrapping, and installation be free of charge to customers?*   []   []

  The alternative is to charge for some or all of these services.

- *Are additional mark-ups called for, because your costs have increased or because an item's low price causes consumers to question its quality?*   []   []

- *Should any groups of customers, such as students or senior citizens, be given purchase discounts?*   []   []

- *Would a schedule of automatic mark-downs after merchandise has been in stock for specified intervals be appropriate?*   []   []

- *Is the size of the mark-down "just enough" to stimulate purchases?*   []   []

  This question is difficult - perhaps impossible - to answer. Nevertheless, it stresses the point that you have to carefully observe the effects of different size mark-downs so that you can eventually acquire some insights into what size mark-downs are "just enough" for different kinds of merchandise.

- *Has cost of the merchandise been considered before setting the markdown price?*   []   []

  This is not to say that a marked down price should never be lower than cost; on the contrary, a price that low may be your only hope of generating some revenue from the item. But cost should be considered to make sure that below-cost mark-down prices are the exception in your store rather than being so common that your total profits are really hurt.

Marketing

In this section we will discuss the role that marketing and advertising play in the development and expansion of a business. We have devoted separate sections to sales; but marketing, advertising and sales are closely interrelated. The way marketing and advertising strategies are being developed and implemented can make the difference between a mediocre and a highly successful enterprise. Here we will give you an overview on what to look for in developing and carrying out these strategies.

Two of the most important functions of marketing are:

• To identify existing markets and search for new ones.

• To search for new products and services to offer your prospects and customers in present and new markets.

New markets are prospective or potential customers to whom you can sell the same products and services as you now sell to your current customers.

Advertising is an information and communications medium. Its objectives are to introduce prospects to your business and its products or services. It must also convince and remind existing customers to keep on doing business with you rather than with your competitors.

Once your customers and prospects have responded to your advertising, it may require an active effort to consummate sales. We will discuss sales later on in this section.

Market Research

Marketing and advertising plans are easier to develop for existing businesses with an established customer base; through experience, owners of these firms know which products and services sell best. A start-up entrepreneur may have to initially rely on research unless he has had previous experience in the field.

One way to understand how marketing works and the impact it can have on your business is to review the following diagrams:

A = Products and services currently offered by your company.
B = New products and services to be developed.
C = Your current customers.
D = New markets (prospective customers).

Your current selling pattern may look like this:

Here, products and services are offered and sold to your present customers.

- Once you have decided to develop new product and service ideas, and start advertising and selling them to your current customers - the pattern changes to:

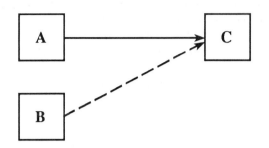

In this case, new products and services are being offered to your customers.

- After you have identified and advertised to new markets, the picture will change as follows;

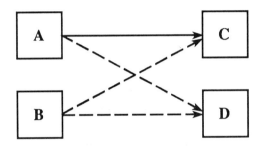

The above illustrates the powerful effects that marketing and advertising can have on the growth of your business. The last diagram demonstrates how both old and new markets can be reached with your existing and new products, resulting in an increase in sales.

The search for new markets

Every business has a number of established customers. To attract new customers you will look for prospects who have characteristics and needs similar to those of your current customers. The purpose of market research is to discover who these prospects are, where they are, and how they can be reached.

Customer analysis can be approached by a number of routes, depending on the type of business involved:

- Published research and statistics, census reports, and reports from trade journals and trade associations.

- Direct customer surveys including analyses of buying patterns from your records.

- Discussions with owners of businesses similar to yours.

- Customer observation, including traffic surveys.

- Statistical research aimed at identifying correlations between types of customers and their buying habits.

Research should also focus on ways to match your product or service as closely as possibly to the needs of your customers. The progress of your business depends upon maintaining and increasing a solid customer base. Customer research is based on the fact that the more you know about your customers, the easier it will be to appeal to and meet their needs. Benefits desired by various customer segments may also differ.

Business-to-Consumer Market Research

One of the objectives of marketing research in a business-to-consumer situation (such as a food or drug store, apparel shop, a neighborhood retailer, service station, etc.) is to determine the size of the business' trading area. The present trading area can be easily outlined on a map by reviewing customer records from the mailing list, credit accounts or customer checks received. This is your primary market. It can be reached by advertising in district or neighborhood newspapers and by direct mail. It's a cost-effective way to let your customers and prospects know who you are, where you are located and what you have to offer.

An effective way to locate new customers is to expand your advertising beyond your current trading area, on a controlled and measurable basis. This can be accomplished through the use of coupons or special offers mailed to residents in these test areas.

By comparing the response in terms of additional sales generated through these mailings, you can easily determine whether it is profitable to include these areas in your advertising efforts on a permanent basis. You also can test coupons in neighborhood papers and shoppers, but will find that they result in a lower response which is more difficult to interpret.

If this test program proves to be successful, the additional trading areas should contribute to an increase in your sales volume. This method can be used by any business which deals with consumers, such as stores and service businesses. Larger businesses can follow the same process, extending their research and tests to wider areas.

Specialty stores like big and small fashions; dietary products; musical instruments; pet supplies; and unique services such as restaurants; art galleries and maid services may have their customers scattered over a larger geographic area. Location is usually not quite as critical a factor to these types of businesses as it is to the ones that depend on heavy local traffic.

Market research techniques for specialty businesses will vary with each type of business. Census information as to income, age and home values will often discover the demographics of the "typical" customers you will be looking for. So are mailings to specialized mailing lists (such as to individuals by age brackets; subscribers to specialty magazines; culturally-oriented people, etc.).

Lower-income demographics would indicate that the people in these groups are unable to pay for high quality merchandise and services. People in higher income groups have the desire and means to afford goods and services on the upper end of the scale (upscale buyers).

It is important to determine whether income levels within a community are stable, or can be expected to change dramatically over time. For example, the makeup of a neighborhood may change as the result of rezoning, population movements, new industries, loss of industries and other events. This may affect the size of your customer base and income levels. It also will determine the type of merchandise and services you should offer as well as upgrades or downgrades of products and services.

Business-to-Business Market Research

A starting point in business-to-business marketing research is to analyze the characteristic (or profile) of your current customer base and inactive accounts. The Standard Industrial Classifications (SIC) Manual, published by the United States government and available at government book stores and libraries, is a useful guide to accomplish this.

The SIC system categorizes every commercial business, organization, and profession into nine major groupings such as manufacturing, retail, financing, services, etc. Each type of business within these major groupings is assigned a four-digit code number. For example, the SIC codes for financial, insurance, and real estate businesses have SIC codes which range from 6000 to 6700. Breaking it down further, banks are coded 6020; Savings and Loan Associations - 6120; Insurance - 6411; Real Estate Appraisers - 6531, and so on.

Once you have decided which market segments are of interest to you, you can order computerized lists from major mailing houses, specifying the codes you need to analyze your market. These listings can be segregated by type of business, size of company, geographic area and many other factors. By assigning SIC numbers to your own customer list, you can determine which codes are, for your purposes, the best ones for prospecting.

Assuming that you have 200 customers with the SIC code of 6531 (Real Estate Appraisers), and there are a total of 800 on the master list in your market area, it would follow that there are 600 who have good potential for your business. By obtaining this list, you can eliminate your own customers and contact the balance who should be good prospects. If you have customers in many different SIC codes, this elimination procedure can be done on a computer by the mailing house. This gives you a print-out of unduplicated prospects. The end result, whether it's done manually or on a computer, is the creation of a new prospect list for personal contacts or direct mailings.

There are more ways of identifying potential markets. By placing advertisements in trade publications that your prospects are likely to read, you will generate both inquiries and achieve name recognition. If the number of responses to your ads seems promising, you will have uncovered new markets which you can contact by telephone, mail, or through continued media advertising.

Telephone surveys and mailed questionnaires can reveal how your company, products or services are perceived by prospects and customers. Based on the results of these surveys, you can make necessary adjustments in a number of areas, resulting in increased sales and the acquisition of new customers.

The Search for New Products and Services

As illustrated earlier in this section, marketing research can uncover opportunities to create and offer new products and services for your present and potential customers. This holds true in almost any type of business. A wholesaler can take on new lines of merchandise or "name brands". A construction company can represent a new line of prefabricated products. An insurance business can offer a new type of policy. A health club can acquire new equipment for new exercise programs. A repair service can expand its scope of operation by servicing additional types of equipment. Manufacturers can create new products, and so forth.

The objective of market research in these situations is to determine if it makes sense to offer something new, and predict whether these products or services will be readily accepted by customers and prospects before a major investment is made.

The chances of succeeding are enhanced when you can offer services that tie in with those you are selling now. For example, you may add accessories to go with your current lines of clothing. Or you can sell computer equipment in connection with your data processing service.

If you add new products or services unrelated to your current business, it is essentially like entering a new business. There is no reason for not considering it, but it will take more effort and capital to accomplish it successfully.

Many businesses have been hurt financially because they invested heavily in innovations, new products and services before conducting adequate feasibility studies to test customer acceptance. The reasons why new goods or services are often difficult to introduce is illustrated by the following example:

A furniture store decided to add a new TV and video department. They had an excellent location, a loyal customer base, and felt that their customers would be good prospects. However the plan failed. One reason was that customers knew the store as a furniture store and were not convinced that the company would have the necessary expertise with the new kind of merchandise.

The lesson to be learned is that before you decide to expand your scope of operation, carefully research your customers' and prospects' willingness to accept new products or services from you.

The basic information you seek for your new product search can often be found in your records and in discussions with your customers and prospects. The alert entrepreneur will quickly recognize where the best opportunities lie, and will understand whether or not the market is ready for changes and innovations.

An analysis of your records will reveal how items with similar or different features and price differentials compare in sales. These are clues that should not be ignored. If acted upon, they can make a big difference in your sales volume.

By adding features and/or modifications to certain products or services, you can increase their appeal to your customers and prospects - and enlarge your market. For example, a health club could offer a free sauna, or a reduced price sauna, with each session. A manufacturer of Do-It-Yourself Kits comes out with a lower-priced version of its standard best seller. A tool manufacturer could re-design the handle of a tool to make it more comfortable to hold and use. This change may have been the result of customer complaints or suggestions.

Product development may also flow from ideas passed from customers to manufacturers. You may receive unsolicited suggestions, or in some cases orders for customized products. If you manufacture customer-specified products, your market research should indicate whether demand for some of them will be high enough to justify producing them on a mass scale.

Occasional changes in a product line by adding or eliminating items can increase sales. A product line can be defined as a number of items which are similar or complement each other and can be sold separately or in sets. Examples are groups of kitchen utensils or tools. The decision to change an item in a product line can be based on the sales volume and profits in each individual item, and taking the pricing structures and profits of potential replacement items into consideration:

Item	Annual Sales Volume (in units)	Gross Profit
1	10,000	50%
2	8,800	25%
3	7,400	60%
4	3,500	35%
5	9,500	62%

In this example, number four should be replaced by an item with more sales appeal. Item number two should be replaced because profits are inadequate. But if such an item is helping to increase the sales of the entire line, it can be retained as a "loss leader". The smart marketer will find many ways of devising new approaches to make profitable changes.

A budget should be prepared after all feasibility studies have been concluded and estimates for marketing have been established. These calculations should include the research; tests; development of new products or services; additional space requirements; equipment; employees; advertising; sales personnel, etc. Also estimate how long it will take for the new or modified products to generate enough profits to re-coup their costs and reach a break-even point. To avoid unpleasant surprises, add 20 to 40 percent to that budget since experience has shown that even the most carefully calculated estimates tend to be too low.

A Five-Step Outline of a Marketing Plan:

Step One. Define your problem. For example: "The purpose of this study is to show whether our customers will prefer a medium sized gas chainsaw, or an electric chainsaw".

Or, conduct a study to determine if family income in your trading area has changed, and now warrants the addition of new products or a change in your advertising approach.

Step Two. Decide what kind of information is necessary and how to collect it. This information can come from trade magazines; industry; consumer and census reports; or from field research; surveys of the competition; traffic studies and sales comparisons.

Field research is often more time-consuming and costly than other types of research. It should only be used if you cannot answer questions to your satisfaction through any other methods. In general, it is not advisable to do your own market field research. Professional market research firms, or university business schools, offer these services and will help you interpret the results. If you do it on your own, customers may be less open in expressing views and opinions than they would in talking to an outside firm.

Step Three. Organize the information you have collected and interpret it. Here again, university business schools can be helpful in this area.

Step Four. Based on an interpretation of the data, make a decision and implement a plan accordingly.

Step Five. Review the results of any changes you have made on the basis of your research, and modify your plans as necessary.

Advertising

Volumes of books have been written and many articles published covering in great detail the advertising media and the techniques of creating and implementing effective promotions. In this manual we are making you aware of how to think about and approach advertising to make it work for you in your business.

There are four basic steps common to all advertising and they are easy to remember. Just think of the opera "AIDA":

A ... Attention - The first step in advertising is to call *attention* to your business.

I .... Interest - The second step, once prospects are aware of your business, is to create *interest* in your product or service.

D ... Desire - Create or increase your prospect's *desire* for the purchase of your products or services.

A ... Action - Encourage customers to take *action* now by either buying from you or by contacting you for further information.

The results of following the AIDA approach are that your prospects and customers should know that your business exists and ready to serve. They also will learn how to locate you in the following ways: By coming to your place of business, through ordering by mail, via telephone, or in requesting the visit of a sales representative. They also want to do business with you because you have projected a favorable image.

Your market research and your experience-based knowledge pinpointed who and where your prospects are. Advertising placed in the right media should do the rest of the job.

Some of the major advertising media are (listed alphabetically):

- Billboards
- Direct Mail
- Magazines
- Newspapers
- Radio
- Television
- Yellow page advertising

Each medium should be used to accomplish specific goals. Contrary to claims made by some people, there is *no* one best medium. Each has its advantages and limitations. It depends on what your advertising is intended to achieve.

Advertising, to be most effective, operates on these two levels:

- Direct action advertising which lets your prospects and customers know who you are, where you are, and what your business has to offer. On this level, you make *specific* offers. It tells of the most desirable qualities or benefits of your products or services, and asks prospects to take action. Their response may result in coming to your place of business; returning a reply card to you; placing a telephone call to you for further information, or asking for a sales representative to visit. Motivating a prospect to take any of these actions can be considered successful advertising.

- The other level of advertising is name recognition or institutional advertising. It works on a more subconscious level than direct action advertising. For example, a neighborhood store may place a small ad in each issue of a local shopper. Larger stores can do the same in the daily newspaper or by using billboards. The message can be just a logo, or a simple statement such as "It pays to shop at Frank's Radio and TV".

A manufacturer with a well-defined market can mail letters and brochures to keep a company name in front of customers, or place institutional advertisements in trade magazines. A gourmet restaurant may advertise regularly in programs which are handed out to theatrical and musical program audiences. The purpose of this advertising is to keep your firm's name in front of the public and not let them forget it.

Institutional advertising can make your newspaper, radio, TV and direct mail advertising more credible because your prospects already know your name and will feel even more confident in dealing with you. Action *and* institutional advertising is a powerful combination. Generally speaking, customers will first contact businesses whose names they are familiar with, particularly in making first-time purchases.

Avoid the mistake of thinking that your old customers and prospects will always have you in mind when they are ready to buy. Even the best customers can forget, especially if they have not purchased from you for a while. Your business must continuously introduce and re-introduce itself to customers and prospects alike. This will jog your inactive customers' memories and let them know that your products or services are still available.

Another reason to advertise regularly is that customers are constantly on the move. New residents may not know that your business is in the area, or what it offers. The rate of residential turnover measured on a national scale ranges from 20 to 25 percent per year. Businesses who sell to other businesses face an even higher turnover rate if you include the number of key people involved. The total turnover in address changes and contacts within these companies such as owners, purchasing agents, and other key personnel, can reach up to 50 percent per year, depending on the industry group. These factors alone make an ongoing advertising program essential to the continued growth of almost any kind of business.

Here are some proven facts on how to think about advertising. It is not an all-inclusive list - but worth your serious consideration:

- Many entrepreneurs make the mistake of advertising inconsistently, or only when sales drop. A crash advertising program is, however, a costly way to revive a declining or failing company. It seldom produces satisfactory results. It is much more productive to control sales and growth with a consistent and well-planned advertising schedule.

- On both the institutional and action advertising levels, consistency in the method and use of the right media will pay off. It is not necessary for advertising to be brilliant or highly creative to be effective. The secret of successful advertising lies in its *continuity*. Informative advertising, even when seemingly dull, seldom fails to outperform flashy ads and copy. To design effective advertisements it is important to know what motivates your customers and how people arrive at buying decisions.

- Customers often comparison shop for price and quality. This is particularly true with repeat purchases like groceries, or with relatively expensive items. It occurs less frequently in impulse buying situations where convenience and emotion play a bigger role than price.

- In creating effective advertising, it is more important to point out product or service benefits than the details of the product or service. People basically buy the benefits they derive from their purchases. For example, a customer may buy a jacket for warmth, style, durability and coordination with other clothing. These are all quality factors you would stress in your advertising.

- Most people return to places where they have bought before. This is true for both consumers and commercial customers.

- Customers may sometimes become unhappy with their present source for one reason or another and start looking around for a new supplier.

- Effective advertising should accomplish a number of things: Remind former customers of your business and keep current customers sold on you; attract new customers or prospects, and point out qualities of your products or services that are superior to those of competitors.

- Advertising influences, but cannot control, customer buying decisions. People are usually more comfortable with the known than with the unknown. They prefer to buy a product of a brand they are familiar with or have heard about. They will more frequently patronize a store, a restaurant or supplier with a known name rather than one they are unfamiliar with. They will hire a service whose name they have seen before rather than trusting a company unknown to them.

- Using more than one advertising medium often compounds the effect of a single medium. In effect, this is like making $1 + 1 = 3$. But, whether you place a single advertisement or a series of advertisements - using one or more media - always be alert to the cost/benefit relationship. Adding one more advertisement to the series or using an additional medium will not always increase sales sufficiently to cover the added cost. You will not know how cost-effective any advertisement will be ahead of time. However, keeping detailed records on costs and resulting sales will allow you to develop approaches and standards which will work well for you.

The following chart gives an overview of how various types of businesses can utilize one or several media. The best approach in finding out which is the most effective for your business is to test different combinations and see which ones yield the best results for the lowest expenditures.

THE ADVERTISING MEDIA AND HOW TO USE THEM

Type of Business	Outdoor	Yellow Pages	Direct Mail	Magazines	Newspapers	Radio	Shoppers	TV
Manufacturing	X		X	X				X
Transportation	X		X	X	X	X		X
Wholesale			X					
Retail		X	X		X	X	X	X
Financial, Insurance, Real Estate	X	X	X		X	X		X
Services		X	X		X	X	X	
Business to Business Services		X	X	X	X	X		X

A brief overview on advertising media follows:

Outdoor

Includes traditional billboards, posters on public transportation (buses, taxicabs, etc.), airports, bus and rail terminals. Offers tremendous exposure opportunities. Message potential is limited as typical exposure to readers is ten seconds or less. For increased effectiveness, the ads at stationary locations should be moved to different sites on a pre-scheduled basis.

Yellow Pages

People who consult directories need specific information and are usually ready to buy. In placing the ads, match the distribution area of the directories as close as possible to your market area and try to avoid gaps and duplicate coverage. Keep in mind that ads in the yellow pages run yearly and cannot be changed or modified once they have been placed. Spend some time reviewing competitors' ads to find out what works best in terms of ad size, layout and copy approach.

Direct Mail

Direct mail is generally effective when you sell your product or service to your own customers, and to prospects that match the profiles of your customers. List selection and accuracy are of prime importance. So is the message which should offer special incentives to bring customers to your place of business - or motivate them to make inquiries or place orders by mail or telephone. This medium can take the form of a simple letter, self-mailer or card, or can be designed as a much more elaborate full-color brochure.

Magazines

They can be classified geographically as being local, regional or national and demographically by types of readership. This information is generally available at no charge from the magazines' advertising departments and can be helpful in defining the demographics and purchasing habits of their readership. Magazines have a longer life than any other advertising media and will generate readership and response for some time.

Newspapers

One of the advantages of newspaper ads is that they convey a sense of immediacy; they also are read on the same day they are published. Readers will often search out advertisements in the area of their interests. There is, however, fierce competition from other ads. When considering newspaper advertising, the size of the ads and circulation information are of prime importance. Generally, it is advisable to use newspapers that provide the highest circulation at the lowest cost, and give you the best coverage in your trading area.

Radio

Radio advertising generally costs less than TV and can be more cost-effective. By selecting appropriate stations and time periods, you can reach specific audiences. In large cities with many radio stations, selecting the best station can be difficult. When considering buying radio time, ask several stations for their ratings that pertain to your target audiences. Make sure that the stations under consideration can be clearly heard in your intended market area.

Shoppers/Weekly papers

Approach this medium *similarly* as you would a newspaper. Shoppers and weekly papers are generally less effective than newspapers but offer lower rates and cover smaller areas.

Television

Advertisers can target their message to specific audiences based on the station's program schedules. TV stations offer elaborate research studies that will enable you to target your ads at specific time periods and programs. Cable TV can add selectivity in targeting audiences - even in local markets. Advertising costs are generally high but must be evaluated in relation to the resulting response.

Telemarketing

Direct mail effectiveness can be tremendously boosted by linking a mailing to a calling program; follow-up calls to all prospects after they receive your letter is a potent one-two punch. Or, "cold" prospecting by phone has been very productive for entrepreneurs in a variety of industries.

Here again, a qualified list is vital. Calls can be used to either close a sale on-the-spot, or to set up face-to-face appointments.

Getting Valuable Free Publicity

Newspapers constantly seek items of interest to print. News of *your* enterprise might represent a good story for readers.

Check your local library for information on how to set up a press release - or ask your ad agency to assist, if applicable. Better yet, call newspapers directly to get an item about your business printed.

Other Proven Ways to Get Customers

Literature packages hung on residential doorknobs; hand-outs in shopping mall parking lots and information drop-offs to companies are all used to generate new sales. And each method can be accomplished at low cost.

Check with appropriate local sources to determine the legalities and limitations of these methods in your area.

Your advertising budget should be allocated as a certain percentage of your current or projected sales volume. It should, however, be flexible enough to provide for occasional special promotions.

Advertising Agencies

Some entrepreneurs prefer to handle their advertising without the help of an advertising agency. Others do some of it by themselves, with agency help. Still others have agencies fully plan and execute their advertising.

Agencies usually require a minimum billing before they accept an account. It may be a flat fee basis, a commission arrangement or a combination of the two.

Select an advertising agency as you would an accountant or attorney and consider their contact person as you would any other consultant (see consultant section). You set the objectives, and they make recommendations, create the strategies and put your advertising plan into action. Media representatives can be helpful in recommending agencies that specialize in your business.

The agency can write your copy and help you decide on what types of media to use (radio, television, newspaper, direct mail, etc.) and how to coordinate them. It is usually best to work with a small agency that can pay closer attention to your business and its needs. Check their references, and get written estimates before agreeing to any program.

The nature of the relationship between advertising agencies and clients can sometimes be difficult because clients' anticipated results are not always met, or the agency does not receive full cooperation from the client. That's why you should engage an agency with people you feel comfortable to work with; aim toward minimizing conflicts.

In working with an agency, you should spend adequate time with their representative to carefully weigh the pros and cons of using various advertising media. Any medium that does not reach your target market - or is not generating sufficient sales in relation to its cost - should be dropped.

Also pay close attention to your competitors' advertising. This will give you an idea of what they are selling, their offers and what customer benefits they are focusing on. Retain copies and records of their advertisements in the print and electronic media, along with the records you are keeping on your own ads. These files are valuable in analyzing your marketing and advertising policies.

Summary

Marketing and advertising are part of the process which leads to sales; each one focuses on the appeal of your product or services and the needs of your customers. Advertising makes customers more receptive to buy from you. It also draws them to your place of business, whether in person, by telephone or mail. Putting together effective advertising takes good planning. It also requires you to carefully compare the results of different media combinations for advertising. Keeping good records of costs and results will be necessary in order to make these comparisons.

Sales and Sales Management

In this section we will discuss the process of selling, and the management of your sales program for increased sales.

You will find that businesses with consistent records of expansion in their product lines or service facilities have carefully planned and executed their marketing and advertising programs, and have superior sales forces. Yet, very few companies are equally strong in all of these areas. In fact, some businesses survive and slowly grow without having any effective programs. Even so, good marketing and advertising programs provide the opportunity for more rapid sales growth, leading to faster expansion and greater profits.

One word of caution: Sales that are expanding too fast can be as perilous to a business as decreasing sales. Quickly expanding sales volume may tax financial and production resources as well as the ability of management and employees to keep up with new demands. In this situation, a business will often have to hire new employees, purchase equipment or inventories and provide additional sales and service support under "pressure-cooker" conditions. This can result in a cash flow problem unless provisions for new financing are being made. This is not to say that a rapid increase in sales is bad. But it must be dealt with promptly to prevent quality control problems, delayed deliveries and inadequate service resulting in customer dissatisfaction and loss of business that may be difficult or impossible to recoup.

Marketing and advertising work together to help place customers in a favorable frame of mind toward your company's products and services. But it still requires salesmanship to sell those products and services.

Types of Sales Situations

There are four basic types of sales situations:

- *Inside sales.* In this type of situation, prospective customers will come to your place of business. This is prevalent in retail businesses and, to a lesser extent in some service, wholesale and industrial supply businesses.

- *Outside sales.* In outside sales, prospects or customers are contacted by your sales representatives. These sales calls are usually done as follow-up to telephone and mail inquiries, or as "cold-calls" or scheduled visits. Outside sales are most common in manufacturing, wholesale, and industrial businesses. Some service businesses also have outside sales forces. Examples are the insurance, real estate and financial fields.

- *Mail and telephone sales.* These methods of selling are most often used in businesses where customers are familiar with the products or services being offered. Mail and telephone sales can be the result of direct mail offers or catalogs and telemarketing programs. They also originate from established customer re-orders.

- *Exhibit Sales.* Commercial or consumer-oriented exhibits can provide opportunities to introduce new products and services. Some exhibits are held in connection with conventions and trade association meetings. Others that cater to the public are sponsored by newspapers, homebuilders, radio and TV stations.

  Exhibits can do an effective job giving you quick exposure to logical prospects, and help you build up a list for future mailings and telemarketing.

We recommend that you study all of the information in this section, regardless of whether your business has "inside" or "outside" sales personnel. They have much in common and the information applies to both.

The Sales Manager and Salesmanship

One of the many responsibilities a small business owner often has is to double as a sales manager.

The sales manager's duties are to:

- Coordinate marketing, advertising and sales efforts.
- Set sales policies and procedures and see that they are followed.
- Hire, train and supervise sales employees.
- Handle administration and follow up on inquiries and sales leads.
- Set the stage for good customer relations.

The sales manager and sales staff should be aware of the kind of impression customers receive from your organization and personnel. Good grooming, personal hygiene and neatly kept attire - appropriate to your sales situation - are absolutely necessary.

Posture, facial expression and tone of voice are also important. Attention to these details will reflect your company's attitude toward its customers. Sales staff behavior should always show friendly respect and concern when communicating with customers. The overall appearance and behavior of your sales personnel strongly affects the image your business presents to customers.

You should also be aware of the strong and weak points in your own sales approach. If you feel that you and your salespeople would benefit by an improvement in this area, don't hesitate to provide further training. Sales are the lifeblood of any business.

There are a great many similarities in sales situations, whether they are in the industrial, retail or service fields. Selling is basically an exchange of information and a negotiating process between a buyer and seller. The same principles apply whether your salesperson visits the buyer, or the buyer comes to your place of business.

Salespeople can be divided into two categories: Order-takers and sales representatives. Both of them are needed in almost every type of business.

Order-takers sometimes have limited knowledge of the products or services a business sells. But they can show customers what they request, and answer general questions. They can finalize a sale and often act as cashiers. Order-takers rarely attempt to sell additional items, or persuade the customer to upgrade a purchase by buying a more expensive item. Good order-takers often develop into effective salespeople as they increase their product knowledge and selling skills.

Sales representatives may work on the inside, such as floor personnel in a retail store. Or they may work outside, calling on customers and prospects at their places of business or homes. Both must have thorough knowledge of products or services offered by your business - and by your competitors. Sales representatives must be capable of approaching customers, determining what their needs are and successfully close sales. They also should stay in touch with their prospects and customers to keep them aware of your business when additional buying needs arise. Sales representatives frequently contact customers in between sales to advise them of new products and services of interest to them.

Effective selling depends upon good product/service knowledge, familiarity with sales techniques, and the proper treatment of customers. They should also be able to explain guarantees or product servicing that the customer may not be aware of, and present them as selling points.

All salespeople should have a solid background in sales techniques and receive continual training through workshops, the reading of sales texts, and thorough close supervision. In outside sales, they should be familiar with customer needs and buying patterns and know when to contact them. It is also advisable in retail situations to keep in touch with the best big ticket customers by mail or telephone.

After a substantial sale has been closed, it is important to review post-purchase aspects with the customer. This includes guarantees, servicing, repairs and follow-up to assure that product performance is satisfactory. These techniques will lay a solid foundation to future sales. You may also use post-sale follow-up occasions to ask about further needs or describe new items and services.

Industrial sales personnel should know as much as possible about the construction, quality and operating procedures of what they are selling. In service businesses, they should be fully familiar with how the service is performed, expected completion times and pricing structures.

Product and service manuals can be of great help. Manufacturers are often willing to demonstrate merchandise or product functions to your sales staff. These instructions are useful as they explain manufacturing processes, the quality of materials used and how to take care of products to keep them in working order.

Salespeople should also be aware of products in the line that might serve as substitutes if the item of first choice is unavailable or fails to meet customer needs or expectations. For example, a certain product may be beyond a customer's price range. A knowledgeable sales person may be able to offer a lower priced item that still meets the customer's needs. For instance, a customer may want high quality skis at a very low price. The salesperson may recommend a relatively inexpensive ski with a high-quality binding. When customer finances permit, he can combine the binding with a higher performance ski.

In selling production machinery, the sales representative could suggest a basic piece of equipment with the option of adding other desirable features when financially feasible.

Salespeople should also be aware of what competitors are offering and how their products and prices compare to yours. This information should be in your files and made available to your sales staff as part of their training. It will help them deal with customer questions or objections. If the price of your product or service is higher than a competitor's, be aware of the reason. Customers will often want to know what benefits the difference in price will buy. A salesperson can highlight quality - if there is a difference, or added benefits you offer such as free delivery, special servicing and guarantees, free assembly, etc. It has been noted in some industries that serious resistance to higher prices begins to develop when the price differential reaches about 10 percent.

If you cannot meet a customer's needs for a particular item or service, it is often a sign of superior salesmanship to obtain it from another supplier, or even a competitor. This saves the customer time and does not expose him directly to the competition. Being helpful in this way gives the customer the clear message that your business cares as much about meeting his needs as making a sale. This approach should result in increased customer satisfaction and more future business.

Generally, it is not necessary or helpful to explain all of the technical details of what you are selling - unless the customer specifically requests the information. Trying to do so may be overwhelming and can result in loss of the sale. Information should always be focused on *benefits to the customer*. If any part of your service operation is performed away from your premises, let the customer know about it. Also, give the customer or prospect an estimate of the usual amount of time required to complete a job, and of the charges. Then advise him of any guarantees and additional benefits available.

Recruiting

When recruiting salespeople, look for *special* traits and characteristics in addition to the normal requirements that apply to new employees. Some of those special attributes are:

- Does the applicant impress you as being sales-oriented?
- Does he/she have previous sales experience?
- Is the applicant capable of understanding your type of business?
- Does the person have an outgoing personality?
- Is he/she self-confident?
- Is he/she persuasive and convincing?
- Does this individual think logically?
- Is he/she good with figures?
- Does the applicant have a strong desire to make money (if the position offers a commission arrangement)?

Don't invest your time and money on tests and training unless you can answer "yes" to most of these questions when you evaluate an applicant.

Sales Training

Effective training for sales personnel should include the following:

- Reading technical and general product or service literature.

- Becoming familiar with your company's history and policies.

- Attending workshops or in-house training sessions.

- Receiving supervised on-the-job training. This can include assignment to an experienced salesperson who will observe the trainee and provide advice on how to improve sales performance.

- Holding frequent progress reviews designed to discover the employee's strengths, weaknesses and areas for improvement.

All aspects of training are important. However, instructions are usually most easily absorbed when put into practice. For example, a technical report will be more easily remembered if backed up by a hands-on demonstration. Personal involvement usually results in faster learning and shorter training periods.

The Small Business Administration lists some steps to help a sales trainee as follows:

- Give more day-to-day help and direction.

- Accompany trainee on sales calls to provide coaching.

- Conduct regular meetings on subjects that you and your representatives want covered.

- Increase sales promotion activities.

- Transfer accounts to other sales representatives if there is insufficient effort or progress.

- Establish tight control over price concessions authorized by representative.

- Increase or revise financial incentives.

- Transfer, replace or discharge.

Steps Toward Closing Sales

In a business where customers come to your place of business, it is important to have sales and display areas carefully laid out, clean and adequately lit, with appropriate decor. You may also consider background music.

Merchandise should be attractively displayed, with related items grouped nearby so they can be easily located by customers. In businesses where major purchases take place, space should be set aside where sales representatives can talk privately to customers without outside distraction.

An effective sales process depends to a great extent upon treating each prospect or customer as an individual with *unique needs*. Here are some of the more important steps involved in making a sale:

- Meet and greet the customer.

- Determine what product/service and benefits are most important to the customer.

- Offer information, and demonstrate the product. Or allow the customer to use it.

- Deal with questions or objections.

- Close the sale.

- Thank the customer for the purchase.

- Follow up on the purchase by checking on customer satisfaction. Discover any additional or unmet needs.

Meeting and greeting customers is the first direct step in making a sale. In a retail situation, if you see a customer just standing around, a simple social greeting such as "Good morning" or "Hello" is appropriate. This should be done promptly. Avoid standard greetings such as "May I help you?" They usually lead to automatic negative responses.

Repeat customers should be greeted by name, if known. If the customer is already looking at merchandise, use a greeting which focuses attention on the product of customer interest. This can be a statement about some feature of the product. Avoid giving an opinion such as "Isn't that a nice color combination?" It's better to stick with facts. For example, "That sleeping bag weighs eight ounces - about as much as a can of soup. It sure cuts down the weight for backpacking." You may also ask how the customer intends to use the product. For example, if a customer is looking at camping tents, the salesperson could ask, "Do you usually hike in, or use a regular camp site? We have a wide selection for both kinds of camping".

Once the customer expresses some interest, the salesperson can ask further questions and lay out the benefits of the product. This can include demonstrating the product or allowing the customer to try it. The salesperson may also help the customer narrow product choices down to one or a few items. This keeps decision-making from becoming overwhelming and impeding the sale. If the customer says "I'm just looking", it is better to let him browse until he asks you for information.

If you can't help a customer immediately, let her know that you will be there shortly. If you have a waiting area, invite her to use it and indicate how long you expect the wait to be. You may give the customer a product to examine or literature to read while waiting. If the wait is longer than expected, check back from time to time to assure her that you have not forgotten. When you are finally able to help the customer, thank her for being so patient.

You can gather clues by watching customer behavior. A customer who moves quickly from item to item checking price tags may be especially concerned with price and looking for a bargain. Another, who goes directly to higher priced items and begins to inspect them carefully, may be more concerned with quality, durability, or construction than price.

A salesperson can determine a customer's needs and desires by asking how the customer intends to use the product, and what features are most important. Questions and objections also provide valuable information about customer motives.

Buying intentions of customers are not always clear in the initial stages of the selling process. A customer may look for a good price, high quality, superior performance, or some combination of those advantages. It is often difficult to offer *all* of them. It's up to the salesperson to resolve such a conflict. If price is a major consideration, point out how the higher cost will save money in the long run. This is true for a number of reasons: Because the product will last longer, wear better and give better performance than a lower priced version. If these factors are not of great importance, a less expensive item may do the job. Similar considerations apply in selling services.

Customer Objections

Sometimes a customer will raise a number of objections. This does not necessarily mean that the sale is going to be lost. A skilled salesperson will take this as a challenge to his sales ability and meet the objections with all available resources.

To do so:

- Take the objection seriously.

- Restate what the customer has said so that you fully understand and clarify the nature of the objection.

- If necessary or permissible, make a concession to settle the objection. Never argue.

- If the objection cannot be resolved, suggest another product or service, or point out special features of this product that overcome any of its drawbacks.

Most objections develop because the buyer is not convinced that a particular product or service will solve his problem. It is up to the salesperson to discover what the real needs are and to prove how this product or service will meet them.

Objections may indicate that the customer needs more information in order to make a decision. They tell you that the customer is seriously considering all aspects of making the purchase, its advantages and drawbacks.

Unreasonable objections may mean that the customer is uncomfortable with the sales approach, or not serious about making the purchase. Concentrate on having more conversation instead of giving a sales pitch. This reduces the pressure and puts the sales process back on track. If a customer clearly does not want a product or service, *do not* push the sale. Trying to force a sale may lose the customer's future business. Your salespeople should be helpful but should not appear too eager or come across too strongly.

There are many approaches in handling objections, but there is one rule that never changes: Under *no* circumstances should the salesperson argue. Often, customers may simply want to air any objection, prove how knowledgeable they are and make sure that they've been heard. Keeping a level head and staying focused on customer needs and benefits will go a long way toward avoiding conflicts.

One way to handle a customer objection is to restate the objection in the customer's words, but removing any emotional sting the customer may have added. You may also turn the objection into a question. An illustration follows:

A customer is shopping for a tricycle. You show him several plastic models, but he says, "What I'm really looking for is one made of metal". You reply, "I have here a small metal bicycle with training wheels." Your customer replies, "I don't like a bicycle with training wheels."

At this point you restate the objection by repeating, "You don't like a bicycle with training wheels" (*not* in form of a question). Or, "You don't like this type at all?" Now the customer will realize he's been heard and that you are sympathetic to his point of view. You proceed by offering a solution: "If you can wait a few days, I will order a tricycle from the wholesaler and call you when it gets here. There is no obligation for you to take it if you don't like it."

You will not always be able to resolve all objections, but you can divert attention to the positive aspects of the product or service and emphasize that you are willing to help solve customer problems.

Should a personality conflict arise between the prospect and a salesperson, consider letting another salesperson handle that particular customer. In outside sales, you can deal with this situation by transferring the account to someone else.

When a salesperson asks for the order, he should avoid giving the customer the choice of a "no" answer. Give only positive choices. For example: "Which of these two items (or services) would you prefer?" "Is there anything else?" "Will this be all?" "Which address shall we send this to?" Start writing the order up for his signature. If a contract sale is involved, call the credit person to finalize the transaction. Then leave quickly and graciously. This reduces the chances that the customer will have a change of mind and back out of the sale. Customers often have second thoughts about purchases. The same principle applies in outside sales. Once you have the signed order, end the conversation as quickly as possible and leave.

Customer Complaints

Customer complaints should be referred to the sales manager. The sales manager can channel complaints to those staff people who are best qualified to resolve them. Or he may personally handle them. Problems must be taken care of as quickly as possible. Whatever the nature of the complaint, customers should be treated courteously. One of the critical tasks in sales management is to monitor complaints or dissatisfaction. A single valid complaint may be a symptom of more widespread dissatisfaction; the problem is likely being experienced by many more of your customers who do not bother to complain.

All personnel must be made aware of the critical importance of handling complaints swiftly. Complaints should be reported to the sales manager because he must -

- Be aware of a troublesome situation in quality, service, pricing, deliveries, or customer relations.

- Resolve the problem.

- Contact the customer in person, by telephone or mail to give assurance that corrective action will be taken.

Inquiry Handling

Almost all businesses receive inquiries about their products or services. Inquiries generally come in by telephone or mail. It is important for the sales manager to establish procedures on how to deal with them. Personnel who handle inquiries should fully understand all aspects of what they are selling. They must also be kept informed of the schedules and contents of all ads currently running. They should be good listeners, plus be articulate on the telephone and in writing letters.

Every inquiry is a new sales opportunity. The sales manager must be in full control of the inquiry handling procedure, particularly when outside sales representatives are designated to follow up.

Handling inquiries includes keeping records, assigning the leads to sales representatives and following up with them after they have made initial contacts with the prospects. A prospect who receives a prompt, courteous, informative response is much more likely to buy from your company than one who receives delayed (or no) response, or incomplete answers. Prompt inquiry handling leads to increased sales.

Direct orders by telephone or mail should be filled promptly and accurately. Late shipments are often cancelled or returned by customers. Errors in filling an order can also mean loss of a sale. Worse, it can result in loss of a customer.

Outside Sales

Much that we have discussed so far applies to both inside and outside sales situations.

The role of the sales manager in training and supervising sales representatives is more critical in outside sales situations because they operate independently, away from home base. By contrast, inside salespeople are generally under close in-house supervision.

An effective sales manager should always be aware what his sales representatives are working on and on whom they are calling. He must also keep track of the sales that are generated.

Sales records should be designed to let representatives track their activities for each established account, and for important prospects they are calling. One of the most important records is the Daily Call Report in which the representative lists the companies and people he sees every day. This form details the results of those calls and of any follow-up plans. The Daily Call Report should also list the more important telephone calls made to customers and prospects. This report is an important working tool for both the sales manager and sales representatives.

It is also advisable for the sales manager to keep in close touch with major accounts to insure that they are handled properly, and to head off any potential problems. He should make occasional sales calls with outside representatives, either for observation and training purposes, or to be of assistance in complex and sensitive sales situations.

Another function of sales managers is to establish priorities for their salespeople regarding the amount of time and effort to be devoted to customers and potential accounts. As a general rule, you can build sales faster by concentrating on high-volume accounts. However, it would be a great mistake to ignore small customers or prospects altogether since many will eventually develop into substantial accounts.

Just as for inside sales, outside sales personnel should be fully familiar with the construction, use, operation, and cost of each product offered. They should also have a wide range of technical information on the finished product or raw materials. This may include electronic, mechanical or chemical engineering information, or other technical information of importance to customers. A strong technical background in the product or service the salesperson is dealing with can be very helpful. However, technical expertise by itself will not make a sale; it still takes superior salesmanship.

Give necessary technical information, but avoid overwhelming your customer with a mass of details. If you do not know the answer to a particular technical question, admit it. Then offer to get back to the customer and follow through promptly.

Your outside salespeople should have a good knowledge of your company's history, organization, philosophy, policies, and procedures. They should know what your competitors are offering. This information will help them emphasize aspects of your products/services that are superior. For example, if your competitor offers a lower price for their product, your sales staff should be able to point out the benefits of your product that more than compensates for the difference. Industrial buyers will usually want to see facts and figures or other documentation that back up your claims.

Never misrepresent a product or service. Be prepared to document any claims you make. If your product or service will not meet a particular need and you cannot offer an acceptable substitute, *say* so. If possible, suggest a compromise or substitute. Making unrealistic claims to a customer will often result in loss of future business.

Outside sales personnel should have as much information as possible about the personal characteristics and habits of the buyers they are calling on. It can be obtained from regular business contacts in and outside of the industry, trade journals, press releases and news clippings, and company literature. It is important to be familiar with their business' goals and present needs. Their career history and personal interests can prove to be valuable information.

Unless an outside sales representative follows a regular schedule with a customer, it is advisable to operate on the basis of formal appointments.

"Dropping in" wastes valuable sales time and can annoy customers. It is a good idea to confirm an appointment shortly before the sales call in order to make sure the customer can see you. It is also imperative to call in advance if you can't keep an appointment. You can reschedule a new appointment at the same time.

If you make an appointment with a new prospect, do not present your complete sales story over the telephone. Give just enough information about the benefits of your product to arouse interest. Your primary objective is to get face-to-face with the prospect. This is particularly true with cold-call appointments; they require a level of persuasiveness that will convince the prospect that time spent with you will be advantageous.

The meeting with a prospect or customer can be divided into six steps.

Step One: When the sales interview begins, discuss with the prospect what you will cover on your visit and approximately how much time it will take. This will put both of you more at ease since you'll both know what to expect from each other.

Step Two: Ask about the customer's needs, and restate those requirements as you understand them. Then ask for the buyer's input. Make sure that your assumptions about his requirements are correct, and determine if the buyer has any additional needs.

Step Three: Present your product or service. Show point by point how it compares to the customer's expectations. If those requirements can't be fully met, offer a compromise, or focus on other features that compensate for the shortcomings. Objections can be handled in the same way. You may use any number of sales aids to present your product or service. These may include product catalogs, photographs, printed material such as charts, audiovisual materials (slides, motion pictures, or video tapes), and product samples or scale models.

Keep in mind that the main emphasis of any sales presentation is focused on customer requirements, and on the benefits offered by the product or service. Sales aids should only be used to show how the product meets those needs. Dwelling on unnecessary details even with sophisticated sales aids - can lose a prospect's attention. You may also take prospects to a site where your product or service is in use. Or, you can furnish references from previous buyers.

Step Four: After you have presented the product and answered questions or objections, restate the customer's needs and how your product or service will meet them. Repeat any concessions or compromises that you have offered, and any additional benefits such as delivery, servicing, or guarantees.

Step Five: Ask for the order, or for an opportunity to place a bid or to make a written proposal, whichever is applicable in this particular sales situation. Then set an appointment to follow-up.

Step Six: If you do not make a sale on the first call, follow up by telephone or in person. Most salespeople give up after the third call. Depending on the size and importance of the sale, statistics show that the most successful salespeople close after the fifth call. Another interesting statistic is that 20 percent of all salespeople create 80 percent of all sales.

Sales Agents

They are also referred to as Manufacturer's Representatives and Commission Agents. Certain types of businesses, particularly small manufacturers, often use independent sales agents. Manufacturers' representatives are business firms which act as sales agents for a number of manufacturers with products that are not competitive to each other. These independent reps have an established customer base on which they make regular sales calls. Rep firms may be one-person operations or employ as many as 100 people. A *commission agent* is usually a one-person business, who frequently operates out of a home or a small office. Commission agents may carry merchandise in their own vehicles, and often collect payments at the time of the sale. If you employ sales agents, you will find significant advantages and disadvantages in using these channels of sales and distribution.

Advantages

There is no fixed sales overhead, payroll, or fringe benefits for sales agents. Sales expense occurs only when a sale takes place. Sales agents operate on a commission basis and do not receive salaries or reimbursements for expenses. Through sales agents, you can achieve quick distribution of your products over large geographic areas.

Disadvantages

Since the sales agent is an independent company, you will have little or no control over this type of sales force, and have only limited contact with your customers. Use of sales agents may reduce your profits since their commissions are higher than those of a regular sales staff. The sales agent may have little or no product knowledge, and is consequently prone to inadvertently misrepresent your business or products.

Also, representatives and agents of this type are in business for themselves and will look out for their own interests first. If they find it advantageous, they may replace your merchandise with that of one of your competitors.

Using agents has its place, but it is important to investigate all aspects of such an arrangement in advance by spelling out all mutual responsibilities in legally binding agreements.

Progress should be regularly monitored and compared to projected sales. To work most successfully with agents, you should treat them like members of your organization. They should have access to your marketing information and be encouraged to make suggestions and recommendations. You should communicate with them frequently to track their activities on your company's behalf.

Section 7

OPERATING YOUR BUSINESS
FOR GROWTH AND PROFITS

Why Day-to-Day Management is Vital

A successful start-up, or - the favorable purchase of an existing business, was the first phase in your life as an entrepreneur. But the real success of your enterprise will depend on the way you think about and manage your business. There is no such thing as a "good" or a "bad" business. However there *is* good and poor management. Experience has shown that good management can do well in so-called "tough" businesses, but poor management will fall short - or fail altogether - in almost *any* kind of business.

The aim of this section is to show you how to recognize the fundamental factors in good management; how to look at them to avoid common pitfalls.

This section covers the following areas:

- Purchasing
- Inventory Control
- Personnel Management
- Production Management
- Business Customs and Conduct
- Use of Consultants

Consider these subjects as an outline from which you can develop an operating procedure for your business. Include finances, sales and marketing in that operating procedure. Each subject represents a vast field of information by itself. You may already have a good working knowledge of some of the operational aspects covered here.

Purchasing

Purchasing is an extremely important function in most businesses. It involves buying items that meet your business needs, whether for resale or internal use. Its aim is to search for the best quality at the lowest possible cost obtainable at the most advantageous terms.

Purchasing of Resale Merchandise

Well organized purchasing procedures and inventory control work together to increase your profits. Small savings in purchasing often create more of an increase in profits than large increases in sales. One very astute entrepreneur said, "I don't make nearly as much money selling as I do in buying and tracking my merchandise".

For example, a 5 percent reduction in costs would generate the same percentage increase in profits as a 10 percent increase in sales. This is illustrated in the following chart:

<u>Reduce costs by 5%</u>

Sales	$10,000	$10,000
Cost (reduction from 60% to 55%)	6,000 (60%)	5,500 (55%)
Gross profit	4,000	4,500
Percentage	40%	45%

<u>Increase sales by 10%</u>

Sales	$11,000 (10,000+1,000)
Cost @ 60%	6,600
Gross profit	4,400
Percentage	44%

Obviously, merchandise selections should reflect customer demands. Those demands should be a known factor to an established business. In a start-up situation, you can benefit from market research which reveals what customers are looking for in quality, features and prices.

You can often increase profits by buying generic products instead of name brands - if they are acceptable to your customers. On the other hand, if the public prefers name brands you must provide them, even if your mark-ups are lower. When buying re-sale merchandise, pay close attention to the following factors. They will help maximize your profits and offer products that meet customer expectations:

- Customer Acceptance.
- Quality.
- Price.
- Credit Terms.
- Discounts for high-volume buying.

Sometimes it can be advantageous to buy merchandise in larger quantities at a lower cost to you, providing that storage or obsolescence do not present problems. The key factor is to determine that the savings are substantially greater than the cost of cash tied up in stock.

The Small Business Administration, in a publication on buying for retail stores, makes the point that the buyers for small stores have advantages over big store buyers. The principal advantages are: Closeness to customers, being in constant touch with the merchandise, and having a finger on the pulse of what is selling. These observations apply equally to businesses outside the retail field. There are two kinds of buying:

- Replenishment buying.
- Anticipation buying.

Replenishment Buying

Replenishment buying is the reordering of staple merchandise as carried in food markets, hardware, liquor, stationery, furniture and similar types of stores. Its concept is to establish adequate inventory levels and constantly replace sold items to keep basic stocks in ample supply. This can be accomplished by recording sales on a master list of these items, either manually or on a computer. Whenever pre-determined stock levels have been reached, orders will be placed.

In many types of businesses, sales representatives of wholesalers or jobbers will take inventory of the items supplied by them. Then they prepare orders based on the rate of current sales. In some cases, the entire store inventory may be represented by a few wholesalers who closely service it.

Anticipation Buying

Anticipation buying involves mainly seasonal merchandise as offered by women's dresses, sportswear, specialty or similar types of businesses. Here, it's a matter of constantly acquiring new goods that may never be available for reorder. In fact, success in this type of business may depend largely on a constant flow of new and different merchandise. New merchandise should be bought with the expectation that it will sell and immediately be replaced.

Some suppliers offer substantial trade discounts for early payment. For example, the commonly used term of "2/10, n30" offers a 2 percent discount for payment in full within 10-days of the invoice date, but allows the customer to take up to 30-days to pay with no discount given. A 2 percent discount on all purchases can add up to considerable savings.

For example, the total of one year's purchases for Quill and Candle is shown below, with a discount for early payment:

Annual Stock Purchase Expenditures
Quill and Candle

Total Purchases	$191,187.50
Less 2% for prompt payment discount	3,823.75
Net Purchase Costs	$187,363.75
Savings	$ 3,823.75

Materials are usually purchased for manufacturing, construction or service-type repair work, which become part of what the customer buys. They are selected either according to specifications or off-the-shelf.

Supply Purchases for Internal Use

These supplies fall into two categories: Supplies that are frequently restocked such as printed matter, cleaning supplies, shipping materials, etc., and those of a one-time nature, or infrequent purchases such as computer software.

Items in continuous use should be regularly inventoried so they can be re-ordered before depletion. You can often save money by buying in bulk if you have adequate storage space. Supplies purchased less frequently need not be inventoried.

It is advisable to check prices with several vendors from time-to-time.

Goods used regularly by your business may also be purchased and delivered on the basis of a single annual contract if you can negotiate an advantageous price.

Equipment Purchases for internal use

Unless there are no alternatives in the selection of a piece of equipment, it will be advantageous to use a bidding process whereby several suppliers submit competitive bids. Your list of specifications for a pick-up truck may read like this example:

- 1/4 ton pickup.
- Automatic transmission.
- Power steering.
- Camper special (heavy duty springs/shocks).
- 1.6 liter engine.
- 4 or 6 cylinder (6 preferred).
- New or used with less than 18,000 miles.

This list of specifications will be submitted to a number of automobile dealers, letting them know it's a competitive bidding situation. If the sale prices offered in the bids are quite close, you may look at differences in service or other advantages available in a vendor. If price is the most important factor, you may select the vendor who offers the lowest bid for a truck that meets the listed specifications.

Service and guarantees on equipment are extremely important factors in equipment purchases since repairs and breakdowns can be costly.

Leasing should be considered as an alternative to outright equipment purchases. Leasing can conserve cash and still give your business quick access to modern equipment. This is especially important in high technology businesses where equipment becomes obsolete rapidly. Leasing conserves operating capital since it usually offers 100 percent financing with no down payment. Installation and shipping are often included in the terms of the lease instead of being charged up-front.

Lease/purchase plans allow you to apply lease payments toward the purchase of equipment if you eventually decide to buy the equipment. In most leases you can also call for competitive bids. The total cost of an outright purchase is usually less than leasing - especially when financing is not a problem and the equipment is unlikely to need upgrading or replacing in the foreseeable future. Consult with your accountant before committing to a lease.

Purchases of made-to-order items such as custom-made equipment

Since these items are built to meet your unique needs, specifications for these purchases must be carefully drafted, covering every aspect of construction including any warranties desired. Whenever possible, get competitive bids on these items, even if they are so specialized that only one vendor is able to supply it. Obtain a firm price quotation and warranty before making any commitments.

Writing specifications can be as simple or complex as the occasion demands. An effective specification will contain some of these requirements as applicable:

- Clear description of product or service.
- Required qualities.
- Purpose.
- By whom used.
- Technical description including -
    Dimensions, colors, weights, chemical formulas, electronic data, etc.
- Performance standards.
- Expected reliability and durability.
- Ease of maintenance.
- Testing requirements.
- Drawings or samples, if required.
- Packing and shipping instructions.

Here's a general example:

In its specifications, the Custom Camper Company sets forth requirements for a rust retardant to be used on certain parts of their products. They expect suppliers to come up with a formula by describing the characteristics they are looking for:

- Safe for use in an area that has some open flame.
- Must not be injurious to operators and end-users.
- Fast-drying.
- Must be safely applied during normal operations.
- Liquid must be translucent and should not require further finishing or painting.
- Must effectively last for at least five years before re-application.
- Anticipated usage: 30 to 50-gallons for the first year.
- Delivery: 30-days from placement of order.

Generally speaking, if a purchase of goods or services represents considerable monetary volume, it is advisable to solicit bids based on a specification. They are, however, usually not necessary for repeat purchases or in the buying of standard products or services.

Purchases of services

Services, such as equipment maintenance and repair, cleaning, deliveries, etc., are often purchased on the basis of competitive bids. This may prove out to be more economical if they are provided through an ongoing contract rather than on a call-basis. A new or unfamiliar service provider may be offered a short-term contract which can later be expanded if services meet your expectations.

Freight-receiving procedures

When receiving freight, it is important to examine the shipment for damages and make certain that the full count of items has been received. The damage inspection should take place at the time the shipment is received. The counts should be verified as soon as possible thereafter. No item should be taken out of the delivery area until it has been inspected. Damaged goods should be kept in this area until they can be inspected by the carrier. Contact the carrier immediately to request an inspection of the damaged items. It is also advisable to send a note confirming the day and time of your call. The inspector will prepare a damage report which you should review carefully. Sign only after you have determined that it describes all damages correctly.

After the inspection, request written authorization from the shipper/supplier to return or dispose of damaged items. Do not use, return, or dispose any items without this authorization.

Inventory Control

The primary goal of inventory control is to keep track of all items, their costs and specifications. One of its objectives is to time purchases for replenishments, and avoid over or under-stocking. Inventory records contain the basic information needed for inventory management. For example, how long it takes to sell certain types of merchandise is vital data in calibrating demand and the timing of re-orders.

The numbers and types of records needed to manage your inventory depend on your particular business. Your accountant can help recommend a system that meets your needs. Very small businesses use visual controls; that is, physically checking what's on-hand, and ordering when items run low.

Each item should have its own stock control card or sheet showing this information:

- Purchase date.
- Quantity ordered.
- Receiving date.
- Quantity received.
- Old total.
- Items sold or used.
- New total.
- Minimum quantity for re-order.
- Specifications, sizes, colors, etc.
- Price
- Delivery costs

These control cards can be purchased at a business stationery store or printed to order. The same information can be kept on a computer for immediate reference on the screen or printed out as hard copy.

There are several types of ready-made stock control systems for use in smaller businesses including tickler, stub, and click sheet control systems.

A tickler file system lists each stock item separately on its own file-sheet or note-card. It is then inventoried as its turn comes up in the file. This allows items to be inventoried on a systematic basis and ordered as needed.

Stub systems use a tear-off portion of the item price-tag to list sold items and subtract them from the stock list.

A click sheet is a running tally, kept by your cashier, of items sold. Tallies are totalled daily and subtracted from beginning stock-on-hand. Computerized inventory management software is also widely available to simplify inventory record-keeping and alert you when to re-order.

Larger businesses may use computerized cash registers ("point-of-sale" terminals) which relay the type of item sold, price, and other information to a central computer. The computer automatically subtracts the item from the listed inventory on hand. Off-line point-of-sale terminals can send this same information directly to the supplier who has authority to automatically restock the items sold.

In some businesses, suppliers make regularly scheduled stock counts, write re-orders and take back unsold merchandise.

If your business changes its type or quantity of stock ordered during different seasons of the year, it is important to develop a seasonal merchandise plan. Such a plan should include estimates of the various merchandise you expect to sell in each period. These estimates will help you decide how much stock to order in meeting expected demand. This will be the case for fashion and other seasonal goods businesses where merchandise periodically changes. Your inventory purchases can be broken down by month or season. For example, the purchasing year may be divided into winter, spring, summer, and fall. You can often stock more economically if you order seasonal items up to six months ahead of your desired delivery date. This can save money, and guarantees that you will have enough stock to last for that season. In-season buying will cost more, and manufacturers will not always be able to fill last-minute orders.

There should be a separate inventory record for each item by size, color or other specification. Accurate inventory control records will help you keep the right quantities of sales merchandise on-hand without having shortages or excess of stock.

In summary, a successful purchasing program depends upon:

- Recognition that different types of items require different purchasing approaches.

- Buying in larger quantities if it does not negatively impact storage capacity and cash flow.

- Taking advantage of trade-credit discount programs when they are available.

- Use of equipment leases where they are advantageous.

- Familiarity with available suppliers, and development of new supply sources.

- Familiarity with freight-receiving procedures.

- Coordination with inventory control.

Employment Management

Employees are among the most valuable assets a business can have. Their cooperation and enthusiasm may spell the difference between having a mediocre or an outstanding business.

In this section we will look at the following topics:

- Your business environment.
- Company policies.
- Job descriptions.
- Job and performance reviews.
- Hiring.
- Training and supervision.
- Delegating authority.
- Motivation/Compensation.
- Problem Employees.
- Dismissals.
- Personnel records.

Your Business Environment is Unique

Small businesses have a great deal to offer in the area of job satisfaction. It is important for you to have a good comprehension of how the environment in a small business differs from that in a larger business. This understanding can help you select employees you will be satisfied with and who will feel comfortable in a small company environment.

A small business will frequently offer its people more diversified jobs than is often possible in a larger company. It allows them to get involved in many aspects of the business, providing more opportunities to learn and stay involved in the operation as a whole. On the other hand, larger businesses can more often allow an employee to specialize in one area. Small companies will develop "generalists", while big business requires and trains "specialists". But regardless of size, most companies will be in need of both generalists and specialists.

A small business can also offer more responsibility and challenge to its employees, but there are relatively fewer people available to fit these requirements than found in many larger businesses. For this reason, employees at all levels in a small business are expected to take on heavier and more varied responsibilities than their counterparts in a larger business.

There are positive and negative aspects to advancement opportunities in small companies. Employees have more room to learn and advance because of greater expansion potential. However, an executive in a small business will rarely command the same salary and benefits as his counterpart in a larger business.

Recent job performance and job satisfaction studies point to two factors which are helpful in increasing employee job performance and satisfaction:

- Being involved with management and participating in planning decisions.

- Working in a group to complete a whole project instead of being a cog in a wheel in a repetitive situation.

When these two factors are combined, employee productivity will rise and losses due to accidents, sickness, or unexcused absences will decrease.

Your business atmosphere will also depend on your management and supervisory skills and attitudes. Workshops, classes, and reading can help you learn and strengthen these skills.

Company Policies

Company policies should be in writing, concise and clear to avoid misunderstandings or abuse of privileges. A written policy is also helpful if you are absent for any period of time and someone else has to make a ruling in the event of a disagreement. Each employee should have a copy and receive updates as policies are changed.

Following is a sample table of contents for an employee handbook.

Personnel Policies and Procedures

Table of Contents

Page

Welcome from the owner (President, Partners, etc.)
Business Philosophy

Employment Policies
Equal Opportunity Employer
Hiring
Probation period
Promotion
Performance reviews
Termination

Salaries and Wages
Work hours
Overtime
Pay dates
Time cards

Benefits   Page
Life, health insurance
Unemployment insurance
Incentive program
Vacations
Leave of absence
Sick leave

Policies
Work rules
Dress code
Security
Tardiness, absenteeism
Settling difficulties
Outside employment
Safety
Changes in address, telephone, marital status

As an employer, it is extremely important that you follow the provisions in the handbook to the letter. There is a growing trend for employees to file complaints against their companies or take legal action if they feel they are not treated according to written policies. This can result in time-consuming and costly proceedings. If you are not sure that you can fully comply with your policy manual, it's better not to have one at all.

Job Descriptions

To write a job description, list the minimum skills or knowledge that the employee filling the position must have. Next, show which additional skills and experience are desirable. Then briefly state what duties the job regularly involves. Spell out what kind of training will be provided and under whose supervision the employee is working. For example, the production manager, sales supervisor, owner, etc.

Following are several sample job descriptions.

Receptionist - Industrial Supply Company

Required Qualifications: Minimum one year experience as receptionist. Typing 50 wpm, filing, high school graduate.

Desired Qualifications: Good conversationalist, likes to deal with people. Self-organizer.

Duties: Answers telephone, keeps records of callers, the time they called and the persons to whom they were referred. Greets customers and other visitors, determines their needs and refers them to the person who can help them. Arranges appointments for sales representatives. When not busy with callers, will type, file. Sort and distribute incoming mail, some simple record keeping.

Supervisor: Office Manager.

                                         * * *

Maintenance Mechanic - Printing Company

Required Qualifications: Five years of general machine maintenance experience on industrial equipment.

Desired Qualifications: Familiarity with printing press equipment. Knowledge of setting up and running presses.

Duties: Repairs presses as quickly as possible. Sets up program for preventative maintenance of all equipment. Periodically cleans parts and checks performance. Keeps complete and up-to-date records of maintenance, tries to anticipate troubles before production is interrupted. Orders and keeps spare parts on hand. Follows factory equipment manual and blueprints.

Supervisor: Pressroom foreman.

                                         * * *

Computer Operator - Insurance Company

Required Qualifications: High school diploma. Will be tested to determine aptitude for computer work. Good in math and ability to reason logically. Previous computer experience or training in community or junior college.

Desired Qualifications: Mechanical aptitude, experience and willingness to work long hours, also evening or night shifts.

Duties: Sets up equipment for printing, monitors each job, following programmer's special instructions. Makes sure computer has been loaded with correct disks. Watches for error lights that could indicate malfunction. Locates problems, solves them or terminates program.

Supervisor: Shift foreperson.

Sales Representative - Electronic Products

Required Qualifications: High school diploma and college degree. Three years of outside sales experience in this or a related field.

Desired Qualifications: Studied engineering, physics or computer sciences. Pleasant personality and appearance. Ability to get along well with people.

Duties: Calls on customers and visits prospective buyers to inform them of products sold. Analyzes buyers' needs and takes orders. Follows up on telephone and mail inquiries. Develops leads by prospecting the markets. Helps to draw up plans for installing newly purchased equipment on customers' premises. Helps negotiate prices and terms. Keeps in touch with customers on a continuing basis.

Supervisor: Sales Manager.

Putting a job description into writing will help you, as an entrepreneur, gain a clearer picture of what the job is like and what type of applicants to look for. The job description is essential to clearly define a new employee's duties. It is also an important help in rating employee performance. It can assist you to identify certain job functions that are no longer required, and enables you to combine job functions more easily and logically for greater efficiency.

Job Performance Reviews

Most of the basic information used to develop a Job Performance Rating and Review can be found in the description for each job. In addition to the required and desired skills, such factors as punctuality, productivity, ambition and the employee's history of voluntary additional training will affect the rating.

The purpose of a rating and review sheet is similar to that of a school report card. It shows employees, in writing, your assessment of their skills and performances. It points out areas for improvement as well as areas of strength. This gives you and your employees a way to measure how job performance changes over time. The rating sheet is completed by the employee's supervisor, discussed with the owner, then reviewed with the employee. Some performance reviews are done without a written report. The approach you take depends on your preference and the needs of your business. Following is a sample Performance Rating and Review:

EMPLOYEE PERFORMANCE RATING AND REVIEW

Employee _____

Position _____

Evaluator _____

Date _____

Date reviewed with supervisor _____

Scale: 0=Unacceptable   N/A Does not apply to this position
                1=Needs Improvement   Columns (A) and (B) to be completed
                2=Standard   by interviewer.
                3=Above Standard
                4=Outstanding

		(A) Ratings	(B) Comments
1.	Invests sufficient time and energy to meet customer needs.	N/A	
2.	Prioritizes tasks and meets deadlines.	4	Excellent
3.	Takes initiative to solve problems with customers.	N/A	
4.	Solves problems independently.	3	Could use refresher course on test equipment, maintenance and trouble-shooting. Other lab skills are excellent.
5.	Maintains good relations with peers and supervisors.	3	Relates well to others, but this position has little direct contact with other staff.
6.	Maintains good relations with customers and prospects.	N/A	
7.	Uses training opportunities within/outside the business.	4	Is in continuing education program.
8.	Attendance.	1	Frequent use of sick leave and other absences. May need to discuss reasons for problem, possibly caused by stress and tensions.

		(A) Ratings	(B) Comments
9.	Adheres to personnel policies and customary business practices.	2	No problems.
10.	Submits reports or work correctly and on time.	4	Excellent.

Additional comments: (Please note any work done especially well; work that needs improvement; factors affecting work performance and attitude. Also, employee comments, significant statements regarding work performance.)

"Employee is an exceptionally hard worker. His work is flawless and completed in timely fashion. He makes good use of supervisory suggestions, and has independently pursued further studies in geochemistry that directly increases his value to the company. He will benefit from further studies or instruction in troubleshooting and maintaining laboratory equipment. He needs a plan to help reduce his use of sick leave. He has had legitimate absences, but they have been increasingly frequent in the past three months. I would like to work out a plan with him to reduce the frequency of absences."

Signature of evaluator   _____

Employee's statement   *I will gladly cooperate in any plan to cut my sick*_____

   *time - reduce tensions, etc.*_____

Signature of employee   _____

You may write either a standard employee performance rating chart which covers many types of jobs, or separate ones for each position.

The prime purpose of the performance review is to give you and the employee feedback that will help improve future performance. It is also an opportunity to acknowledge good work. Performance reviews should occur on a regular basis (annually or semi-annually) and be conducted privately, at a leisurely pace. A review should not be a one-way street. It should also give the employee an opportunity to offer opinions and ask questions.

Hiring

There are two major avenues available to the small entrepreneur for finding new employees. One is through placing classified advertisements in local newspapers. The other is by going through private or public employment agencies. Alternative ways are through referrals from present employees, friends, business contacts, service clubs, and should be used only when appropriate.

In placing newspaper ads, you can list your company name, address and telephone number with a name of a person to ask for. Or, you can list a box number provided by the paper. Your choice will depend on the kind of response you expect. The less skill the job requires, the *greater* the response will be. If you want to avoid being swamped with telephone calls or drop-in applicants, it is better to use a box number and pre-screen applications before conducting interviews.

On the other hand, if you are trying to fill a high salaried, technical, managerial or sales position, it is better to use your telephone number and name in your ad. Applicants of this kind are hesitant to send a reply to a blind box number.

Private employment agencies can be a good source of qualified applicants. They will collect a fee from you or your employee if you hire an applicant they have referred. In some cases, you can split this fee with your employee.

Public employment services can also furnish job applicants. If you advise them of the skills you are looking for, they will screen applicants through aptitude testing. Their services are usually free.

All applicants should fill out your employment application, even if they have their own resumes. Don't interview any applicant until you have reviewed the completed application.

The application should be simple, yet capture all the information you need to screen applicants for your requirements. It should focus on previous schooling, work experience and references. You should go over your application form with your attorney in order to make sure it does not discriminate on the basis of age, sex, race, religion, national origin, or physical handicaps. Following is a sample application.

EMPLOYMENT APPLICATION

Name:_____ Date:_____

Address:_____

Home Telephone:_____ Business Telephone:_____

Social Security Number:_____ Driver's License #:_____

Other Licenses:_____

High School Location:_____ Degree:_____ G.E.D.:____

Other Schools or Training:_____ Degree:_____

_____ Degree:_____

_____ Degree:_____

Do you plan to attend additional schools?_____

List Past and Present Employment, Beginning with Most Recent Job

Company Name:_____ Address:_____

Supervisor:_____ Telephone:_____

Dates Worked:_____ Salary:_____

Reason for Leaving:_____

Job Title and Duties:_____

_____

_____

May we contact this employer?   Yes ( ) No ( )

Previous Job:_____

Company Name:_____ Address:_____

Supervisor:_____ Telephone:_____

Dates Worked:_____ Salary:_____

Reason for Leaving:_____

Job Title and Duties:_____

_____

_____

May we contact this employer?   Yes ( ) No ( )

Previous Job:_____

Company Name:_____ Address:_____

Supervisor:_____ Telephone:_____

Dates Worked:_____ Salary:_____

Reason for Leaving:_____

Job Title and Duties:_____

_____

_____

May we contact this employer?   Yes ( ) No ( )

Previous Job:_____
Company Name:_____ Address:_____
Supervisor:_____ Telephone:_____
Dates Worked:_____ Salary:_____
Reason for Leaving:_____
Job Title and Duties:_____
_____
_____
_____

May we contact this employer?   Yes ( ) No ( )

Personal or Job References

Name:_____
Address:_____
Telephone:_____Relationship:_____

Name:_____
Address:_____
Telephone:_____Relationship:_____

Name:_____
Address:_____
Telephone:_____Relationship:_____

The above information is true and correct. I understand that false statements may be grounds for dismissal.

_____   _____
         Applicant   Date

Your interview should concentrate on the applicant's required and desired skills to determine the level of experience gained in previous jobs. This should also reveal attitudes toward work in general. It is helpful to work from a checklist of interview questions so you can cover all necessary areas to assure you ask each applicant similar questions. This makes it easier to draw comparisons.

Use the telephone to contact the references of applicants you are thinking of hiring. Letters rarely give the quantity or quality of information needed. In addition, many people are reluctant to respond to letters. Ask for specific information about the applicant's skills; work record and reliability; ability to learn tasks and work independently, and ability to accept supervision and get along with co-workers. You may also ask the applicant for copies of any pertinent licenses or degrees.

When filling more critical positions, it's advisable to hold more than one interview with more promising applicants. Each succeeding interview will give you a better picture of what the candidates are like and how they may fit into your company.

When you hire an employee, lay out the steps you or your supervisors will take to train this person. Take time to go over the policy manual with a new employee. Also, review the job description and expectations. Then take care of any paperwork necessary for payroll, tax reporting, emergencies, or other use. The employee should be introduced to fellow workers on the first day of employment.

Federal Fair Employment Standards require that employees and applicants be treated equally, regardless of race, religion, sex, age, or handicaps. Be careful not to ask questions that discriminate on job applications or in interviews. State and local laws sometimes expand Equal Opportunity Laws to include non-discrimination on the basis of other factors.

Retain all employment applications, references, and any tests of those who are *not* hired. There are two reasons for this: First, it gives you all the documentation you need to defend yourself in case a former applicant files a complaint against you claiming discrimination. Second, should there be another job opening - or if you decide to interview certain applicants again at a later date - you won't have to advertise until you have reviewed the old applications.

The application is also useful if a former employee reapplies for a job. Employment applications and performance rating sheets from employees and ex-employees should be kept for a minimum of three years. They can prove helpful when you are asked to respond to requests for references. And they are valuable in possible disputes which may arise later.

Here are some general observations regarding the hiring of new people: When business is moving fast, there is often a tendency to hire more people than you actually need. Many times entrepreneurs have learned that when the rush period is over, they are overstaffed and reluctant to lay-off.

There are some alternatives to over-hiring:

- Insist that your present employees produce more. This may sound callous, but it's a fact that almost anyone - including the boss - can put. forth an additional 10 to 20 percent effort without difficulty.

- Authorize overtime until the peak has passed.

- Hire part-time people if possible.

- Employ qualified temporary help from an agency.

These measures will increase your efficiency and profits. Should the increase in the business' activity prove to be permanent, you can take the necessary time to screen and hire permanent people and phase out the stop-gap measures in the process.

Training and Supervision

The objective of training is to familiarize employees with the policies of your business, plus the special procedures that may be used in a particular job. To ease the transition, a new employee can initially be assigned to work with an experienced employee on a "buddy-system" basis to orient him to the workplace, the environment, and co-workers.

After the training period, the new employee should be closely supervised. He also should be encouraged to ask questions about his work and be given hands-on guidance until he develops the necessary skills and confidence to function on his own. To offer effective training, someone in your company should be qualified to setup and monitor the procedures used during the indoctrination period. The pay-off in terms of increased productivity and efficiency can be rewarding.

Delegating Authority

In order for you to devote more time and energy to major projects, you must share responsibilities with your managers and other employees. They must be given sufficient authority to initiate and complete their assignments - whether you are there or not.

When you assign a certain task or project to a supervisor or an employee, that person should have the authority over those working on it. The individual you select should also be able to obtain necessary supplies and other essentials in order to complete the job. Depending on the circumstances, he should be given an overall outline - preferably in writing -spelling out which actions can be taken on his initiative and which require your prior approval.

He also should be required to report to you regularly on the progress of work. The emphasis should be on results first and methods second. Your manager may approach a problem from a different direction than you would take. Unless you have strong objections to any particular approach, continue to focus on results. Try not to inhibit anyone. By stepping in to change things that have been working, you may squelch creativity and make your people reluctant to accept delegation.

If you strongly prefer using a specific method to solve a particular problem, make that clear from the beginning. Changing a plan *after* a manager has invested time and thought in making it work can lead to frustration and resentment as well as waste of time and money.

Motivation/Compensation

Different employees are motivated to work for different reasons. These include sense of accomplishment, recognition, challenge, money and competition. For many people, job satisfaction means having the freedom to make decisions, and to implement them. Others may find financial compensations more satisfying; raises, bonuses, and other incentives can be used as tools to boost morale and productivity. For salespeople, commissions are the most effective way to demonstrate the connection between performance and results. But all people like to know that what they accomplish is noticed and rewarded.

Problem Employees

Problem employees usually fall into one of three categories:

- Employees who are poor performers.
- Employees who are disruptive and affect the working environment.
- Employees who fall into both categories.

To minimize the impact of problem employees in your business, take action *before* they get out of hand. First, investigate. Talk to the employee's supervisor and observe the situation yourself before deciding how to handle the situation. Call the employee in for a confidential meeting to determine the cause of the problem. The causes can be personal conflicts at work, or problems outside of the job such as family or health concerns. Also, look for personal conflict or dissatisfaction within the job setting, including the inability to perform the required duties. Determine if you can help solve the problem, or if it's beyond remedy. The action you take can include holding confidential meetings; suggesting that the employee seek counseling; changing job duties and other appropriate measures. In some cases it will require outright dismissal, or suggesting that the employee terminate for his own good and that of the company.

Be certain to document any corrective action you take by recording it in the employee's personnel file.

Dismissals

Dismissal or termination may be necessary for any number of reasons:

- Unacceptable behavior.
- Unsatisfactory work performance.
- Phase-out of the job.
- Slow-down in business.

The first two items listed above fall into procedures for dealing with problem employees. For terminations due to phase-outs or slow-downs, discuss the situation and the need for termination with the employee. Where possible, offer paid time-off to find another job. Also provide a letter of reference and other assistance.

Termination can be very painful for employees since it almost always involves loss of income and self-esteem. Sometimes terminated employees file complaints. In order to prevail in any resulting hearings or legal action, take these precautions in the dismissal procedure:

- Follow the steps normally used to deal with problem employees.
- Carefully explain the reasons for termination.
- Where possible, offer assistance in finding other employment.
- Consider termination as carefully as you would hiring.

Personnel Records

Personnel files enable you to follow the employment history of each employee. These records should include salary structure and raises, promotions, recommendations, disciplinary action, and other important aspects of employee involvement in your business. Prepackaged personnel record systems are available in business stationery stores to simplify this recordkeeping.

General Comments

Good personnel management involves setting clear and understandable policies. It also involves giving good training and providing consistent supervision. Since employee satisfaction and productivity go hand in hand, effective managers pay close attention to employee motivation and compensation plans. Personnel records give you a way to judge your investment in your employees at all times.

Production Management in Manufacturing and Service Operations

The aim of effective production management is to produce goods or services of acceptable or superior quality in a timely manner, at the lowest possible cost. The key factor in superior production management is a smooth and harmonious interaction between the human element and machines. In practical terms, this means machines should be designed and built to operate with minimum down-time and relative ease of operation.

Machines must be staffed by people who are trained, skilled and motivated to turn out quality products in the shortest possible time. It is the job of production management to make this happen. Our discussion of production management applies to the whole range of machinery and equipment used in the production of goods and services. This includes typewriters, word processors, computers, copiers, etc. Also, service equipment such as chainsaws, drill and punch presses, forklifts,, cranes, equipment on wheels, etc. And production machinery like industrial sewing machines, printing presses, computers, extruding equipment, etc. In studying this section, you can adapt the ideas to the type of machinery you use in your operating environment.

Effective production management will bring together the right kind of equipment with well-trained and experienced operators, and provide for superior planning and supervision. This should result in the production of better goods and services at lower costs. If these elements are in place, then the ultimate goal of production management has been reached.

We will now discuss the individual factors that are important in reaching these objectives. We have divided the information into the following categories:

- Equipment and machinery
- Operation of equipment
- Material handling
- Scheduling
- Maintenance
- Production labor
- Manual labor
- Control of labor costs
- Quality control

When deciding what kind of production equipment to buy or replace, consider the following:

Calculate your current production requirements and estimate the increase of the production requirements you anticipate at the end of the machine's useful life.

If your estimates show that the production requirements will reach the machine's capacity long before the end of its useful life, you have two options:

Option 1 -   Buy a machine to take care of your present requirements now, and replace it with a more productive unit when the need arises.

Option 2 -   Buy a larger capacity machine right now.

Your choice between option 1 and 2 will also be influenced by factors such as financing, obsolescence of equipment, future demands for your products and other applicable considerations.

Production Requirements

The equipment available to you now may be subject to improvements in future models. Some machines can be modified to meet these needs, while other equipment will have to be replaced. In general, you will save money by buying equipment that can be modified rather than replaced. Compare the investment in your initial equipment acquisition with subsequent modifications and upgrades of the anticipated replacement costs in the future. For example, you may plan to use a fork lift full-time, day-in and day-out. In this case, a higher-priced model with longer life may save money over a lower-priced but limited-life model. However, if the fork lift will only be used occasionally, you may save money by buying the lower priced model.

Operating Ease

One of the important considerations, when making equipment buying decisions, is the operating ease and skill levels required for its safe and efficient use. The price is important of course, but low-priced equipment is often more difficult to operate and may have a history of frequent breakdowns, higher maintenance costs and lower productivity. By contrast, higher-priced equipment may offer more features, fewer problems and can often be operated by less skilled personnel.

Warranties and Maintenance

The kind of warranties and maintenance contracts manufacturers offer on their equipment is an important consideration in making a purchase decision. Repairs, parts and downtime are expensive both in terms of costs and production delays. Compare carefully what different manufacturers offer in that respect.

Price

Finally, consider the price. It must be within the limits of your budget and should be considered alongside other factors such as:

- Production requirements.
- Ease-of-use.
- Downtime history.
- Servicing.
- Warranties.
- Required maintenance.
- The equipment's useful life expectancy.
- Obsolescence, in the event that a more productive model makes its appearance on the market in the foreseeable future.

The Buying Decision

Become thoroughly familiar with the equipment before you consider buying it. See it demonstrated under *actual working conditions*. This could be a site where it's installed and operating. Talk to that company's management and their operators about their experiences. Get as much first-hand information as you can before making a decision. Be careful when dealing with a piece of equipment which incorporates brand new or revolutionary approaches. Equipment or machinery offered with such features will often have unexpected problems, or otherwise prove disappointing.

Operation of Equipment

Once you have selected the right equipment, the next step toward a profitable operation will be to hire or train experienced operators. Even the best equipment will not be profitable if operated ineptly.

In most production situations the cost of labor far exceeds the investment in equipment. If a machine costs $30,000 and its useful life is ten years, the average annual cost is $3,000. Based on 2,000 annual hours of operation, the hourly cost will be $1.50.

The following example illustrates how the labor cost affects the relative importance of the equipment cost. We assume that the labor rates in Company "A" is $5.00 per hour and in Company "B" $13.50 per hour. The hourly equipment cost is identical — $1.50.

Industry		A	B
Hourly Labor Costs		$5.00	$13.50
Hourly Equipment Costs	(e)	1.50	1.50
Total Hourly Costs*	(t)	$6.50	$15.00
Percentage Cost of Equipment per hour	$\frac{e}{t}$	23%	10%

*Excluding overhead, power, maintenance, etc.

This shows that the actual equipment cost represents a relatively small part of your total production cost. It also demonstrates that as the labor cost increases, the percentage of the hourly operating cost of the equipment decreases.

For this reason, the price of the equipment is usually not the most important factor in a profitable operation. The amount of down-time a machine can have due to breakdowns or maintenance problems can be a significant factor since the operator will still be paid whether or not the machine is in operation.

Downtime which is due to equipment failure or operator inexperience, brings into focus the importance of hiring, training and retaining qualified and productive workers. The higher wages commanded by skilled operators can be justified only if their productivity is superior.

For example:

Operator	Wage rate	Units produced	Cost per unit
A	$10.00/hr.	200/hr.	$ .50
B	15.00/hr.	400/hr.	.375

This illustrates how the more skilled and higher paid operator can be 100 percent more productive and save 25 percent in production cost at the same time.

Material Handling

Material handling procedures depend upon your plant layout and your requirements for movement of components or materials into, within, and out of your plant. The best layout is a ground-floor facility with truck-level loading dock and ceilings with heights up to 20 feet. High ceilings allow for more freedom in placing utility lines so that machinery can be installed and moved almost anywhere within the building. High ceilings are also ideal for stacked storage of materials and finished goods.

Working space that is divided into small areas - or broken up by steps or floors - has less open space and necessitates more material handling. You can overcome some of these disadvantages by arranging people and equipment in a logical workflow system that minimizes "moving" or "carrying" time. Well-placed conveyors can save money and labor hours. Materials and products can also be moved more quickly and efficiently by using hand carts, forklifts, or other wheeled equipment.

Scheduling

The best way to schedule production or service jobs is to begin with the day the job has to be completed and work backwards from there to set all necessary production deadlines.

For example, if your deadline to complete a project is January 15, begin by marking that date on your production schedule. Then back-track from that date to show when each necessary project step will be started and completed.

January 2	January 5	January 9	January 15	January 15
Place material order.	Deliver to prep. department.	Complete material prep. Deliver to production equipment.	Complete final quality control check.	Load, deliver.

Your production schedule should show when various machines will be in use. This enables you to schedule jobs on available equipment, avoiding delays and idle operators or machines. Also take into account when materials or components will be available from outside suppliers.

When a number of different products are in production at the same time, scheduling becomes more complex and priorities should be established to meet delivery commitments.

Maintenance

Regularly scheduled equipment maintenance is a *must*. Just like servicing your car on a regular basis, the critical parts of equipment and machinery must be inspected and serviced and records maintained. A broken down piece of equipment can raise havoc with production schedules and will increase production costs. It also can result in customers becoming unhappy with delays, and may cause lost business.

Production Labor

The wages paid to production employees are a saleable commodity. Each productive hour worked must be sold at a profit. It makes little difference if the wages are straight labor such as mechanics' time in an automobile repair shop, or time spent by machine operators that goes into a finished product.

In contrast to production work, activities performed by office and sales personnel are geared to the completion of a certain fixed amount of work. This may include processing invoices, preparing statements, writing advertising copy, etc. If employees complete their work in less than their regular working hours, their pace may slow down to stretch the time. If the workload is more than they can handle, they will work faster, stay late or spend weekends to meet deadlines.

For that reason, this category of employee is often paid on a fixed monthly or annual basis. Their jobs are also more secure, with less likelihood of lay-off. In most cases their earnings are lower than those of production employees at corresponding levels.

The production labor cost for each hour not worked due to equipment failure, faulty scheduling, reworking poorly done jobs, or loafing represents a loss to the company. For this reason, it is very important to make production labor as efficient as possible.

One approach in achieving this goal is to conduct time and motion studies which measure and compare production processes for their efficiencies. These studies will, for instance, measure the distance over which materials have to be moved and operators have to travel in the production process. From machine to machine, from floor to floor, from the finishing process station to shipping, and so forth. As a result of these studies, equipment and people can be relocated into more logical and productive arrangements, saving time and increasing efficiencies.

Measuring and recording each employee's machine and hand labor output can help in establishing reasonable production standards, and in comparing operators to each other. The results of such observations and studies can be used as a basis to train or retrain employees and to adjust locations of materials and equipment for increased efficiency.

Encourage employee involvement in the productivity improvement process. Experience has shown that this is a highly important step in increasing productivity.

Employees whose suggestions and ideas lead to significant increases in productivity can be rewarded in a number of ways:

- Money.
- Increased responsibility.
- Public recognition.
- Increased opportunities for advancement or special training.

In some situations it may be advisable to consult an industrial engineer to study your production situation. This should generate recommendations on the most cost-effective ways to increase productivity. These consulting costs often pay for themselves hundreds of times over in terms of labor savings and quality improvements.

Manual Labor

Manual labor involves production work using small machines, hand tools or hands only. The production cost here is basically labor plus materials. Manual labor usually demands fewer skills than machine labor except for work requiring a high degree of craftsmanship. Machine-produced products require larger investments in equipment and higher operator skill-levels. But it is just as important to pay close attention to material handling procedures and the skills of employees in manual operations.

Controlling Labor Costs

Prudent overtime management, use of part-time help, and farm-outs of certain operations can each take you a long way to controlling costs.

Overtime Management

Most businesses avoid overtime because it increases labor costs. But there are situations when overtime can't be avoided; it may even result in *additional* profits. In deciding when to authorize overtime work, it should be kept in mind that materials, basic overhead expenses, equipment depreciation and fringe benefits remain unchanged.

For example:

	Job requiring five hours	
	Performed on regular time	Performed on overtime
Material costs	$50.00	$50.00
Cost of overhead (5.00/hr.)	25.00	25.00
Machine depreciation (1.50/hr.)	7.50	7.50
Wages - $10.00/hr. ($15.00 on overtime)	50.00	75.00
Fringe benefits (3.00/hr.)	15.00	15.00
Total cost of job	$147.50	$172.50

Here, the additional cost for performing the job on overtime is $25.00 or about 17 percent.

When to authorize overtime depends on the situation at hand. If you are behind in your schedule and customers are unhappy, you will have to decide between the possibility of losing the business, or producing the work on overtime. In another situation, the sales department sells more than you can handle on a regular schedule and still meet the delivery deadline. Here, the decision is whether to turn the orders away or produce them on overtime. Or, your work load may fluctuate heavily, resulting in a "feast or famine" situation. If your work force has enough people to cover peak loads, then you are probably overstaffed during other times, including down periods. Now you will have to decide whether it makes sense to keep non-productive people on the payroll or employ fewer people who will work overtime during peak periods. In each case, the business will usually show higher profits by virtue of overtime labor.

One word of caution: If overtime extends over long periods of time, employees will eventually become fatigued and production output will suffer. Watch this situation closely.

Part-time Help

Much of what was discussed under overtime applies here as well. Part-time or on-call employees can be used to help handle peak production periods. They obviously should be trained and called in only as-needed. There are some individuals who prefer to work part-time or on an on-call basis, while others see it as an opportunity to learn. With proper training they sometimes become full-time employees.

Farm-outs

In some industrial and service-type businesses it is often customary to send part of the work to another company capable of performing the work. To determine whether this is advisable, consider the following factors:

- Cost.
- Quality, speed and reliability of service.
- Non-competitive status of suppliers.
- Effect of farm-out on the profitability of your product or service.

When analyzing the pros and cons of producing certain parts or services in-house, you may discover that there are qualified outside suppliers who can furnish them faster, at a lower cost and, frequently, of a better quality.

If outside suppliers cannot reliably supply needed parts or materials when your company needs them, then producing your own components may be necessary even if the costs are higher. Component cost, quality, and availability are all-important factors in your make-or-buy decision.

Quality Control

Quality is a state of mind. Expecting high quality is the first step toward achieving it. What is acceptable quality is a matter of opinion. You, your customers and your competitors will set the standards for acceptable quality in what you are selling. Regardless of the nature of your product or service, the work must be inspected or tested. Inspections are performed during production and after completion. This can be accomplished by supervisors or quality control employees. When inspecting during the production process, sample every 10th, 100th, or 1000th unit - or whatever makes sense in your situation. This saves time, and alerts you to any problems.

You will need to set clear standards for quality against which sample units can be compared. If quality drops below acceptable standards, you must take steps to identify and solve the problem. The source of a problem may be defective materials; machine malfunction; poor workmanship caused by unqualified employees; accidents, or sometimes deliberate action.

In a business offering repair services, the service person and the customer should test repaired items and agree that the work is satisfactory before signing off on it.

In summary, it can be stated that in the complex process and interaction of ideas, people and machinery, there is no simple solution to achieve all the objectives of production management in a single bold stroke. Instead, it takes careful coordination and supervision in a number of areas.

It takes ongoing involvement by the production supervisor, who in many instances will be the business owner. Laying out a procedure and expecting it to be followed without careful supervision and follow-through invites disaster. There is a chain that links equipment, operating procedures, material handling, scheduling, maintenance and labor costs to quality. The more efficient each component is, the more successful and profitable your business will be. A broken or weak link in this chain will lead to trouble.

A production process which is continuously monitored presents a tremendous challenge to the production manager. The results of improving, revising, and enhancing any part of the production process will be reflected in increased profits.

Business Customs and Conduct

Business customs and conduct - like social etiquette - is a set of flexible rules which vary widely from business to business. Here we'll discuss appearance, communications, telephone practices and generally provide guidelines of what is customary and acceptable in business. By reviewing and applying some of these suggestions, you can improve your relationships with your customers, suppliers and employees. After all, how you and your employees act in the office and interrelate with others will affect the image your business presents to the outside world.

Dress and Grooming

One of the most easily noticed aspects of office behavior is employee dress and grooming. Appropriate dress depends on job type. You may set a dress code to spell out the types of clothing your employees are expected to wear in a general way. For example, ties for men, no jeans, etc. You can set a strict policy that describes specific clothing, or one that gives employees more room to express personal tastes. You may also decide to leave clothing choices open, except to rule out certain unacceptable attire.

Grooming is also an area that can differ widely. An absolute must is to pay close attention to personal hygiene. Whatever their clothing or hair style, employees should be neat and clean. Appearance counts as a way of expressing individual and company attitudes toward business.

Decor

Another easily noticed aspect of appearance is how employees take care of their work areas. Office areas which are visible to buyers, customers, or clients should always be kept tidy. There is a wide range of appropriate decor and furnishings. This choice will depend upon the needs of your business and, if possible, reflect the tastes of your customers. The office should be comfortable to visit and work in, and convey a business-like environment. Clutter can distract employees and customers, and office areas should be simply decorated and neatly kept.

Frequency and length of customer and supplier visits will be a factor in determining decor and furnishings. The money allocated for this purpose should be kept modest, particularly in a start-up business. On the other hand, if your business requires a display of showmanship to impress visitors and create a favorable image, your budget should make the necessary provisions for it. For example:

An auto collision repair office will have frequent customer visits, but for brief contacts only. A law office will normally have fewer customer visits, but for longer periods. It is important to plan decor and furnishings to allow for customer comfort and expectations.

Your waiting area should not be used as an employee or supplier interview area if customers may be present. Customers should always be allowed the courtesy of keeping their business private. The presence of other customers can be distracting. If smokers and non-smokers must share this space, strongly consider a no-smoking policy along with the necessary signs. Your contact area for outsiders should be pleasant and as free of confusion as possible.

Conversation

Employees should also be aware of the negative impact that unnecessary conversations have. Continuous talk - even between two people - can upset the entire atmosphere. Conversations should be carried on at normal voice levels. Whispers or shouts will distract employees and customers. Employees should never discuss personal business within the hearing of customers. If there is an employee lounge, you can suggest it as the place to discuss personal matters during regular break periods. Even some business-related conversations can be distracting or inappropriate. Conversations that concern sensitive or confidential information should be conducted only in private offices, or during times when no customers or suppliers are present.

Playing radios, singing, humming and whistling can be very disturbing. These activities should not take place in the office or shop. Eating or drinking should not be permitted during working hours, and limited to designated areas during regular rest periods.

Telephone Procedures

You and your employees represent your business when using the telephone. Tone of voice and distinctive, clear speech is important. Talk directly into the mouthpiece. Your lips should be no more than one-half inch from the mouthpiece. Speak as clearly as possible, with the tone and loudness you would use in a face-to-face conversation. If the person you are talking to asks you to speak louder, try moving your lips slightly closer to the mouthpiece. Chewing gum, eating or drinking, or trying to talk with any other object in your mouth can make it very difficult for you to be understood.

Numbers can be easily misunderstood over the telephone. Pronounce them slowly and carefully, repeating them if necessary. Ask your listener to do the same so you are certain they have been heard correctly.

If you are not able to reach the person you asked for, leave a message. Give your name, the name of your business and a number and time you can be reached. If you need a prompt response from the person you are trying to reach, ask what time is best to call again. When you reach a receptionist or switchboard operator, introduce· yourself, explain what company you are representing and who you would like to speak to. For example, "This is Nelson Briggs from Icron Electronics. Is Angela Niel in please?"

When you answer a call, give your name and, if necessary, your department. Make a note of the caller's name, number, business and any action you need to take on the call. If you cannot take a call immediately, tell the caller that you can't talk at this time. Offer to call back, or say it's okay for him to remain on "hold" - if the delay will not exceed one-minute. If you say that you'll call at a certain time, be sure to follow through promptly.

Wrong-number calls should be treated courteously, they are minor inconveniences. Ask the caller what number he was trying to reach. This helps him to determine whether he has an incorrect number, or has dialed incorrectly. This can save you from receiving a repeat call; it also will save the caller the embarrassment of making the same mistake twice. Courtesy can pay in unexpected ways; today's wrong number can become tomorrow's customer.

If a call is accidentally cut off, hang up immediately. If you are the caller, re-dial without delay. If you are the one who was called, wait for the caller to re-dial. This saves the irritation of calling back only to get a busy signal as the other person tries to reach you.

The name of the company should always be given in answering calls from the outside. This applies whether it's the switchboard operator or some other employee who answers the telephone. It can be preceded by "Good morning/Afternoon," and may be followed by "May I help you?" or a similar expression. If the caller asks for specific information, put him on "hold" and connect him with the right party. It is not generally a good idea to ask who the caller is.

If the call has been transferred from the switchboard to some other person, it may only be necessary to give one's name and department.

Exact greetings will depend upon the customs in your area. Language can be "formal" using full sentences, or "telegraphic". Either greeting may be acceptable, depending on your business and local customs.

Formal: "This is Doran's Nursery. I'm Edna Doran. How can I help you?"

Telegraphic: "Doran's Nursery"

Whether you address callers on a first-name basis, or by title will depend on how well you know them, your own preferences, the customs in your area, and the nature of your business.

Conversations are usually terminated by the caller. If the called person wishes to end the conversation, thank the caller for telephoning and encourage him to call again. A conversation that drags on can be difficult to end tactfully, particularly if you are not the caller. However, the same skills you use in face-to-face contact can also be applied here. You may close the call in the same way you would close a sale. You can be quite direct, but keeping your tone friendly, with a phrase such as "Will that be all?"

Or you can restate the customer's needs, the action you will take, and ask if they have other needs. For example:

"You've really had some problems with that lawn mower. If you can bring it in by three p.m., I'm sure we can fix it by five, or give you a loaner. Is there anything else I can do for you now?"

When you finish a call, put the receiver down gently. Make a note of any action you need to make, and be sure to follow up.

Conversations should focus on the business at hand. Language should be as formal as necessary. In general, avoid slang. As for humor, what is acceptable to one person may be offensive to another. So caution is recommended. All conversations should be clear, brief and courteous. The same skills used for face-to-face dealings with customers can also be quite effective by telephone.

Your business may set either a strict or lenient policy on employees receiving personal calls in the office. The freedom to make or accept personal calls during business hours may be highly important to some employees and less to others. Encourage employees to use their breaks for these calls. They should not expect to be paid for time used on personal business. Abuses can tie up lines when customers are trying to reach you.

An important point of courtesy in calling or dealing with customers or business contacts is to remember and use their names. Be especially careful to make certain that you have heard the name correctly. *Use* the customer's name in conversation with him. Be careful not to overuse the name, and pay special attention to pronunciation. When in doubt, ask the customer if you are pronouncing his name correctly. The difference in "Carlson" and "Carson" may be small to you, but will be important to your customer.

Receptionists

Receptionists and switchboard operators are often the most "visible" employees to the outside world. They are frequently responsible for the first contacts customers and other callers experience with your company. Because of this, receptionists should be especially well-groomed, courteous, knowledgeable and tactful. Since receptionists do present the initial image of your business, they should be highly skilled in telephone communications. They should know when to screen incoming calls before connecting them, when to take messages and when to put them through promptly.

It can be helpful to give new receptionists or switchboard operators a chart that shows departments, extension numbers, names of supervisors and areas of responsibility. This makes it easier to properly direct a call when a prospect or customer is unsure who may be able to help him. Receptionists should greet customers visiting the office by name, if possible. Offer coffee if the customer must wait for a lengthy period, and try to let the customer know about how long the wait will be.

Like other employees, receptionists and switchboard operators should help keep the customer comfortable in a business-like manner. Check back frequently if a customer must be kept waiting on the telephone. Some telephone systems use music to make waiting more pleasant. Use these systems with caution, since musical tastes vary from person to person.

Receptionists should also have a list of scheduled appointments so they can give customers or other contacts accurate information as to when they should call back or visit.

Cashiers

Since mistakes are easily made in cash transactions, special care should be taken to count change to the customer, and announce aloud what denomination of bill ($1.00, $5.00, $10.00, etc.) the customer has given you. If change to a single bill is given, the bill should be left visible at the cash register while the change is being counted. This saves confusion if the customer mistakenly or purposely claims that the bill was actually a higher denomination. Change should be counted back to the customer, and not simply handed to him. This cuts down on the possibility of over-paying or short-changing a customer.

Cashiers should be alerted to counterfeit bills and be aware of check cashing policies. If you can't accept a check - or if a customer is in possession of counterfeit bills - call a manager over to talk with the customer privately. The manager should explain the situation to the customer and ask for any information that can help establish whether the customer was unaware of a problem, or purposely offered a problem check or counterfeit bills. The point of this conversation is *not* to establish guilt, but to lay the situation out clearly. If you feel that the customer intended to pass a bad check or counterfeit bills, you should call the police. In this case, the customer should be advised - not forced - to stay until the police arrive. If the customer tries to leave, do not physically prevent him from doing so.

Complaints

Individuals who complain about purchases should be treated with special courtesy, particularly when they appear to be quite irate. The best way to handle these people - whether on the telephone or in person - is to listen to them without interruption. Be sympathetic and re-assure them that every attempt will be made to get to the bottom of the problem. Make every effort to give the customer the benefit of the doubt. Offer a solution, or ask what kind of solution the customer would be happiest with. Having the customer's continued business will often make up for a loss or compromise on a single item. Review the section on customer complaints.

Meetings Outside of the Business

It is advisable to not meet too frequently with the same customer or customer's employee over lunch, dinner, at a sports event or similar occasion. Such meetings should have a clear business purpose, and not be just entertainment or relaxation. Avoid ordering alcoholic drinks during these meetings, or use in moderation. The same rules apply if you are asked out by a supplier or a sales representative.

Sexual Harassment

Plan ahead to avoid this problem. Within the office, stick to business and avoid after hours activities not related to business. It is difficult and costly to clear yourself or your staff of sexual harassment charges. Whether proven or not, such charges can hurt the reputation of your company.

Employee Policies

You and your managers should set personal examples for all desirable qualities and behavior patterns you expect your employees to follow. Encourage them to come forth with ideas for improving procedures, production and sales techniques. This leads to increased productivity and fewer losses due to sickness, accidents, or staff turnover. The best employee management relations come from dealing with employees directly. Recognize good performance publicly. Any personally sensitive matters, problems in behavior or job performance should be handled in privacy and confidentially. Put emphasis on *solving* the problem rather than taking punitive actions. The consequences of failing to solve the problem should also be clearly laid out. Conflict resolution seminars can also help build the skills needed for employees and managers to work well together.

You are responsible for keeping all aspects of the work setting focused on business. Emotional conflicts "back-biting", personal attacks and power struggles are destructive. They result in dissatisfaction, productivity losses and turnover. Open communication is essential. So are seminars, workshops, and use of mediators if the occasion demands it.

Employees should be given clear work guidelines and expectations, yet be allowed to exercise their judgment as often as possible to accomplish tasks. As owner and manager, you will be responsible for setting up those guidelines and expectations. It is also important to balance fair, equal treatment of employees while taking individual needs and differences into consideration.

As an entrepreneur, your business reflects *you*. It should demonstrate your own values for quality, fairness, honesty and treatment of people, whether they're your customer, suppliers or employees.

About Consultants

No entrepreneur should be expected to have all the expertise it takes to deal successfully with every aspect of the business.

In engaging the services of consultants, you buy knowledge and experience that is not available within your organization. There are basically two reasons for hiring consultants:

- To keep you from making and continuing with wrong decisions and business practices that are costing you money.

- To help you develop and implement new ideas and approaches that will make more money for you.

As an outsider - but with your company's interest at heart - a consultant should have unbiased views that enables him to identify problems and recognize opportunities you may be unaware of.

Here's a partial listing of fields where consultants operate:

- Accounting
- Advertising/Public relations
- Architecture
- Chemistry
- Child Care
- Computers
- Construction
- Engineering
- Finance
- Freight
- Import/Export
- Industrial
- Labor Relations
- Legal
- Management
- Manufacturing
- Marketing
- Material Handling
- Packaging
- Research/Development
- Restaurants
- Safety
- Security
- Speech Writers
- Transportation
- Warehousing

Using a consultant does not in any way reflect negatively on your capabilities as an entrepreneur. Consultants are used by multi-billion dollar corporations as well as one-person businesses. The basic reason consultants are beneficial is that they bring specialized skills, experiences and an outsider's view to certain situations and problems. They are not constricted by conventional and often outdated thinking which frequently inhibits an owner in his approach to the resolution of problems.

When consultants are working on problems or new ideas, they may also want to talk things over with your managers and employees. Keep in mind that these discussions can be more effective if the business owner is not present; it will encourage employees to express their views and opinions more freely.

In engaging a consultant, you buy experience and advice that, ideally, will provide solutions to your problems and challenges. The entrepreneur-consultant relationship should be a stimulating one and result in new ideas and approaches, which in turn leads to the creation and implementation of effective new plans.

Fees for consulting services may appear high at times until you consider the two reasons for engaging a consultant: One is to help you *save money*. The other, to help you *make more money*. The cost of consulting services should be more than covered by the benefits they bring.

You can make the best use of consultants by keeping them informed on what is happening in your business, and particularly on the projects in which they are involved.

Consultants can also help you implement decisions, make outside contacts, and introduce you to other people who can be helpful. Personal compatibility is extremely important in an entrepreneur-consultant relationship. You and the consultant must feel comfortable in dealing with each other.

A good consultant will outline options on how to approach problems, projects or planning, but should *not* make decisions for you. It is your job to accept, reject or modify recommendations presented by a consultant.

But before you decide to engage the services of a consultant, it is prudent to obtain information, advice, and recommendations from sources which are free or low-cost. The SBA (Small Business Administration) has highly experienced, usually retired business people and executives who are available for interviews and advice. This service is free through their SCORE program (Service Corps of Retired Executives). The SBA also maintains an elaborate library which contains books and pamphlets on many aspects of operating start-up and existing businesses. Some of them are free or available at nominal cost.

Public libraries and bookstores also offer a wide range of choices on books on almost any business subject. Trade organizations are often equipped to answer specific questions, or refer you to individuals who can. Suppliers of goods and services also may have good insight into the nature of your business and can answer many of your questions.

Government agencies and university schools of business can also provide excellent consulting services including low-cost assistance with market research and analysis.

This is not to say that these sources can substitute for professional consultants. But they go a long way toward getting you better acquainted with all of the aspects of your planning and problem-solving. They will enable you to ask more incisive and pertinent questions when you begin to talk with a consultant. This alone can save on consulting fees and make your investment in consultants more productive.

There are a number of ways in which the services of consultants can be utilized:

- On a case-by-case basis.
- For a specified time-period.
- For a certain number of hours-per-month.
- For a special project or problem.

Fees can be set by the hour, by the project, or on a monthly retainer. Any combination of these can be worked out. There is usually no charge for the first exploratory meeting.

You can find consultants through recommendations from accountants, attorneys, bankers, business and personal acquaintances and trade organizations. One word of caution: Do *not* use a friend or relative.

The search for consultants usually begins on the telephone. Briefly outline your ideas, then ask the consultant about his experiences and background, and decide whether he has the qualifications to be of help to you. If you believe he shows good potential, ask about fee schedules and set up an appointment for an exploratory meeting. Determine the kind of information or papers you should have ready for this occasion. If the consultant impresses you favorably, ask for references but make no commitment to engage him at this meeting. Check the references. Then request a written proposal which outlines your objectives, the fee structure, and the time required to complete the job. Do not move too fast in making a decision. You may wish to check out more than one consultant.

Accountants, advertising agencies and attorneys can also be considered as consultants. But for the most part, their services are utilized on an ongoing basis. The selection procedure can be conducted along similar lines as previously discussed, but should be even more thorough since these professionals will be deeply involved in your business over a long period of time. Replacing them can often be time-consuming, costly and disruptive. The utmost care and caution is advised in making a good choice in the first place.

To arrive at a good decision in affiliating with a professional firm, take the sizes of both your company and their organization into consideration. The difference in size should not be so pronounced that your company gets lost in theirs. In some cases - especially where you want continuing individual attention - it will be to your advantage to deal with the principal of a small accounting, advertising or law firm. Ideally, it should have two or three partners. If your regular contact leaves or is otherwise unavailable to you, one of the other members of the firm could step into the breach. This would not be possible in a one-person company.

Next, we will discuss the role which accountants, advertising agencies and attorneys should play in your business.

Accountants are needed for small businesses, beginning with the start-up phase. They can design an accounting/bookkeeping system tailored to your unique needs; keep books; prepare financial statements and help you interpret them, and prepare your tax returns. They can be helpful in spotting problem areas. Their advice is also critical in guiding the general well-being of your business which includes the review of expansion plans, and estimating cash requirements and sources. Using a qualified accountant should give you more accurate records and informative financial statements that can help in your business planning and in dealing with lenders. Well-structured financial statements will yield clues to new opportunities or trouble spots in your business, and help you formulate strategies for dealing with them.

Advertising agencies can help you identify your marketing needs; devise advertising plans; create copy; select and place advertising in the appropriate media. They will advise you on how to measure the effectiveness of your advertisements, and make recommendations for revisions in your plans.

They will be able to supply you with references and samples of their work. Periodic consultations may be based on a flat fee basis, while other services such as writing copy, preparing artwork and typesetting will be billed separately. Smaller agencies will often charge less and give your account more attention.

A competent attorney is another invaluable member on your advisory team. The legal aspects of today's business world are becoming increasingly complex, even for a small business. There is hardly a business activity that does not present legal pitfalls. In some cases, a wrong move or faulty decision by an entrepreneur may result in considerable losses - or even threaten the existence of the business itself. Here is a partial list of areas in which it is highly advisable to consult an attorney:

- Incorporation.
- Contracts.
- Leases (real estate, facilities, or equipment).
- Employee disputes.
- Sales and purchase agreements.
- Liability and libel problems.
- Collection problems.
- Government regulations.

The best time to consult an attorney is before problems arise; when serious difficulties are still preventable. It is important to recognize potentially dangerous situations and act decisively. As with other consultants, an attorney should be selected on the basis of his experience with businesses similar to yours.

The matter of fees should be discussed, resolved, and put into writing before *any* work is done. A common type of fee arrangement is based on a retainer, that is, a flat monthly fee. It ordinarily covers day-to-day legal questions and problems with suppliers; customers; collections; contracts; purchase and sales agreements, and writing letters with legal implications on your company's behalf. This retainer fee does not usually include representing you or your company in legal actions of any kind. It should be reviewed periodically to determine whether it still fairly represents the work done by the attorney. Other methods of compensation are based on hourly rates, fixed fees for specific situations or contingency fees in the collection of past-due accounts. That is, a percentage of the amount collected.

In order to make the best use of your attorney -

- Advise him of any changes or new information that might affect your case.

- Insist that you be regularly informed on any developments.

- Ask for copies of any document that is prepared on your behalf.

- Sign legal documents only after you have gone over them with him.

Generally speaking, if you have any doubt about advice received when dealing with any consultant or other professional, do not hesitate to get a second opinion. And be prepared, if necessary, to look for a replacement. However, staying with one consultant may give that person a better idea of your business history and make him more valuable to you as time goes on.

Section 8

WHEN AND HOW TO SELL YOUR BUSINESS
AT A PROFIT

In this section we will discuss reasons for selling a business by exploring an entrepreneur's motivation and the steps to be taken in planning for and formulating a sale strategy.

If you are planning to buy a business, this information can also be helpful in your negotiation techniques.

This information is divided into the following topics:

• Reasons for selling your business.

• Developing ideas for selling.

• Determining the worth of your business.

• Preparing your business for the sale.

• Finding a buyer.

• Negotiating the sale.

• Handling the after-sale transition period.

Reasons for Selling your Business

The decision to sell your business is in many ways as soul-searching and complex a process as starting or buying a business; perhaps even more so. In both situations, nothing less than your future is at stake.

The decision to sell a business may be based on a number of considerations. They could be personal, financial or management reasons - or some combination of these factors. For example:

Some entrepreneurs who are involved in more than one business - or have a regular job on the side, or are involved in other time-consuming projects - may discover that they can't do justice to all of these activities. They may realize that they have overextended themselves and need a change of pace. Consequently, they consider selling.

Others, after being in business for a number of years, lose interest in their enterprise and discover another type of business that they believe to be more exciting or profitable. So they decide to sell out in order to make that change.

Another personal reason to sell is due to stress or "burn-out" which manifests itself by:

- A feeling of being overwhelmed or preoccupied by problems.

- No longer enjoying or being challenged by a particular kind of work.

- Having a sense of being trapped.

- Spending less time at work or at least wishing that they could.

- Having difficulty concentrating or being easily distracted.

- Poor health and anxiety about not being able to handle the fast pace, tensions and future demands of the business motivates many entrepreneurs to start thinking about selling.

Other entrepreneurs decide to sell while the business is doing well and making a profit. They believe that while they're in good health and in full charge it's an opportune time to get out. Or, they may simply wish to retire and "cash in the chips".

There are also a number of financial reasons that motivate entrepreneurs to sell. An unexpected, attractive offer may be made for your business. Even though you had not planned on selling, you may now be tempted to do so. There is nothing wrong with pursuing such an offer, but make sure you have or will develop future financial plans that will ensure your continued economic and emotional well-being. Also, take another careful look at your business with the aid of qualified consultants. Perhaps the buyer sees great opportunities that you may have overlooked.

Another reason to sell is that the business is not doing well. This can be due to your management style; deterioration of the neighborhood where you are located; competition in your product line or services you are offering, and other factors. Obviously, you will not get top dollars for this business, but there are always buyers around who have the money, ability and will to overcome adversities.

Sometimes a business is sold quickly in order to raise cash to deal with an emergency situation. When a "fire sale" like this occurs, it can be costly to the seller. It does not allow sufficient time to properly prepare the business for sale, to find the best buyer, or to obtain the best price or terms. If a buyer cannot be found in short order, the owner may have to liquidate. This amounts to selling the equipment, fixtures and other assets, including merchandise, then collecting the accounts receivable, and closing the doors.

A need to make major changes in your business can be a valid reason to sell. These changes include remodeling, retooling, buying up-to-date equipment or other improvements. These are long-term investments. If you are near retirement or plan to leave the business in the foreseeable future, you may not recover your investment. That may be a good time to sell. Your buyer can then do what's necessary and benefit in the long term.

You also may decide to sell if your lease is about to expire and its new terms are not acceptable to you. Still, a lease that's not acceptable to you may very well be satisfactory to a buyer.

Developing Ideas for Selling

An initial discussion about selling your business should be held with your closest, most trusted contacts. If you have a spouse or business partner, make certain they are the first ones to know about your ideas. You will need their approval and support. Other contacts may be your attorney, accountant, selected friends and relatives or other special individuals. Make sure these people understand the importance of keeping this information confidential. Such information can hurt your business if it gets out prematurely. It can be especially damaging if you fail to sell. Also let this group of confidants know that you are in the thinking stage and don't yet have firm plans. Fewer than one in ten businesses on the market sell within one year.

Such deliberations allow you to think out loud and have sounding boards for your ideas. When initially talking with your close contacts, do not divulge any more information than is necessary, and stress that it be kept confidential. Where possible, limit what you discuss in this very early stage to -

- Reasons for selling.

- Future potential of the business.

- Your future plans.

Opinions differ on just when to tell your employees of your plans to sell. Timing is important. As just mentioned, if news of your plans are leaked prematurely, your business could be hurt. Particularly if your competitors learn about it. On the other hand, saving news of a sale until the last minute may be discouraging to your employees. Also, you may find that one of them would have been an interested and qualified buyer, given the opportunity.

Determining the Worth of Your Business

The value of your business is the worth of its tangible and intangible assets. Tangible assets, which have specific dollar values, include the following:

- Market or replacement value of equipment, supplies and inventory.

- Cash value of accounts receivable, minus a percentage to cover uncollectible accounts.

- Value of real estate or buildings.

- Value of transferrable licenses or deposits.

- Cash-on-hand.

Intangible assets are usually referred to as "good will." Such assets include the reputation of your business; your work force and customer base; location; trademarks; patents, etc. There is no clear dollar value for these assets, but they heavily contribute to the expected profits of a business.

The general formula for pricing a business is:

Target or asking price = Tangible assets + good will

But there are many pricing approaches. Your accountant can give you advice on which approach makes the most sense in your situation. There are no iron-clad rules for arriving at a price.

You can base your asking price on the net worth of your business which is the value of your assets minus your debts and other liabilities. Net worth = assets - liabilities. This approach does not take good will into account. Your tangible assets can be priced according to their fair market value (replacement value) or the depreciated value. A price approach that includes tangible assets and good will is obviously to your advantage. One factor that can determine your price is the expected future earnings.

Your business may also be priced based on sales prices of similar businesses.

Whatever pricing approach you use, keep in mind that an annual return on investment of 20 to 30 percent - not including the owner's salary - will be acceptable to most buyers.

Before you finalize your asking price, add a percentage to give yourself room for negotiation and compromise with the buyer.

The final price which you and the buyer agree to will also be influenced by terms of the sale.

You may be willing to accept a lower price if you need to sell quickly, or if the buyer can offer all cash-in-full. You may ask more if you carry a contract on the balance owed you. You should also expect the general economy to influence the price; if the economy is sluggish, the price for your business may be lower than when business is booming. A slower economy usually means higher risk and lower profits.

In order to negotiate a price to your advantage, carefully consider any problems, risks, or liabilities that will be of concern to your buyer. Then be prepared to explain your rationale and assumptions for placing a value on the business. This should be based on the following factors:

- Tangible assets.

- Age of your business. An established business (over five years old) is considered less risky than a newer business.

- Experienced personnel.

- Strong industry future.

- Strong predicted sales growth.

- Established customer base.

- Tax advantages to the buyer.

You will usually reveal your asking price when potential buyers inquire. This tends to discourage unqualified parties. Only rarely will your initial figure be the final sale price. It is merely a starting point for negotiations. In order to set a final price, it may be advisable to have your business appraised.

Your appraiser should be a specialist in business and real estate. An appraiser will usually submit several prices based on different formulas. They are most helpful once you start negotiating with interested buyers.

The primary concern for most buyers is how well the business will return profits on their investment. There are numerous formulas based on the value of assets and expected returns by which to calculate the price of a business.

Appraisals, various formulas, and earnings projections give only approximate estimates. The market value of your business is a number modified by the effects of supply and demand. How many businesses similar to yours are available, and how *much* they are in demand will determine whether its market value is higher or lower than a price established by formula.

Other factors affecting the price of a business are:

- Liquidation value.

- Ease of resale.

- Availability of financing and the initial investments required.

- Condition and value of facilities, equipment and inventory.

- Quality of current management.

- Location.

- Availability of labor and costs for training.

- Time, energy demands on management.

- Strength and nature of competing businesses.

- Expected costs of expansion, necessary renovation.

- Condition of the local, state and national economy.

Preparing Your Business for Sale

The first step in preparing your business for sale is to sit down with your accountant and an attorney who has had extensive experience in negotiating the buying and selling of businesses. If a business broker is involved, that person should also be involved. Remember, however, that *you* should maintain control over the process, just as you would do with any consultant.

As you prepare for the sale, be careful not to neglect ongoing business. It will need more rather than less attention than usual. You should keep its external and internal appearance at its best - just as when you put your home up for sale. Focus on the positive aspects of your operations and resolve as many problems as possible before negotiations with buyers begin.

You will need to prepare financial statements for potential buyers. These include profit and loss statements; balance statements; cash flow statements; inventory reports; payroll records; customer and accounts receivable lists, etc. Sometimes a market analysis can be included to show the present situation of the market and the strength and nature of your competition.

Be careful when you release information. Know your potential buyers as well as possible. In some cases you may ask for a good faith deposit or have potential buyers sign non-disclosure agreements to assure that they will handle this information confidentially and return it to you. Your attorney will advise you at which stages of the negotiating process to make various documents available. You may also develop an improvement or expansion plan for potential buyers. It is similar to a business plan based on your experience with the business.

As previously discussed, you will also have to decide when to let your employees know about your plans to sell. Information leaks can upset them unnecessarily and used by your competitors to your disadvantage. For that reason, it is critical to give serious thought to the timing of when to reveal this information. Opinions differ on what the best timing is. We recommend making information available only as necessary - ideally not before the sale has been closed.

Finding a Buyer

Once you have made a definite decision to sell, begin searching for buyers. There are many ways to go about it. Here's a partial list:

- Regular business contacts.

- Trade/business association contacts.

- Sales personnel in similar businesses.

- Referrals from your attorney, banker, accountant, or other consultant.

- Friends, relatives and employees — if applicable.

- Advertising the business in local or regional publications. Ads may be placed in the business opportunities section of newspapers, trade magazines or in national/regional publications such as the Wall Street Journal. Advertisements with blind box numbers should create enough interest in your business to elicit responses. But these ads should not be too explicit to reveal your firm's identity.

- Business Brokers. Unless you are skilled in negotiating and selling businesses, it is advisable to make use of a business broker. The broker should be well-acquainted with the market for your business. He can screen potential buyers, help you prepare your business for the sale and assist in closing the sale. Brokers charge a commission based on a percentage of the sale price. The commission can pay for itself as brokers can bring more prospective buyers to you and obtain better selling prices.

Unless it is a cash sale, look for these important qualities in a buyer:

- Financial stability.

- Good or superior management abilities.

- Experience in your type of business.

- Compatibility with you, your customers and employees.

How to Negotiate the Sale

There is no set routine on how to conduct your negotiations. They will usually take place in your attorney's office with you, the buyer, the accountants and attorneys for both parties present. Also, a business broker if one is involved. Depending on the complexity of the transaction, it may take from one week to several months to close a sale. There may also be times when you meet the buyer informally at your place of business or at lunch or dinner.

The most important steps toward successful negotiations are as follows:

Get to know your buyer well. This enables you to create an atmosphere of trust in which compromises can take place. Be ready to support your position - but also be flexible.

Come prepared with facts and figures to back up your statements and claims. Never present anything that you cannot substantiate.

Be willing to take time to carefully consider price and sale terms point by point. Take notes as each point is discussed. Compare notes with your consultants and the other parties involved in order to avoid misunderstandings. Take breaks as needed. Go into negotiations well-rested.

Be aware of the tax implications of the sale for yourself, your business, and the buyer.

When your negotiations are completed and the price and terms of the sale have been agreed upon to everyone's satisfaction, the attorneys will draft all necessary papers. This may involve quite a number of documents and financial instruments, too numerous to describe since they vary from one situation to another.

How to Handle the After-Sale Transition Period

With careful planning, your business can have a smooth transition to new ownership and management. If the new owners are members of your family, you may be able to reduce your taxes by giving them portions of the company's equity over a number of years. If two or more partners are involved in selling a business, it can be extremely difficult to negotiate a sale if the buyer is closely related to one of the partners. In such cases, more negotiating time may be needed. Or it may be wiser to sell to an outsider. Another option is to buy out the partner(s), then negotiate a transfer of ownership to the relative.

Most sale agreements require the seller to assist the buyer for a period that can vary from three months to two years. Arrangements range from a full-time employment contract to an "on-call" consulting relationship. This contract will spell out the terms that both parties agree to. Some sellers find it difficult to function properly or feel comfortable in these situations because the buyer will have his own ideas on how the business should be operated. Also, the seller may not always agree with these new approaches.

It's up to the seller to adjust to these changes, and that can be emotionally difficult. The former owner also has to be extremely tactful when dealing with the employees. Many employees may still feel more loyal to the seller than to the buyer. In fact, some employees may consider the new owner to be an intruder. The seller must plan and carry out a tactful withdrawal from former employees, suppliers and customers. He must also do everything possible to make the transition period as stress-free and pleasant as possible for everyone concerned. This will make the seller's equity in the business - the balance still owed to him - more secure. So in the final analysis, it *is* in your best interest to do everything in your power to assist in the transition. The faster and more trouble-free the transition, the better the business will weather the inevitable changes.

Section 9

ENTREPRENEURIAL TRAITS: HOW DO YOU COMPARE WITH THE LEADERS?

The Entrepreneurial Self Test

Taking this test will help you learn more about your qualifications to become a successful entrepreneur. Your answers will reveal strengths and weaknesses and show the areas where improvements are needed.

Successful entrepreneurs show a similar pattern of answers, but no two can be expected to answer in exactly the same way. So a high score will not guarantee that you'll be successful. Nor does a low score mean that you wouldn't be successful. This test is simply a guide to help you identify qualities that are important to entrepreneurs. It will identify the areas in which you should make changes and improvements in order to increase your chance for success. With that information, you can make the decision that will have a great effect on your future.

One word of advice: When you answer the questions, be honest with yourself. No one else needs to see the results of this test. Do not peek at the answers until completed. Do not change your answers as you compare them with the test score. Your first answer usually reveals the most about your thinking. Find a quiet place where you can complete the questionnaire without interruption. Take as much time as you need, and finish the test in one sitting if at all possible.

For easy interpretation of the test, look under *Analysis* following the test. We wish you Good Luck . . . now go for it!

YES NO

☐ ☐ **1.** Have you ever been employed in a small business (one with 50 or less employees)?

☐ ☐ **2.** Are you comfortable with most of the decisions you make on the basis of a hunch (intuition)?

☐ ☐ **3.** Do you have difficulties with your personal finances?

☐ ☐ **4.** Did your parents (or other family members) own or operate a small business?

☐ ☐ **5.** Is your marriage difficult or unstable? (If you are not married, answer NO.)

☐ ☐ **6.** Have you ever attended a stress-management class or read about stress management?

☐ ☐ **7.** Do people seldom come to you for advice?

☐ ☐ **8.** Do you act quickly on projects that involve difficult decisions?

☐ ☐ **9.** Have you enjoyed most of your jobs in the past?

☐ ☐ **10.** When you want to change someone's idea, are you often afraid that that person will not accept your idea?

☐ ☐ **11.** Do you frequently put off projects that involve difficult decisions?

☐ ☐ **12.** Have you been successful in reaching some of your long-term goals (five years or longer)?

☐ ☐ **13.** Do your friends or family support your decision to start a business?

☐ ☐ **14.** Do you have a college degree in business or a good understanding of economics and finance?

☐ ☐ **15.** Is drinking a problem for you?

YES NO

☐ ☐ **16.** Do you have a Ph.D. in a business field or some other field?

☐ ☐ **17.** Do high blood pressure, ulcers, or heart problems run in your family?

☐ ☐ **18.** Do you believe you usually have good hunches (or intuition) about making decisions?

☐ ☐ **19.** Did you have one or more paying jobs as a child (or teenager)?

☐ ☐ **20.** Do you enjoy working with people, rather than working alone?

☐ ☐ **21.** Were you born in a foreign country?

☐ ☐ **22.** Does it bother you to make a decision when there is more than one good answer to a problem?

☐ ☐ **23.** Do you believe it is all right to change a goal once a plan has been made and a project has been started?

☐ ☐ **24.** Have there been times when you thought of yourself as not "fitting in" at work or school?

☐ ☐ **25.** If your business succeeded, would you feel the most important benefit was an escape from workplace politics?

☐ ☐ **26.** Do you feel that you work harder and have more drive than most people?

☐ ☐ **27.** Do you prefer highly varied work to routine work?

☐ ☐ **28.** Do you need more sleep than other people?

☐ ☐ **29.** Do you feel overwhelmed when you must review a lot of information to make a decision?

☐ ☐ **30.** Do you often meet or beat deadlines?

YES NO

☐ ☐ **31.** Do you have marketing or sales experience?

☐ ☐ **32.** Do you have a budget, and usually stay within it?

☐ ☐ **33.** Do you usually solve problems carefully, but quickly?

☐ ☐ **34.** Do you feel that you do your work more slowly than the people around you?

☐ ☐ **35.** When you must act immediately (without a lot of information), can you make a quick decision?

☐ ☐ **36.** In sports, do you prefer active participation over watching the activity?

☐ ☐ **37.** Do you find it easy to let important projects pile up, without being able to get to them?

☐ ☐ **38.** Has it been hard to get along with your supervisors/superiors in the past?

☐ ☐ **39.** Do you seldom or never use street drugs or prescription drugs?

☐ ☐ **40.** In your opinion, are you more cautious in risk taking than other people are?

☐ ☐ **41.** Would you have difficulty giving up a lot of time with your family if your business required it?

☐ ☐ **42.** Do you believe that you could work easily with workers who made independent decisions?

☐ ☐ **43.** Are you comfortable changing a plan once a project has started?

☐ ☐ **44.** Do you believe that more businesses fail because of bad luck than because of poor sales?

☐ ☐ **45.** Would you have difficulty working long hours and/or weekends?

YES NO

☐ ☐ **46.** Do you have a hard time making a decision when it is necessary to review a lot of information?

☐ ☐ **47.** Could you work easily with employees who needed to be told what to do?

☐ ☐ **48.** Do you prefer being alone to being with people when making an important decision?

☐ ☐ **49.** Do you have debts that are problems for you?

☐ ☐ **50.** Has your drinking been a problem for other people?

☐ ☐ **51.** Do most people consider you a leader?

☐ ☐ **52.** Do you often let problems "slide," and hope that they will work themselves out without your help?

☐ ☐ **53.** Can you usually convince someone to accept your ideas, even though that person may have a different opinion?

☐ ☐ **54.** Have you had major health problems in the past five years?

☐ ☐ **55.** Do you _always_ think of yourself as someone who does not "fit in" in work or school situations?

☐ ☐ **56.** Do you feel you get enough sleep?

☐ ☐ **57.** Do you believe your family (or dependents) could take frequent "neglect" if your business made that necessary?

☐ ☐ **58.** When you succeed, is it more often because something was "meant to be" than because of your hard work?

☐ ☐ **59.** Do you feel that many of the goals you set for yourself are too difficult to attain?

☐ ☐ **60.** Do you feel that you make better decisions than other people around you?

YES NO

61. Making a lot of money is not the most important aspect of being in business!

62. Do you worry about changing your eating or sleeping habits?

63. Have you been unsuccessful in reaching most of your long-term goals (five years or longer)?

64. Have you ever started a business of your own?

65. Do you believe you would not be content or satisfied working for someone else?

66. Do you believe that more businesses fail because of bad luck than because of bad management?

67. Do you feel you have a quick temper?

68. Do you often find yourself speaking before you've really thought something through?

69. Do you prefer routine work to highly varied work?

70. Do you feel that you set higher (or more difficult) standards than other people?

71. Would it bother you to dismiss a popular employee?

72. If you are planning to enter a high-tech business, do you have previous training or experience?

73. Are you often absent from work because of illness?

74. Have you taken courses in your business field (continuing education, correspondence, etc.)?

75. Do you often read business or news journals (or articles)?

YES NO

76. Do you have average or below-average skills in mathematics?

77. Were your parents immigrants?

78. a. If you are male, are you often uncomfortable dealing with businesswomen?

    b. If you are female, are you often uncomfortable dealing with businessmen?

79. Have your past job, school, or training experiences given you many opportunities to make decisions?

80. Do you usually prefer being with people to being alone when you are involved in recreation or leisure-time activities?

81. Do you prefer working independently to working under supervision?

82. Would you hesitate to leave a job before you found another one?

83. Are you uncomfortable speaking to a group?

84. If under great pressure, do you usually solve problems slowly and carefully?

85. Do you prefer sales work over manual labor?

86. Are you debt-free?

87. Do your mistakes come back to haunt you over and over?

88. Would you hesitate to ask consultants for advice?

89. Have you had management experience in a small business?

90. Are your strongest relationships with people difficult or unstable?

YES NO

☐ ☐ 91. If it appears a plan is unworkable will you still pursue it?

☐ ☐ 92. Would you be willing to complete a 25-hour project in 2 days?

☐ ☐ 93. Do you see yourself as a leader?

☐ ☐ 94. Would you be embarrassed to ask a relative for a loan to start a business?

☐ ☐ 95. Would you rather carry out a project than plan it?

☐ ☐ 96. Is it difficult for you to change other people's ideas to your way of thinking?

☐ ☐ 97. When you have an idea, is it difficult for others to make you change your mind?

☐ ☐ 98. If you have to make a rapid decision without much information, do you usually delay the decision until more information can be collected?

☐ ☐ 99. Do you often read non-technical/non-business literature (books, magazines, etc.)?

☐ ☐ 100. Do you believe that more businesses fail because of poor management than because of competition?

☐ ☐ 101. Is it better to take a bank loan for past due bills than making arrangements with the creditors for payment?

☐ ☐ 102. Have you had problems dealing with job stress in the past?

☐ ☐ 103. Do you hesitate to talk with people you don't know?

☐ ☐ 104. If your business succeeded, would you feel that the most important benefit was complete independence?

☐ ☐ 105. Do you set a plan and stick to it, no matter what?

YES NO

☐ ☐ 106. Do you have no difficulty concentrating, even with many distractions?

☐ ☐ 107. Do you have very firm opinions on most subjects, and therefore have difficulty dealing with people with different views?

☐ ☐ 108. Have you enjoyed most of your sales experience? (If you have no sales experience, answer No.)

☐ ☐ 109. Have you ever "blown up" with a difficult or "impossible" customer?

☐ ☐ 110. In your opinion, is the customer "always right"?

☐ ☐ 111. Do people often come to you for advice?

☐ ☐ 112. Have you had problems with your credit rating?

☐ ☐ 113. Do you have experience operating and maintaining the equipment your business will need?

☐ ☐ 114. Do you have a local criminal record that could hurt or jeopardize your business?

☐ ☐ 115. Did you finish high school or get a G.E.D.? (Answer Yes if you are still in school and intend to finish.)

☐ ☐ 116. Have you quit jobs because of dissatisfaction?

☐ ☐ 117. Do you often miss deadlines or appointments?

☐ ☐ 118. If your business failed, would your personal relationships also fail?

☐ ☐ 119. Should you discuss your plans to go into business with your family and friends?

☐ ☐ 120. If your business succeeded, would you feel that the most important benefit was your sense of accomplishment?

Test Answers and Categories

QUESTION	ANSWER	CATEGORY	QUESTION	ANSWER	CATEGORY	QUESTION	ANSWER	CATEGORY	QUESTION	ANSWER	CATEGORY
1.	Y	D	31.	Y	D	61.	Y	H	91.	N	E
2.	Y	F	32.	Y	H	62.	N	A	92.	Y	A,F
3.	N	B,H,	33.	Y	F	63.	N	E	93.	Y	G
4.	Y	A	34.	N	D,F	64.	Y	D,H	94.	N	C
5.	N	B	35.	Y	F	65.	Y	G,H	95.	N	G
6.	Y	A	36.	Y	G	66.	N	G	96.	N	G
7.	N	G	37.	N	F	67.	N	G	97.	Y	G
8.	Y	F	38.	Y	D	68.	N	G	98.	N	F
9.	N	D,H	39.	Y	A	69.	N	D	99.	Y	C
10.	N	G	40.	N	G,H	70.	Y	E,G	100.	Y	G
11.	N	F	41.	N	B	71.	N	G	101.	N	F
12.	Y	E,H	42.	Y	G	72.	Y	C	102.	N	A
13.	Y	B	43.	Y	E,F	73.	N	A	103.	N	G
14.	Y	C	44.	N	G	74.	Y	C	104.	N	H
15.	N	A	45.	N	B	75.	Y	C	105.	N	F
16.	N	C	46.	N	F	76.	N	C	106.	Y	G
17.	N	A	47.	Y	G	77.	Y	A	107.	N	G
18.	Y	F	48.	N	G	78.	N	G	108.	Y	D
19.	Y	A,D	49.	N	H	79.	Y	C,D	109.	N	G
20.	Y	G	50.	N	A	80.	Y	G	110.	N	G
21.	Y	A	51.	Y	G	81.	Y	D	111.	Y	G
22.	N	F	52.	N	F	82.	N	D	112.	N	B
23.	Y	E	53.	Y	G	83.	N	G	113.	Y	D
24.	Y	D,G,H	54.	N	A	84.	Y	F	114.	N	A
25.	N	G,H	55.	N	G	85.	Y	D	115.	Y	C
26.	Y	D,G,H	56.	Y	A	86.	N	H	116.	Y	D
27.	Y	D	57.	Y	B	87.	N	G	117.	N	G
28.	N	A	58.	N	G	88.	N	G	118.	N	B
29.	N	F	59.	N	E	89.	Y	D,H	119.	Y	E
30.	Y	F	60.	Y	G,H	90.	N	B	120.	Y	H

Here Is How You Score The Test

Compare your answers with the Answer Sheet. Add the correct answers to find your percentage score as follows:

1. Multiply the number of correct answers by 100. Then divide by 120.

2. For example, if you answered 90 questions correctly, you proceed as follows:

$$\frac{\text{Numbers correct} \times 100}{120} \quad \text{or} \quad \frac{90 \times 100}{120} = 75$$

3. Your score is then 75%.

The higher you scored, the more closely your answers match those of successful entrepreneurs, and the better you may be prepared for being an entrepreneur. If you scored above 70%, your answers were very much like those of successful entrepreneurs. If you scored lower, you may benefit from going back over your answers to see which areas are weakest, and then consider getting some additional information, or training before you make a final decision. If you are already in business, you may identify some areas you could strengthen by seeking additional training or making use of employees or consultants who have strength in those areas.

Categories

Category A. Health, Personal and Family Background.   Entrepreneurs must often work long hours with less sleep than other people, and handle the most stressful problems of running a business; so assessing your health and ability to deal with stress is one highly important part of your decision to become an entrepreneur. If drug or alcohol use is a problem to you (or a problem to other people), that may be one reason to believe that you have difficulty dealing with stress and could benefit by learning stress-management techniques before you start your business.

Entrepreneurs are most often the first child born to a family, and are often immigrants or the children of immigrants. They are willing to put in long hours to achieve their objectives. They also usually have some childhood or teenage experience in working independently — operating a lemonade stand, delivering newspapers, etc. — and have parents who were entrepreneurs at some time.

Questions: 4, 6, 15, 17, 19, 21, 28, 39, 50, 54, 56, 62, 73, 77, 92, 102, 114

Category B. Personal Stability.   Personal relationships are critical to success as an entrepreneur. Family support when faced with daily uncertainties about the business, can mean the difference of taking the business through difficult times, or giving up.

Questions: 3, 5, 13, 41, 45, 57, 90, 112, 118

Category C. Formal and Self-Education.   Entrepreneurs in technical fields usually have a bachelors or masters degree in their field — rarely a doctorate. Successful entrepreneurs are not often debt-free, but they know how to use indebtedness to save or make money. It is therefore important to have a good understanding of bookkeeping, accounting and finances regardless of the type of business you plan to enter. One way to obtain the necessary knowledge is through self-study (books, tapes, etc.) and by attending continuing education classes and taking self-improvement courses.

Questions: 14, 16, 72, 74, 75, 76, 79, 94, 99, 115

Category D. Employment Experience.   Successful entrepreneurs generally have some small business management experience before starting their own businesses, and have sales and marketing experience. They are often people who weren't satisfied working for others; felt that they could do their jobs better than their co-workers and supervisors; and left one or more well paying jobs because of dissatisfaction.

Questions: 1, 9, 19, 24, 26, 27, 31, 34, 38, 64, 69, 79, 81, 82, 85, 89, 108, 113, 116

Category E. Goal Setting.   Entrepreneurs constantly set, change, and try to reach their short and long-term goals. They are comfortable with changing goals even while a project is underway, and set high but not unreasonable goals. They enjoy project planning as much as carrying out projects.

Questions: 12, 23, 43, 59, 63, 70, 91, 119

Category F. Problem Solving.   New businesses must move quickly to survive, and this means that entrepreneurs must often make decisions based on their hunches, instead of waiting for a lot of further information. Good intuition, willingness to make a decision with limited information, and fast decision-making are all important to success in a small business. Perhaps most important is being able to decide when to move quickly, and when to wait for further information. How well your business succeeds will also depend upon how adaptable you are — how easily and quickly you can change a plan or activity that isn't routine.

Questions: 2, 8, 11, 18, 22, 29, 30, 33, 34, 35, 37, 43, 46, 52, 84, 92, 98, 101, 105

Category G. Psychological Characteristics. Successful entrepreneurs enjoy dealing with people; are comfortable talking to them in a group or individually; and believe that they can convince people to accept their ideas. They are persuasive; aggressive; willing to take risks; have more than average drive and ability; are curious; and are almost always seen as leaders or advisors. They believe that they control what happens in their business and personal lives, regardless of luck or chance. Most also can deal comfortably with a wide range of employees — those who can act quite independently, and those who need more instruction in completing job-tasks.

Questions: 7, 10, 20, 24, 26, 36, 40, 42, 44, 47, 48, 51, 53, 55, 58, 60, 65, 66, 67, 68, 70, 71, 78, 80, 83, 87, 88, 93, 95, 96, 97, 100, 103, 106, 107, 109, 110, 111, 117

Category H. Motivation for Being An Entrepreneur. Most successful entrepreneurs give "a sense of accomplishment or pride" as their main reason for starting a small business. They enjoy problem-solving; have a history of successful problem-solving; and believe that they are in control. They usually have not been content working for someone else, often because of a feeling of lack of personal freedom. The possibility of a greater income is seldom given as a reason for wanting to be an entrepreneur — perhaps because the personal investment is so high and the risks are so great. Because the risks are very real, escape from financial difficulties may be one of the poorest reasons to choose an entrepreneurial role.

Questions: 3, 9, 12, 24, 25, 26, 32, 40, 49, 60, 61, 64, 65, 86, 89, 104, 120

What follows now is a general discussion of important entrepreneurial traits. It covers such areas as education; experience; family background; personality factors; natural characteristics; motivation; investigative and organizational skills. You can profit by reviewing your Self-Test answers with the observations that follow.

Are Entrepreneurs Born or Made?

This is an often-asked question. If you've ever met a "natural", you know that she or he is the sales representative with little experience who goes out into the territory and quickly out-produces the old pro's. Or, the inventor whose concept and ideas about a new widget come together overnight -without going through the usual trials and errors.

There are indeed a few "born" entrepreneurs . . . "naturals" . . . who succeed in small business. But, for the most of us, natural ability goes only so far. The "natural" entrepreneur, without adequate training and experience, can only develop haphazardly - if at all.

At the other extreme is the person who seems absolutely unsuited to a particular role - apparently born to lose; the kind who "snatches defeat from the jaws of victory." Fortunately, these people are rare. In some instances, they can do well when they find the right slot in life.

It goes without saying that not *everyone* is cut out to be an entrepreneur. But the vast majority of people considering this step will have at least some, and perhaps many, of the traits that lead to success. Attitudes can be changed, skills can be sharpened, and experience can be broadened to "make" an entrepreneur.

If you do not feel you are a natural, take an extra moment to consider the personal cost of changing. The rewards and risks can have a lasting effect on your life. *Whatever you decide, the fact that you have made the effort to learn more about yourself and Small Business indicates that you have the interest and motivation to become an entrepreneur!* And that is a *very* positive sign.

As you are evaluating yourself, you may discover you lack certain desirable entrepreneurial traits. For example, in most small businesses it is important for you to be persuasive to share your ideas by talking with individuals and groups of people. The test points out that successful entrepreneurs are usually persuasive and comfortable with sharing their ideas. If you see yourself as shy, you'll have to consider how that might affect your particular business. In some businesses, such as direct sales, it could be a major handicap. But in businesses that require less public contact, as for example in an industrial supply business, it would matter less.

It is important that the business you eventually go into is compatible with your personal characteristics. If you decide that shyness is a problem, you can handle it in a number of ways. You can take assertiveness training or other personal growth classes or workshops. You may also want to consider taking on a more outgoing partner or employee to do some of your talking. Another option is to change your business plans instead of trying to change yourself. There are businesses where shyness is not a major hurdle. Or, you may come to grips with the fact that shyness is a handicap that can present problems, but you can acquire the determination to overcome that shortcoming through superior talents in other areas.

A less obvious but very important physical trait of successful entrepreneurs is good health and plenty of energy. Start-up entrepreneurs cannot readily afford loss of time for sickness, especially in the early stages of the enterprise. Entrepreneurs also have - and need - higher than ordinary levels of energy to meet around-the-clock demands, deal with emergencies and work long hours. The more energy you put into your business, the more rewards you can expect to get in return. Also, the harder you work, the harder your employees will be likely to work. Your energy level and stamina depend on how well your body handles stress. So in the area of physical stamina and health, entrepreneurs appear to be born instead of made. The encouraging part is that, within limits, you may have some control in improving your energy levels through exercise, diet and attention to your general well-being. Taking good care of your body gives you another edge for success.

In summary, begin by looking at yourself. What are your strengths? Your weaknesses? Establish a priority sequence for making changes and use all the tools at your disposal for implementing them. Use results of your Self-Test as your guide.

Prepare yourself to succeed by getting training and information from workshops; books; trade journals and associations; successful entrepreneurs and consultants. Also, acquire whatever additional education is required. Preparing yourself to be a successful entrepreneur involves keen self-analysis and the self-discipline to make plans that will deal with your weak points.

There is no simple answer to the question of whether entrepreneurs are born or made. What is clear, however, is that all entrepreneurs must invest time and energy to make the most of their natural abilities, and use all available tools to remedy weaknesses.

Education and the Successful Entrepreneur

Formal business education is certainly helpful to a fledgling entrepreneur, but it isn't by any means the only way to acquire entrepreneurial know-how. A growing number of university business schools are offering entrepreneurial courses. But in general, M.B.A. programs are directed toward turning out corporate leaders. One characteristic of traditional M.B.A. programs has been their focus on big business strategies, which may not necessarily apply to small business. But there are also courses for entrepreneurs available at community or junior colleges - with more practical approaches for learning the ins and outs of small business.

There is no single program that has *all* the answers, but you can choose from a number of courses that can fill in the gaps in your knowledge and strengthen some of your weaknesses.

Successful entrepreneurs' education are varied. Most of these are at least high school graduates. In technical fields they may have a bachelor's or master's degree. Doctorates are uncommon, in part because holders of these degrees most often focus on research instead of immediate practical applications.

Not all successful entrepreneurs were glowing successes in school. Some positive traits that are important for success as an entrepreneur may have actually kept some future entrepreneurs from succeeding in school. For example, successful entrepreneurs are often described as "high-energy" people. Their "perpetual motion" style is similar in some ways to "hyperactive" children's behavior in school. In the classroom, the successful future entrepreneur may have been tagged as a problem. In a corporate environment this person is the "maverick" or loner who avoids conventional channels and is easily bored with company politics. He either settles down to wait for retirement, or faces punishment just as a "problem child" might.

Many problems with accepting authority - that successful entrepreneurs sometimes experience when working for someone else - may also have been experienced during earlier days in school. *Accepting authority* often means taking someone else's ideas at face value, without question. Again, this is *not* characteristic of the successful entrepreneur. He believes strongly in his own ideas. High energy level and strong personal opinions, which are common traits in successful entrepreneurs, may in some cases have actually blocked success in school.

By the same token, success in school will not guarantee success as an entrepreneur. School or academic intelligence can be helpful, especially in technical fields. However, if your IQ, education and experience are not supplemented by a lot of common sense, then you might be in trouble.

Experience and the Successful Entrepreneur

It takes total involvement to learn the ins and outs of small business. Business experience plays a very important role in your success as an entrepreneur. It is important here to make it clear what we mean by "Big Business" and "Small Business".

By U.S. government standards, a small manufacturing business has less than 500 employees. Other types of small businesses are based on annual sales. For example, less than $500,000 for nursery products, or up to $13 million for department stores. This is, however, too simple a definition to help us here. For our purposes, it is more helpful to think of big and small business as organizations run according to two distinctively different management styles.

But there are exceptions: A department store with 150 employees; several vice-presidents; buyers and a personnel department may be operated more like a big business. On the other hand, a chain of fast-food restaurants with 1,000 employees, owned and operated by entrepreneurial-type management that makes all the important decisions, may be considered a small business as far as their management style is concerned.

Changes in small business can be made frequently and quickly. Decision-making channels are short, and very few people are involved. The owner may make all decisions and delegate tasks to a manager. Also, because there are fewer people involved, the environment in a small business is more personal and offers employees more contact with management. Policies can be changed with comparative ease and speed. This may also allow employees to be more creative and innovative. Small business, however, can be as vulnerable as big business to problems between people, and conflicts of ideas and policies. Because big business involves many more people in decision-making processes, it is often necessary to have very precise policies for making and implementing these decisions. This means that change usually takes longer.

Since big businesses are usually well established, their well-defined policies may not provide as much leeway for necessary changes and creative input. This can be frustrating for some employees, while others will feel quite comfortable in this kind of an environment; those who work and play by the rules. In a small business, most employees feel more free to be themselves and work closely with the entrepreneur.

Previous experience working for a small business can be most helpful in becoming a successful entrepreneur. If you had managerial background, this experience will be helpful in any type of business you may want to enter. Experience in marketing and sales will be advantageous in sales-intensive enterprises such as insurance, real estate and in almost any type of business where you visit prospects or customers at their place of business. Production experience will be useful if the main thrust of the business is manufacturing or providing services to businesses on a continuing basis - such as supplying parts, repair services, etc.

There are, of course, exceptions: You will find "seat-of-the-pants flyers" who enter a business without any experience and manage to make a go of it. These individuals have the ability to get things done by delegating and learning quickly. They are usually very perceptive and make up for lack of experience by surrounding themselves with people who do have the know-how.

But entrepreneurs who do not fit this particular mold can still succeed by acquiring the experience and by taking the necessary time to acquire the skills. You may pay dearly for jumping the gun and rushing into a business with too little experience. So be careful and take a hard look at your situation. The choice is between applying your limited experience in the hope to gain quick success, or to better prepare yourself and make your move when you feel ready. This is a decision no one can make for you, and deserves a lot of thought.

What are some of the backgrounds successful entrepreneurs have in common? One is childhood or teenage experiences such as newspaper carriers, lemonade stand or "liquid fast-food" operators, lawn mowing tycoons, and other more unusual jobs. Also, they often had part-time jobs working for themselves or others in high school or college.

Another common trait is that of having difficulty working for others; dissatisfaction on the job, and poor or strained relations with superiors.

Big Business Background of Successful Entrepreneurs

Entrepreneurially-oriented people working in big business will often experience frustrations. Many of the problems are due to the structure and philosophy of big business. Other problems relate to entrepreneurs' emotional needs and psychological makeup. Big business can be restrictive; it may mean handling repetitive tasks or very narrow responsibilities, making it difficult to see the big picture and understand just where one fits in. This "lack of fit" can lead to a sense of personal insignificance and less desire to be involved. Also, the limited chances to be in contact with management can lead to frustration. If you are not in touch with the people making the decisions, you have little opportunity to make your views and ideas known.

Entrepreneurs often feel trapped by the slowness of change and the limits it puts on creativity and innovation. An entrepreneur's need to be part of change - and to see it happen *now* is not something big business can satisfy. Corporate structures are too complex to bring about rapid changes since they depend on consensus and moving decisions through management channels. Most entrepreneurs feel that if they cannot participate in all aspects of a business, they at least want as much control as possible over their particular part of the operation. This dissatisfaction motivates many future entrepreneurs to leave well-paid positions in favor of smaller enterprises . . . or, they start their own businesses.

History has demonstrated that many of those dissatisfied, less successful employees who left big business have succeeded as entrepreneurs. What are the prospects for *successful* employees or managers who make the same move? Perhaps surprisingly, these people do not always succeed as entrepreneurs. This is because big and small business are worlds apart in structure and style; the skills necessary for survival in one does not necessarily guarantee success in the other. For example, slow, conservative decision-making works well in big businesses where policies change gradually. But that same decision-making style can spell disaster in a small business which is faced with changes and has no set policies to deal with them. However, many people successfully manage that change and carry over their record of success into a small operation.

Small Business Backgrounds of Successful Entrepreneurs

Many successful entrepreneurs quit their jobs in *small* businesses because of dissatisfaction. What are the major difficulties here?

Small business usually moves at a fast pace, allowing employees to be involved in more areas of the operation. This provides more opportunity for creativity, and recognizes and rewards individual efforts. These aspects are very appealing to entrepreneurs. So the question is, why continue to work for someone else if you are convinced you can succeed on your own? Another plausible answer follows:

Successful entrepreneurs sometimes experience discontent in even the most ideal small business situations for one major reason: *They had such strong opinions on business decisions and direction, they were often at odds with management.* This is a two-fold problem. First, management feels threatened by an outspoken employee who holds different views on how to run the business. Second, the employee is frustrated because he has definite ideas of how to do things better, but can't put these ideas into action. Added to this, the employee may see little opportunity to advance in the company. Or, he may be offered advancement only to have it later taken over by the owner's son-in-law. However, it *sometimes* happens that an "irreplaceable" employee becomes a partner in the business.

Another commonality of some successful entrepreneurs is having experienced one or more business failures. Since a business failure makes it more difficult to regain the wherewithal for the next venture, each try shows a strong spirit of determination. Entrepreneurs are more likely than anyone else to consider failures as "learning experiences". By having carefully studied this handbook and followed its recommendations, you can go a long way in avoiding those costly reverses.

In summary, successful entrepreneurs commonly have background which include:

- Childhood or teenage job experience.

- Experience in small business management, sales, marketing and production.

- A history of difficulty in working for others, as well as general job dissatisfaction.

- Determination to keep trying until success is reached.

Family Backgrounds of Successful Entrepreneurs

There is no one family type common to successful entrepreneurs. But there are some family-patterns that seem to go along with success.

Immigrants or children of immigrants are more likely to become entrepreneurs than are children of native-born parents. There are many explanations for this phenomenon: One is that immigrants are ambitious and encourage their children to make their own opportunities. Another is that immigrants often feel insecure since they may have felt economical or political pressure in their native countries, and encourage their children to plan and make their own security. Children of immigrants whose parents are also entrepreneurs have not one, but two favorable factors to succeed in their favor: Their parents are both immigrants and entrepreneurs.

Generally, one's chances for success as an entrepreneur increases by having one or more family members who are entrepreneurs. This increases the likelihood of success in at least two ways:

- First, it offers the opportunity for early experience in working in or being exposed to small business.

- Second, the family member can help as an advisor in starting and operating the business, and introduce important business contacts.

Successful entrepreneurs also show a birth-order pattern. Most are the first-born, or oldest child in a family. Some birth-order studies indicate that first-borns in general have higher IQs and appear to be more aggressive than later-born brothers and sisters. Why this trend seems to hold is unclear, but it makes sense that these relatively more intelligent, aggressive individuals would have an edge for success over other children, all other things being equal.

A less scientific explanation is that the oldest child is born to a natural leadership position, and overseeing the activities of a group of children provides a form of early leadership and management training. Parents often have more time to spend with first-borns and only children. Whatever the reason, being the oldest child in a family is one predictor for success as an entrepreneur.

At present, a majority of entrepreneurs are men, and the most successful are evidently backed by emotionally supportive wives. During recent years, however, an ever-increasing number of women have joined the ranks of entrepreneurs. Most entrepreneurs, married or not, appear to be homebodies rather than party boys or girls. Family relations and home atmosphere seem to be highly important to them. A majority also have one or more children.

Studies show that while successful entrepreneurs place high value on supportive families, they seldom say they would be willing to neglect work in favor of their families. How do we make sense of this? Since divorce rates for successful entrepreneurs are no higher than for other groups, a possible explanation may be that these people believe that their supportive families are smooth-running and self-sufficient. The entrepreneur focuses on the business and expects and rest of the family to handle home crises more or less independently.

Another theory suggests that entrepreneurs' need for self-esteem overshadows or crowds out their need for love and social life. If this is correct, it also explains their greater concentration on business over family.

Summarizing, family patterns common to many successful entrepreneurs include the likelihood of being an immigrant or child of an immigrant; having another member of the family who is an entrepreneur; being the oldest child; having supportive families; and concentration on the business, with the family sometimes "taking a back seat."

Common Personality Factors in Successful Entrepreneurs

Successful entrepreneurs stand out from the crowd in at least three broad personality trait areas. First, in their unique personal style, and in self-confidence evidenced by drive and motivation. Second, in the way they act toward other people, as well as in their needs or desires to relate to others. Third, on how they solve problems and approach problem-solving.

How are successful entrepreneurs different from others in personal style?

They differ in self-confidence. They are sold on themselves, and believe in their abilities to succeed. Because they trust their own instincts, they can be very persuasive in swaying others to accept their ideas. Their confidence seems almost contagious, thus inspiring the trust of other people. They believe in themselves, and they can make others believe in them as well. But most are not perfectionists. Perfectionists constantly worry, change products and procedures and often fail to see the big picture. The entrepreneur's self-confidence can accomplish many important objectives. It helps them convince others to accept their ideas. This can be crucial when they persuade others to back their businesses financially, or to buy their products or services. It can also be important when they share their business dreams and directions with their families and employees. Their self-confidence increases the faith of anyone who listens that they will share in the success of the entrepreneur's venture. This, in turn, increases the willingness of others to invest more energy and effort in making the business succeed.

No one likes to back a losing cause. If you can give a clear, convincing and realistic picture of upcoming success, people will be ready to invest time, money, and energy to be a part of that picture.

Besides having high self-confidence, successful entrepreneurs also have good communications skills. They can be clear and persuasive in talking to groups or individuals. They have strong ideas, and enjoy sharing those ideas. They are direct and do not easily back down if others disagree or have different views. Your ability to be persuasive and stand your own ground when others disagree - or are unwilling to listen to your views - is important. This ability to be assertive is critical to your success as an entrepreneur since you will have to make your points heard no matter what the opposition. Successful entrepreneurs also need to be good writers; you will need to come up with clear, easily understood business letters, memos, responses to complaints, and other communications. If you have something important to say, take the time to say it well. Equally important is your ability to be a good listener - to capture good ideas and sort through complex or obscure messages to get at the heart of matters.

Successful entrepreneurs are also characterized by having "shatter-proof" egos. They may be temporarily slowed by failure, but are rarely stopped by it. The ability to pick themselves up when things have gone wrong and try again is essential to their future success. This psychological staying-power and drive is as important as their physical health and stamina. Failure is never final, but only a temporary setback.

Successful entrepreneurs crave the feeling of being appreciated by others. They need to test their personal worth and want to feel valued and important in the eyes of others.

Could any part of this personal style get in the way of your success? The answer is yes. Overconfidence can create major problems. For example, it may lead you to underestimate the financial requirements for your business. The problem here is in expecting your success to come too quickly - misjudging the time it will take for your business to grow and show profits. This may result into cash short-falls, leaving you unable to pay bills or meet your payroll; a serious threat to your business.

Another danger in overconfidence is glossing over or failing to take a careful look at areas of weakness for the start-up and operation of the business. You cannot solve a problem you are unaware of. The Self-Test gives you a chance to identify weak areas and deal with them before they hurt your chances to succeed. Reviewing the results of the test can help you identify some of these problems. Confidence is a strong asset for success, but it must have a solid foundation in reality.

What Traits Successful Entrepreneurs Show in Relating to Others

Successful entrepreneurs are almost always considered leaders by other people. Their styles of leadership may vary from quiet technical wizards to back-slapping entertainers. But most have a background as leaders or advisors in school clubs, organizations and businesses.

What methods do successful entrepreneurs employ in their affiliation with other people or social connections?

Where it helps to meet a business or personal goal, successful entrepreneurs are friendly, outgoing, and enjoy talking to and being with people. These relationships are often self-serving. For example, they may join a club or organization if they expect to obtain some business or connections from club members. If they do not see this potential, they are not as likely to be interested. So where these goals are not present, entrepreneurs show less need or desire for social contact. This is not a Jekyll and Hyde change; entrepreneurs simply seem to be extremely selective in what they will do to reach a business goal.

Successful entrepreneurs also enjoy competing with others and with themselves. They will often participate in competitive individual sports, and see business as a competitive game in which they expect to win. They make little distinction between work and play, so are often labeled "workaholics" by those around them, although they are the last ones to recognize it.

Also common to some entrepreneurs is a strong desire to exercise power over people they are in contact with. This trait manifests itself by a drive to run the whole show; an inability to delegate tasks, and the need to make all the decisions in their lives and work. Yet most entrepreneurs are not power-hungry. They simply expect to call their own shots and insist on being in control. But they will let other people have their way if it is to the benefit of their business. They instinctively know that it's necessary to cooperate with others in order to achieve their objectives. They are persistent in problem-solving and patient when there are obstacles to overcome. Successful entrepreneurs will commit themselves to projects which may take years to complete. They are not discouraged by failures. They view them as a learning opportunity and challenge to start over with improved plans.

Most successful entrepreneurs also have a firm conviction that they are not totally influenced by outside forces such as "luck", "fate", the economy or other people. While they may indeed appear to others to be very lucky people, most of them credit their success to experience, intuition, and careful decision-making. They believe that luck often comes to those who do things right in the first place.

Another important trait of successful entrepreneurs is their skill in analyzing problems. They are expert in making rapid but well thought-out decisions using limited or incomplete information. They seem to have an instinct for sorting out the irrelevant and going directly to the heart of the matter. They are highly creative in their solution to problems. This means that they don't just recognize a good idea, but find ways to *implement* it. It is one thing to have good ideas, another to be able to put them into successful action.

Does this quickness at making decisions based on incomplete or ambiguous information also imply that successful entrepreneurs are willing risk-takers? In a sense, risk and entrepreneurship go hand-in-hand. However, they seldom classify themselves as big risk-takers. Rarely are they attracted by the "sure thing" - that entails few risks and thrills. But they will balance a moderate risk against the chance for an inviting reward. Most see some aspects of their business as risky, but not the business as a whole.

What traits do successful entrepreneurs possess in the area of planning projects and problem-solving?

Successful entrepreneurs are always reaching for new goals, and keep on competing with themselves by setting ever higher goals. It is important, however, to set long-term goals first. For example: A plan that calls for an increase in sales volume by $5 million within five years, or expansion of sales representation to all of the states west of the Mississippi. There also could be intermediate goals - like guideposts - moving toward the final objective. Be sure to set your next long-term goal long before reaching the previous one. Do not make the mistake of setting goals too low, making them too easy to reach. This could result in disappointments and let-downs. What will you do for an encore?

It has been said there are two kinds of tragedies in life. One is to never achieve your ultimate objectives. The other is to achieve them. Something to think about.

Because entrepreneurs are self-motivated, they plan their own projects and establish the steps necessary to complete them. Their projects often involve long-term commitments of time, energy and funds. They expect to make sacrifices and forego immediate rewards. This willingness to be patient is another mark of a successful entrepreneur. They are not only able to understand the necessity for patience, but also do what is necessary, on a systematic step-by-step basis, to reach a set goal.

Let us examine how to approach projects and problems. What is a project? It can be described as anything you do that will benefit the business and ultimately increase profits. For example, expansion can encompass -

- Adding a new line of merchandise.

- Manufacturing new products.

- Increasing the sales force.

- Developing new markets.

- Taking cost reduction measures.

What is a problem? A simple way to define it is: *Anything that can go and will go wrong presents a problem.* Problems will occur in the ordinary course of business as well as during the implementation of plans.

Because the number of hours in each day are limited, and are taken up by managerial or sales responsibilities, the successful entrepreneur will have to set priorities carefully. He will have to determine how much time can be personally devoted to projects and problems and how much time should be delegated.

Once you have established the sequence for handling projects and problems, you have to think about *how* you will deal with them. Big projects or problems are best approached by creating a written step-by-step outline. Define each step and how to approach it. You will find that by doing so, big problems will become smaller and more manageable. This will make it easier for you to delegate parts of tasks to others in your company for quicker and more efficient completion.

Follow-through is extremely important. Guided by your outline, you can assure that you and others on the project are doing their tasks on schedule and correctly. By keeping a log for each person and each responsibility involved, you can control and oversee the progress without losing sight of the final objective.

In summary, successful entrepreneurs display a number of traits in problem solving:

- High need for achievement.

- Ongoing desire to set and reach increasingly challenging goals.

- High self-motivation.

- Willingness to be patient.

- Belief in self-control instead of control from outside forces such as fate or the economy.

- Ability to make rapid decisions with limited information.

- Skill in analyzing information.

- Willingness to take risks.

- Belief that money is the best measure of success, rather than the ultimate reward.

The Ability to Investigate

Limitless curiosity is one of the successful entrepreneur's most impressive traits. Entrepreneurs are information magnets. They collect information everywhere, on business and non-business subjects alike.

There are rewards in collecting a wide variety of information. People whose interests and knowledge are limited to highly specialized areas of expertise and information face serious trouble as entrepreneurs. As an entrepreneur, you will deal with all aspects of your business. Having a wide variety of information is important. For example, if you decide to start an equipment repair service - and are an expert on machinery but inexperienced in customer relations, collections, and financing - your expertise in one area may not be sufficient to carry your business through to success, unless you have the assistance of qualified employees or a partner.

There is often a childlike quality to an entrepreneur's eagerness to continually question. These seemingly naive but pointed questions set people at ease. By making yourself non-threatening, you'll be able to collect a vast amount of information. Asking questions of people in your field helps you gather direct information on trends, problems and problem-solving. It also allows you to establish future business contacts and open doors to new opportunities.

Sometimes an opportunity is ready and waiting for you. A good technique for questioning is to start low-key and gradually move to more complex questions. At the same time, gather information on other people and resources to keep the questioning process going. If you listen carefully and ask good questions, you can get a feel for different kinds of markets and ways of doing things.

Listen to all kinds of people including customers, competitors and suppliers. These contacts can give you clues to winning business ideas.

You'll be pleasantly surprised at the way most people go out of their way to share useful information. In talking with people in your field you also will get a "feel" for the business of your choice, and a knowledge of the "trade lingo". As you pick up on this language, your conversations will carry more credibility as you go along in the questioning process.

Successful entrepreneurs also acquire information by doing a lot of reading. In their usual efficient and somewhat impatient style, they go to the core of information and skip trivial details. While they do not read everything from cover to cover, they quickly grasp the essence and the most useful information. They compare what they read to the facts as they know them. When they instinctively disbelieve a piece of information, they simply ignore it.

Successful entrepreneurs also try hard to be objective. This means they concentrate on getting facts instead of trying to look for information to back an opinion or pre-conceived idea. The entrepreneur needs and prefers information on the way things are rather than on a collection of opinions on how they should be. Analyzing information and trying to see how it relates to reality is all part of being objective.

But it is difficult to be objective all the time. Hopes, dreams and feelings can make it hard to see facts clearly. This can, at times, lead entrepreneurs to believe that they are being objective when they really are not. Of course if they make important decisions based on faulty belief, the results can be disastrous. How can you test whether you are being objective or not? You never can be absolutely sure. But by discussing your ideas with unbiased experts in your field - with people who do not have personal reasons for wanting facts to be one way or the other - you can achieve a high degree of objectivity.

Summarizing, entrepreneurs show some of these common traits in investigation:

- Limitless curiosity.

- Childlike eagerness to question.

- Motivation to research books and magazines for useful information.

- High objectivity.

- An instinct for detecting faulty or misleading information.

The Importance of Self-Organization

Successful entrepreneurs combine the best of two worlds in their self-organization. They are careful thinkers as well as forceful "do-ers".

What makes their approaches different from other people's? First, they do not take things for granted. They believe that what was true in the business world 30 years ago - or even three years ago - may not be true for all time. They are not afraid of change and they welcome the opportunities it can bring. Successful entrepreneurs must be able to tolerate change and the confusion and chaos that sometimes come with it. Beyond this, they need the capacity and ability to look beyond the turmoil which changes sometimes bring, and not lose sight of the big picture. They know how to bring order out of chaos.

How do they accomplish this feat? Probably some of the talent is inborn or related to their way of looking at people and events. The rest is more clearly a result of practice and experience - like learning to skim a book for important ideas rather than reading it cover to cover, a skill that can be sharpened with practice. It may also be helpful to list page numbers and paragraphs of special importance, then go back later to mark or photocopy these sections. The same applies to taking notes in trade meetings, lectures and other listening situations.

The successful entrepreneur is able to extract the important from a mass of trivial or non-essential matter. He is able to concentrate not only on the big picture, but on the fine points as well.

Concerns with detail touch many areas in your life as an entrepreneur. Attention to detail helps your ability to solve problems. For example, when you and your competitors are faced with industry-wide problems (government regulations, etc.)

and you can sort through a lot of information and come up with the answers more quickly than the rest, you will be way ahead of them. And that should be to your advantage. Also, careful attention to details in developing plans and implementing decisions means that you'll have fewer unpleasant surprises in these areas. The ability to identify what is important and essential - and what is not - helps prepare you to make the right decisions. This will help you on most projects, from trimming your business expenses to increasing your sales.

For example, your choice of office furnishings and decor will depend to a large extent on how much importance you attach to the outward physical appearance of your particular business. If your customers and suppliers will regularly be visiting the office, you will have different requirements for decor than if their visits occur infrequently. Often, the cost of making an impression will be made up for in increased business. Your attention to details in this matter will determine whether you will see your decision as spending money to make money, or cutting unnecessary expenses to reach the same goal.

In summary, successful entrepreneurs are information magnets who collect ideas and facts from wide-ranging sources. Among these sources are:

- Business contacts in the community. Also information obtained from trade organizations in the field of business you are interested in.

- Written materials such as trade magazines, books, local and government publications, national business weeklies, newspapers and business newsletters.

- Owners and managers of existing businesses.

This collection of knowledge, obtained by listening and reading, is the foundation of your information base. It is invaluable if organized for easy access when the need arises.

Traits successful entrepreneurs show in self-organization include:

- Flexible self-organization that adapts to continuing changes.

- High tolerance for these changes and new information.

- Ability to create order from chaos.

- Methodical attention to details.

- Ability to distinguish important details.

Motivation to Enter the World of Business

A sense of pride and the need for accomplishment are the two factors most often mentioned by top enterprisers as the basic objectives for starting their own ventures. Also, dissatisfaction in working for others - a feeling of being trapped, and powerless to bring about change or advance in their careers. Entering small business ownership solely as a vehicle of escape carries some dangers, particularly when it leads to entering a venture without having spent sufficient time to evaluate overall readiness.

The key to success is preparedness. This handbook brought you specific recommendations for helping you achieve your goals. The prospect of a comfortable or exceptional income is inviting. But money in itself is seldom considered the prime objective. It more often serves as a benchmark or proof of success rather than the end objective. Considering the risks and high personal investment involved in becoming an entrepreneur, attempting to escape financial problems by this route may be one of the wrong reasons for starting a small business. It is true, however, that the sense of pride, need for accomplishment and desire for personal freedom and expression are the fuels that drive successful entrepreneurs toward achievement.

Even though becoming an entrepreneur is not a cure-all, it can lead to a very rewarding lifestyle, with far greater opportunities for creativity and personal freedom. Plus the opportunity to make your own security, and the potential for excellent income and ultimately - wealth.

Taking a Close Look at Yourself as an Entrepreneur

In the previous section we discussed the traits and characteristics common to successful start-up entrepreneurs. Now you are about to discover, through a Personal Inventory, how you can move toward more specific areas of business. Those you should avoid will also be indicated.

The Personal Inventory covers the following areas:

- Personal qualifications.

- Capabilities.

- Product/service experience.

- Basic business knowledge.

- Survey of the personal inventory.

Take your time as you read and work on this section. It may be the most important part of your study. The Personal Inventory, like a merchandise inventory, will disclose to you what you have on the "shelf". It will give you an insight into your strong and weak areas.

Your Personal Inventory - a Self Survey

The purpose of the Entrepreneurial Self-Test was to establish your general suitability and qualifications to become an entrepreneur. The purpose of taking the Personal Inventory is to discover your strong and weak points. They too can affect your success in the business of your choice.

If you have taken time to complete and review the Entrepreneurial Self-Test and made careful notes during the discussion of traits in successful entrepreneurs, you will have a head-start in completing your Personal Inventory and Survey. Neither the Entrepreneurial Self-Test nor your Personal Inventory resemble tests you may have had in school. They are simply aids to help you collect more information about yourself. Since there are often no right or wrong answers, you will be able to draw your own conclusions as to your strengths and weaknesses.

To accomplish the objective of appraising yourself, we urge you to complete the following five worksheets conscientiously.

WORKSHEET I

Identifying Personal Qualifications

This worksheet deals with your work-related background and includes your paid and unpaid work experiences such as jobs, volunteer work and other activities inside or outside of the business field. If you have a prepared employment resume, it can serve as a useful guide.

The worksheet is divided into two columns. On the left side you will see how an aspiring entrepreneur, Kim Smith, approached the situation. His proposed business is a sheet music, music supply and band instrument store. On the right side are spaces for *your* answers. Your comments will obviously be completely different. But Kim's responses will give you an idea on how to go about it.

Categories A to D deal with your educational and general experiences. The purpose here is to look at the big picture highlighting your background and interests, and not just job history alone.

The left column shows how Kim listed his paid and unpaid activities. It includes his education, hobbies and interests, volunteer and business background. Use it as a guide as you make your own list on the right.

If you have had a job that involved widely different kinds of duties, you may want to list it more than once. For example, Kim has listed three symphony related jobs: Ticket sales, librarian and computer programming. As a single job may involve a wide variety of tasks, recording your experience this way will bring out the areas of most importance.

Categories E to G. Here Kim has broken down his business experience into three areas. They are small business management experience, direct experience in his business field and experience in sales/marketing. His activities include some jobs that involve practical knowledge in more than one category. For example, Kim has listed his background as a musician in all three categories. This shows that as a musician he had acquired experience in small business management in the same type of business he wants to own (a music store) and in sales/marketing.

Simply eyeballing the length of these lists and comparing them to each other may give you some useful information about which areas you will need to strengthen. Adding specific information will be even more helpful. For example, if you show two years of experience at the Far East Export Company in the Small Business Management Experience category, describe your duties fully - such as personnel management, shipping management or dealing with suppliers.

In *Category H*, Kim recorded his own conclusions about his strengths, weaknesses, and the things he has enjoyed most and least. The list below gives you an idea of some areas to think about as you write down your conclusions:

- Money management, including your experience dealing with banks and other lenders, bookkeeping and collections.

- Purchasing and inventory.

- Pricing.

- Marketing, including advertising, selling, and public relations.

- Personnel management, including how well you set priorities and manage your own time.

Keep in mind that this worksheet is for *your own information*. It is not necessary for anyone else to see it. So be honest with yourself as you identify your strengths as well as your weaknesses.

As you review Worksheet I, pay close attention to the patterns of strengths and weaknesses, likes and dislikes that show up frequently. Activities listed in Categories A to G are important to your future as an entrepreneur. If you don't have much experience in a certain area, think of ways to increase it. Two good alternatives are further training and on-the-job experience to acquire needed skills.

You can also use this inventory to help identify and build on your strengths. If you are especially strong in one area, consider the edge you could have over competitors by developing it further.

In starting your own business, you are like a racecar driver trying to enter a field of already moving cars. You face handicaps right at the start. If you expect to compete, you will need to have a solid background and experience to help your business get moving quickly to catch up with the competition.

Entrepreneur: KIM SMITH   MY EXPERIENCE
                                            (Fill in below)

EDUCATION AND GENERAL EXPERIENCE

A. Education/Training   Education/Training

    High School Band -   Librarian
                    Musician

    Jr. College - Computer Science

B. Hobbies and Interests: Hobbies and Interests:

    Community Orchestra
    Acting in Theater
    Collecting rare books
    Photography
    Personal computer programming

C. Volunteer experience: Volunteer Experience:

    Ticket sales - community theater
    Clown, juggler - Children's Hospital
    Grant writing - United Way

D. Paid Experience: Paid Experience:

    Childhood: Shoeshine, carwash, dog-
                  walking

    College: Ticket sales, door-to-door
              book sales

    Adult: Sheet music, band instrument
             sales
        Symphony ticket sales (home
             solicitation)
        Symphony librarian
        Symphony computer programming
             and data entry - payroll
        Dance band manager

BUSINESS EXPERIENCE

E. Small Business Management   Small Business Management
    Experience: Experience:

    Young-person's jobs: 6-8 months, customer
        relations and self-management

    Direct Book Sales, 1 year - purchasing,
        customer relations, collections,
        self-management

    Musician, 6 years - managed dance band,
        personnel management, financial
        planning, bookkeeping, marketing,
        collections - limited

F. Experience in My Business Field: Experience in My Field:

    Musician, 6 years - hands-on knowledge
        of instruments, instruction, and
        repair

    Music Librarian, 3 years in high school;
        2 years in the symphony; purchasing;
        filing

G. Sales/Marketing Experience: Sales/Marketing Experience:

    Direct Book Sales, 1 year

    Ticket Sales, 4 years; box office and
        direct, also by phone

    Musician, 6 years; Booked engagements

    Symphony Librarian, 2 years; marketing
        research, promotional booklet design

CONCLUSIONS

H. Most enjoyed: Most enjoyed:
    Customer relations, marketing/advertising,
        direct sales

    Strongest areas: Strongest areas:
    Customer relations, marketing/advertising

    Least enjoyed: Least enjoyed:
    Phone ticket-sales, collections

    Weakest areas: Weakest areas:
    Purchasing, financial planning

WORKSHEET II

Your Capabilities

Worksheet II compares your traits to those of successful entrepreneurs in the areas of investigative skills and problem-solving. The first column of Worksheet II lists traits successful entrepreneurs show in those two areas. Kim Smith has used the second column to show his traits compared to those of successful entrepreneurs. After thinking about each trait listed in the first column, and recording them, Kim has added his conclusions at the end of the worksheet. You will put your comments in the third column.

After you have compared your capabilities to those of successful entrepreneurs in column 1, go back through the list and identify not only the areas where you have strong ability, but also those you enjoy doing. For example, if you can deal well with making decisions based on rapidly changing complex (or limited) information - but you don't enjoy doing so -it's important that you mention that in your conclusions on the bottom of Worksheet II.

PERSONAL TRAITS IN PROBLEM SOLVING
AND INVESTIGATING

1	2	3 (Fill in below)
Traits of Successful Entrepreneurs	Kim Smith's Traits	My Traits
Constantly set higher and higher goals	Usually set reachable long-term goals but sometimes take on too many short-term goals at one time	
Choose their own projects	Choose my own projects, but listen to advice on ways to complete those projects	
Breaking down large projects and deal with them, one step at a time	I can break a project down and deal with it in smaller steps	
Prioritize projects - do first things first	I do this easily, and often write things down on a calendar so I can check back to see that they are started and completed on time	
Look before leaping - take time to plan, and are willing to wait and work for the ultimate rewards	I'm often impatient, but I take enough time to plan well, and complete what I start	
Can make decisions and change plans quickly	I can make fast, usually good decisions but I prefer to take my time	

1	2	3
Traits of Successful Entrepreneurs	Kim Smith's Traits	My Traits
Can quickly sort through information to find the most important points	I do this easily - I enjoy listening, talking, and reading	
Can make good decisions even with incomplete information	I'm not comfortable with this, but I do it well	
Enjoy making independent decis- ions	I enjoy this	
Can delegate or share tasks	I usually work alone, so I don't have much experience in this area	
Take moderate risks	I like a challenge, but I do not usually think of what I do as a risk taker	

CONCLUSIONS

KIM SMITH
I most enjoy:

Choosing my own projects, planning how to
carry them out, and actually making them work

I am strongest in:

Analyzing, or sorting information to find
the most important pieces

I am most uncomfortable in:

Making quick decisions with relatively
little information

My weakest area is:

Delegating/sharing tasks

MY EXPERIENCE
I most enjoy:

I am strongest in:

I am most uncomfortable in:

My weakest area is:

Here is one important point to think about: It is possible to have many of the capabilities that go along with success in a certain field, and still not be "right" for it. For example, you may possess all the skills you need to be a competent, successful computer programmer. But starting a computer programming service may not be a good choice if you don't enjoy using those skills - or dislike the pressures that go with that work. Your capabilities are important, but it's crucial that your interests follow hand-in-hand with your abilities.

WORKSHEET III

Product/Service Experience

This worksheet deals with the experience you have in your specific business field. It is designed to show the extent of knowledge you have in your chosen field. For example, if you intend to start a canoe-manufacturing business, you should know about the performance of natural fabric and wooden canoes as compared to aluminum and fiberglass. You must be knowledgeable about engineering and construction. Being familiar with the pricing and quality of your competitor's lines is extremely important.

Ask yourself if your experience in canoe-making is sufficient for you to create higher quality or lower cost products than those of your competitors. Do you have a good "feel" for this field, as well as a command of its "language"? Do you really know enough about it to establish credibility with knowledgeable customers?

Once again, we have used Kim Smith's experience as an example. Notice that Kim's business involves services (instrument repair and music lessons) as well as products. This may or may not be the case for your business. You would fit best in a business that involves either products or services, but not necessarily both.

Worksheet III examines the specific experience you have in your field. The left column divides Kim's experience in his business field into two parts - products and services. You will record your answers in the spaces to the right.

First, you will list your experience with each product and/or service your business involves. For example, Kim has shown sheet music as a product his business will carry. He has also noted what types of sheet music he has strong background in, and the ones he is less experienced in. Be sure to analyze the areas which you feel should be improved. Review your answers to identify your strongest areas and the ones you are most comfortable with.

This part of your Personal Inventory will help you decide on your level of in-field business knowledge and what further training or experience is advisable. Most entrepreneurs continue learning in seminars and workshops even after their business is well-established. You can never know all there is to know in your field, but you should have a "feel" for your business that goes well beyond simply knowing the basics.

KIM SMITH
Proposed Business: Music Store

My Proposed Business
(Fill in below)

Products:

Products:

1. Sheet music - I have a good background
    in classical music and soft rock; I am
    much weaker in other types of music.

2. Music supplies - good background in pre-
    ferred supplies for beginning and ad-
    vanced musicians; weakest in electronic
    accessories.

3. Pre-band instruments - very little back-
    ground.

4. Band/Orchestra instruments - strongest
    in woodwinds, brass, strings, percussion
    (including piano); much weaker in synth-
    esizers and other electronic systems.

Comments:

Comments:

I am familiar with pricing, performance
standards and quality comparisons for
most of these items, except for some
electronic systems.

Services:

Services:

1. Instrument repair and selection - strong
    in all but electronic systems.

2. Work easily with very young and older
    customers, and can offer lessons on
    all band instruments.

Comments:

Comments:

I feel comfortable talking with either
inexperienced or expert customers. Except for unfamiliarity with some forms
of popular music and electronic instruments and accessories, I know the
field well.

WORKSHEET IV

Basic Business Knowledge

This Worksheet deals with your knowledge in basic business principles and practice. Most business failures are caused by poor management, lack of financial expertise and problems in the area of sales and marketing. This part of your inventory focuses on your skills and experience in:

- Money management.

- Purchasing and inventory control.

- Pricing.

- Sales and marketing.

- Personnel and self-management.

- Using outside consultants and other resources.

The Worksheet explores experience in business skills gained from previous jobs and activities. Kim once managed a dance band. He checked off the spaces in the first column to show his experience level. His previous jobs did not involve pricing, so Kim has put an "x" in the none/some experience column. He did, however, have advertising experience and indicated that with an "x" in the medium/high experience column. Now complete the second column.

BASIC BUSINESS KNOWLEDGE

	1 Kim Smith's Experience		2 My Experience (Fill in below)	
Type of Experience	None/Some	Med./High	None/Some	Med./High
Money management:				
1. Dealing with banks, lenders	x			
2. Bookkeeping		x		
3. Collections		x		
4. Credit for Customers		x		
Credit for this business	x			
5. Cash flow		x		
6. Insurance and Employee Benefits	x			
7. Purchasing/ Inventory Control	x			
Pricing Experience:	x			
Marketing Experience:				
1. Advertising		x		
2. Selling		x		
3. Public relations		x		
Personnel Management:	x			
Use of Consultants:	x			

WORKSHEET V

Survey of the Personal Inventory

This Worksheet will help you summarize your experiences in each area. It will help to give you a complete overview of your skills, experiences and personal attitudes in each of the areas that are important to success. Your ratings will place you in a better position to judge for yourself where your strengths and weaknesses are.

Rate yourself based on your answers from Worksheet I to IV on a scale of 1 to 10. The higher the number, the greater the experience or skill-level. A total score of 89 or less indicates that additional study, training or work experience is desirable.

	Scale (1-10)
Education and Training	_____
Hobbies and Interests	_____
Volunteer Work	_____
Job Experience	_____
Management Experience	_____
Experience in chosen field	_____
Sales and Marketing	_____
Goal Setting	_____
Self-organization	_____
Decision making	_____
Risk taking	_____
Product and Service know-how	_____
Money Management	_____
Personnel Management	_____
Use of Consultants	_____
Total	_____

Your answers will serve as guideposts to the additional steps in training and information-gathering you must take to supplement your qualifications as an entrepreneur in the field of your choice.

The Financial Side of Your Personal Inventory

The following pages recap material you have already covered in the financial section of this handbook This review will serve to reinforce some vitally important facts on money issues.

The amount of money you personally have available or are able to raise will have a definite bearing on the type and size of business you will start.

In studying this section, you will obtain a picture on how to view the money aspects of starting a business.

First take a look at your current financial situation. How much of your liquid assets (cash available from savings, stocks and bonds, receivables, and cash on hand) could you invest in a business? How much could you obtain from sales of properties? How much could you expect to borrow from friends and relatives? Most lenders require that you put up a good part of the needed start-up funds for your enterprise. You'll need an approximation of what those costs will be. The details of how to arrive at these estimates were discussed earlier in this handbook.

Begin your personal financial inventory by carefully reviewing your credit history. Is it spotless? Or have you ever been delinquent or defaulted in repaying a loan? Have you ever declared bankruptcy? What are the largest loans you have received and paid off? What loans or other debts are you still responsible for paying? If you were a lender, would you consider loaning money to a person who had your identical credit history? Would this person be a good, a questionable, or a poor risk?

Consider how you will back your loans and what collaterals you could offer. Look at the importance of the assets you will be pledging as collaterals; what would the effect on you be if you were unable to make good on your loans and lost your collaterals?

In starting or buying a business there are a number of expenditures involved before you even open the doors. Some of these are operating expenses such as rent, utilities, insurance, lease deposits, remodelling, renovating, etc. Others are purchase of equipment; supplies; interior furnishings; start-up inventory; legal fees; accounting and consulting services; salaries for yourself and your employees from the day you open until the business begins to show a profit.

You will want to go over these figures with your accountant, banker, or SBA counselor to make sure your estimates are complete, accurate and reflect a representative picture of the unique start-up needs for your business.

You may have to develop a business plan which is an outline of your business goals and explains your strategy for reaching those goals; also your projections for sales and expenses and expected growth and profits. This plan is useful in gaining an overview of the business as a whole and gives potential lenders more information about your venture's growth possibilities and repayment capabilities.

Business plans were previously discussed in detail. You should be thinking about all possible sources of funding now. There is a wide range of choices available. The first and foremost source is money which you have saved for your venture. Others are equity loans on your home or other properties you may own, including notes or contracts in your possession which you can offer as collaterals. Friends or relatives may be another source of financing.

Aside from loans from lending institutions, it may be possible to obtain funds from business development corporations, state and federal programs. Sometimes other successful entrepreneurs, clubs, religious organizations and alumni associations will make loans. Taking in one or more partners can present a solution to your financing problem. In larger undertakings, money supplied by venture capitalists is an acceptable way to finance a business.

If you are dealing now with an accountant, banker and attorney, talk to them about your ideas. Try to explain and "sell" them on your business dreams. Keep them advised of your plans while you remain in the planning stage and can still be flexible. Make sure these people follow your logic and reasoning and take their comments and suggestions seriously. Let them know not only of the potential rewards of your venture, but also of the risks as you see them. Also keep in mind that these professionals may not be the same ones you will ultimately deal with when you have started in business.

Ask yourself the following questions: Do these people know you well enough to trust you? Are they respected in their fields? How much do you trust their judgment? Are they readily available to you when you need to consult them? Would you feel comfortable letting them know that you were seeking additional information and advice from other consultants? Are you prepared to change to other consultants if you find it difficult to work with any of them?

Also consider what institutional ties these consultants have. A banker in a small, independent bank may be just as knowledgeable as a branch manager of a large bank, but may give your account more weight and personalized attention than you could get in a larger institution. On the other hand, the large bank may have more funds available or better terms to offer you. The choice depends on your unique needs.

The financial part of your Personal Inventory will give you an initial overview into these areas. First, determine what kind of income you can expect until the time your business breaks even and becomes profitable. Will you be able to get by financially during this period? Are you ready and willing to make sacrifices? How about your family? Will they understand and accept the situation as well? What is the minimum income you can subsist on? Have your financing plans made allowances to cover this?

Next, determine what kind of personal financial investment your business will require. Is this level of investment realistic for you? What's the average rate of return on this type of business? What could you predict as a return on your investment within one year? Five years? Ten? Could you expect a less risky, higher return by investing the same money elsewhere, such as stocks or in real estate? Could you expect to do better financially by working for someone else?

Finally, explore the potential financial rewards of your business as compared to its risks. Does the earnings potential outweigh the risk of losing your business, your credit rating and your collateral? Is this risk something that both you and your family are willing to take? Do you have any concerns about the emotional impact of such a loss on yourself and your family?

The questions posed are not intended to discourage you from starting a business. Millions of entrepreneurs have faced them before and took all of the necessary steps to overcome these potential pitfalls. This handbook provides most of the answers.

In summary, your Personal Inventory can be of great help in evaluating yourself for your role as an entrepreneur. But there are also elements which cannot be assessed objectively by yourself, such as the strength and staying power of your motivation to succeed; your belief and dedication to carry out your plans. These are difficult factors to measure or compare with other entrepreneurs who have gone into business before. They are, however, necessary ingredients which, when combined with experience, aptitude and devotion to your ideas, will lead to success.

Good luck!

Bibliography

The following books are resources used in writing this handbook:

Albert, Kenneth J. -   Straight Talk about Small Business
                             New York: McGraw-Hill Book Company

Comiskey, James C. -   How to Start, Expand & Sell a Business
                             California: Venture Perspectives Press

Feldstein, Stuart -   Home, Inc.
                             New York: Grosset & Dunlop

Fierro, Robert -   The New American Entrepreneur
                             New York: William Morrow & Company, Inc.

Flexman, Nancy A. -   Small Business Management
Scanlan, Thomas J.   Texas: Argus Communications

Gaedeke, Ralph M. -   Small Business Management
Tootelian, Dennis H.   Illinois: Scott, Foresman and Company

Goldstein, Arnold S. -   Starting on a Shoestring
                             New York: John Wiley & Sons

Smith, Brian R. -   How to Prosper in Your Own Business
                             Vermont: The Stephen Greene Press

Tarrant, John J. -   Making it Big on Your Own -
                             Playboy Press

Van Voorhis, -   Entrepreneurship and Small Business Management
  Kenneth R.   Massachusetts: Allyn and Bacon, Inc.

Wallace, Dr. Melvin -   Partners in Business
                             Delaware: Enterprise Publishing Company

Witt, Scott -   Spare-time Businesses You can Start and Run for
                               Less Than $1,500
                             New York: Parker Publishing Co., Inc.

Various publications by the Small Business Administration and other U.S. Government publications.

Index

Page numbers follow section numbers

About the Author

Fred Klein has had a lifetime of involvement in the world of business as an entrepreneur and counselor to other entrepreneurs. He started a small service business on a shoestring, then expanded it into other profitable mutimillion-dollar businesses in the graphic arts and marketing fields. He has written manuals and newsletters in the sales, administrative, and marketing areas.

He accumulated his vast knowledge and experience in all phases of business while being actively involved in the promotion of products and services, negotiating leases, sales and purchasing contracts as well as dealing with customers, suppliers, accountants, attorneys and the hiring and firing of employees. He experienced many of the triumphs and setbacks which most entrepreneurs encounter during the various stages of progress of their businesses.

By the time one of his companies, Dinner & Klein, a direct mail, printing and marketing firm, expanded its operation on a national scale, he and his wife Vera, who worked with him in an executive position, assisted owners and managers of retail stores, service establishments, manufacturing plants, publishers, and mail order operators, in their marketing and promotional efforts.

Since the sale of his companies, he counsels business owners and start-up entrepreneurs on marketing research and planning, day-to-day management problems, and start-up techniques - with an emphasis on the key word of business success - PROFITS.

NOTES

NOTES

NOTES

NOTES

NOTES

NOTES